WE'D HAVE A GREAT
RELATIONSHIP
IF IT WEREN'T FOR
YOU

REGAINING LOVE AND
INTIMACY THROUGH MUTUALITY

Bruce Derman, Ph.D.
with Michael Hauge

Mutual Connection Press
Woodland Hills, California

Library of Congress Cataloging-in-Publication Data

Derman, Bruce
   We'd have a great relationship if it weren't for you: regaining love and
intimacy through mutuality/Bruce Derman with Michael Hauge.
      p.   cm.
   Includes bibliographical references (p. 303).
   ISBN 0-9663704-0-6
   1. Marriage. 2. Unmarried couples. 3. Mutualism. 4. Intimacy
(Psychology) I. Hauge, Michael. II. Title.
HQ734.D525   1994   94-23088
306.81—dc20   CIP

©1994 Bruce Derman with Michael Hauge
ISBN 0-9663704-0-6

Originally published by Health Communications, Inc.

MUTUAL CONNECTION PRESS
22817 Ventura Blvd., Suite 806
Woodland Hills, CA 91364

Cover design by Andrea Perrine Brower

To my father,
George Derman,
who until he died, lived every step of my life with me

and

To my mother,
Fay Derman,
who still does.

Acknowledgments

I would like to thank all the people who have been part of my life over the past 20 years, and who waited patiently for me to fulfill my life-long dream of seeing a book with my name on it.

I wish to express my deepest appreciation to my wife Karen, whose presence and sharing inspired me to write this book.

I also want to thank my clients, who have been my relationship teachers throughout this process. Both Michael and I want to thank Christine Belleris, Matthew Diener and Christine Winter, our editors at Health Communications, for their input and guidance, as well as our first editor, Barbara Nichols, who played a big part in making this book a reality. We're deeply grateful to Barbara Alexander, Marlene Dantzer, Mitchell Group, Dianne Haak, Lori Kaplan, Al Ludington, Judith Siegfried and Frederic Wiedemann for their very helpful comments and suggestions, as well as to Bob Bass for his technical support, to Vicki Arthur for her insight and guidance regarding publicity and promotion, and to Stephen Johnson and Robert Strock for their valuable contributions. And we both offer a special heartfelt thanks to Shirley Bass and Nancy Lynn-Pearson for their invaluable time, input and commitment to this book.

I want to give a special thank-you to my sons, Derek, Jason and Adam, to whom I offer this book as my legacy. And to my father and mother, who gave me their legacy.

And a final appreciation to my collaborator Michael Hauge, who not only wrote this with me every step of the way, but who lived the essence and meaning of this book with me throughout the entire process.

Acknowledgments from Michael Hauge

In addition to all my friends and family, for their continued love and support, I would especially like to offer my thanks to two people:

To Bruce Derman, not only for letting me be a part of this wonderful project, but also for making the mutual process of leaving our comfort zones, extending our limits, and finding our sameness so fulfilling and so much fun.

And to my wife Vicki, whose unending love, support and belief in me is more than I could ever repay.

Contents

Acknowledgments vii

Introduction ix

Prologue   THE BOTTOMLESS HOLE
A Fable of the Unknown xxi

PART I: JUDGMENT

Chapter 1   LIFE ON THE SEESAW
The Difference Game 3

Chapter 2   PROTECTION FROM THE UNKNOWN
The Goal of the Difference Game 27

Chapter 3   PLAYING THE GAME
The Rules of the Difference Game 45

Chapter 4   LIVING IN THE COMFORT ZONE
The Consequences of the Difference Game 63

PART II: ACCEPTANCE

Chapter 5   ACCEPTING THE UNACCEPTABLE
Mutuality 75

Chapter 6   A LONGING TO JOIN
The Goal of Mutuality 117

Chapter 7   THROUGH THE EYES OF SAMENESS
The Rules of Mutuality 131

Chapter 8   LIVING IN EQUALITY AND ACCEPTANCE
             The Consequences of Mutuality 141

PART III: JOINING

Chapter 9   FROM DENIAL TO ACCEPTANCE
             The Mutuality Continuum 147

Chapter 10   MOVING INTO SAMENESS
             The Steps to Intimacy 155

PART IV: OBSTACLES

Chapter 11   THE JOY OF UNSATISFACTORY SEX
             Mutuality in the Bedroom 195

Chapter 12   OTHER TOUGH ISSUES
             Threats to Mutuality 239

PART V: ENDINGS AND NEW BEGINNINGS

Chapter 13   COOPERATIVE SEPARATION
             Mutuality and Divorce 257

Chapter 14   NEW RELATIONSHIPS
             Finding a Mutual Partner 273

PART VI: INTEGRATION

Chapter 15   SEEING THE SAMENESS IN EVERYONE
             Universal Mutuality 291

Bibliography 307

Introduction

Two people meet and fall in love. The love grows and they create a life together. Each believes—or wants to believe—that they are both interested in the same kind of relationship. Certainly, each believes that they are mutually committed to a partnership that will sustain and grow for a long time, maybe forever. And each believes that he or she has found a partner, a companion and a friend, as well as a spouse and a lover.

But then something happens . . .

Over time, this wonderful relationship begins to struggle and falter as problems, confrontations and crises emerge. More and more, the partners seem to be going their own separate ways. Each partner's behavior appears increasingly unfamiliar to the other, and pretty soon they are each privately longing for the good old days, when romance blossomed, communication was complete and differences seemed nonexistent.

They work to recapture the rapture of falling in love, but its failure to reappear only magnifies the differences and conflicts that are beginning to seem insurmountable.

Each feels betrayed by the other for failing to fulfill his or her dreams, and they both become disillusioned and angry as their hope for a satisfying relationship unravels. So they struggle through some form of physical or emotional separation, awkwardly and angrily confronting each other, with long periods of silence separating the trivial arguments from the earth-shaking crises.

Other people are soon brought into the picture, as relatives, friends and therapists listen to all the battle reports, offer sympathy and advice, and begin taking sides.

And finally, if the relationship becomes too intolerable, the couple will bring in two other people who care very little about love and connection, but who know a lot about divorce law.

And as the partners look at each other through the smoke and haze of all the legal jargon, each may ask, "How could I have ever selected this person as my mate? What became of the lover I fell head-over-heels for? **What happened . . .?!***"*

What happened was that as they moved from the romantic bliss of falling in love to the harsh reality of building a relationship, they began to expose their own humanity.

And it terrified them.

Living together, experiencing their sexual vulnerability, creating a home, having and raising children, and confronting work, finances, illness, friends, relatives, and all the other stresses of everyday life became overwhelming. Because with each new conflict and crisis, they were exposed to their own shortcomings, limitations and helplessness.

All the physical, mental and emotional qualities and feelings they consciously or unconsciously regarded as weak, unacceptable and unfamiliar were now staring them in the face. And experiencing this fear, anger, boredom, impotence, helplessness, selfishness, arrogance, disappointment, failure, success and the hundred other very human qualities they regarded as unacceptable in either themselves or their spouses created a tension that seemed intolerable.

Unconsciously, the partners asked themselves, "What am I going to do with these unsuitable feelings? I don't want to expose all this stuff, even to myself. And I *certainly* don't want my partner to see them. More than anything else, *I've got to protect myself.*"

So, to shield themselves against the exposure and vulnerability that would come with real closeness and intimacy, the couple began focusing on all the differences that would keep them at a comfortable distance. As long as their energy was devoted to proving how different they were, how much better—or even less—than each other, there was little risk that either partner would truly be seen.

This couple began the inescapable process of using their differences to prevent themselves from experiencing an uncomfortable level of intimacy, exposure and vulnerability. This is the process I call *the difference game*.

As long as we can use our differences to stay superior or inferior to our partners, we may experience pain, conflict and separation, but we won't have to confront the much more terrifying prospect of moving closer and revealing our own fear and weakness.

"I try to communicate, but you just won't open up." "I try to understand you, but your logic is beyond belief." "When it comes to handling money, we're like night and day." There's little chance of real connection or exposure under a barrage of judgments such as these.

In the difference game, both partners accumulate outside evidence to verify their inequality, focusing more and more on negative beliefs that will justify their separation. Beliefs such as "Men will never take care of you" or "Women will never hear your needs" become dominant for each of them.

Now a vicious circle develops: the more the couple plays the game, the more their distance and antagonism grow. And in turn, the more difficult the relationship becomes, the more helpless and threatened they feel, and the harder each partner plays the game.

After awhile, the partners are no longer in control of their relationship, but instead are using every interaction to prove that each is better or less than the other. And because they aren't fully conscious of playing the difference game, they ultimately become its victims.

But what choice do they have? What can couples do when romance fades, when intimacy frightens, and when relationships begin to turn? How can we possibly find our love relationships under all the protective layers we carry with us to cover our wounds and scars?

As they search for answers, couples today are bombarded with information and advice. Books, tapes, seminars and talk shows create a chorus of voices telling us why our relationships are unsatisfying or nonexistent.

Men can't commit . . . Women are angry . . . Men and women can't communicate . . . You're incompatible . . . He's going to abandon you . . .

She doesn't understand you . . . You'll never find the right guy . . . All the good ones are married or gay . . .

Couples are left floundering in a sea of labels and jargon, worrying that they may be co-dependent, love addicts, food addicts, drug addicts, toxic parents, abandoned children, Peter Pans, Cinderellas, narcissistic, borderline, feminist, misogynist or politically incorrect. When we're not consumed by these characterizations, we're searching for our inner child, wild man, wild woman, core self or true self.

All of these voices and labels carry the same underlying message: *the problems in your relationship are due to the failure of you or your partner to overcome some weakness or difference.* If you'd only communicate better, be more assertive, be less selfish, be more responsive in bed, get rid of your co-dependency, heal the wounds of childhood, love more, love less, or get in touch with your true nature, then you could find, keep and improve your marriage. If you don't somehow eliminate these differences with your partner, you'll never have the relationship you want.

But despite all these apparent solutions, couples continue to struggle with conflict, unhappiness and emotional numbness. And when the pain and distance become great enough, they confront the eternal couples' dilemma: *Do we give up on this relationship, or do we make a new commitment to each other?* Should we stay together and keep battling to fix this relationship? Or should we accept that our differences are just too great to overcome, write it off as a big mistake and move on?

For many years as a psychotherapist, I struggled with this same dilemma. Are the troubled couples who come to see me truly incompatible? Do I accept their belief that they just don't belong together, or do I invite them to take the difficult journey of working on their relationship?

I once worked with a couple on the verge of divorce. The wife would tell me with tearful conviction how her husband was impossible to talk to, constantly moody, a liar who would manipulate every interaction. He would repeatedly interrupt her, elucidating in great detail that she was an emotional basket case who could change from sweet and loving to yelling and screaming in a split second. I counseled a gay couple who had only two modes of relating: bursts of contained hostility or endless periods of dead silence. And I saw another couple whose nearly nonexistent lovemaking occurred only when he was demanding enough, or she felt obligated enough.

Yet these obviously "incompatible" couples, like so many I worked with, were able to turn their relationships around and regain the love and intimacy they had lost, while other couples with much less striking differences gave up on therapy in favor of painful, acrimonious breakups. What was making the difference? When did these troubled couples change their direction from separation to connection?

For each couple the key was going beneath all their obvious differences to truly experience the sameness that they shared. When they stopped focussing on the unacceptable qualities in their partners, they were able to find a basis for intimacy and joining.

How many times have you been around a particular couple and asked, "Why are they still together? As different as they are, why did they even get together in the first place? I can barely tolerate their constant arguing and complaining, how can they?"

The problem is, you're asking the wrong question. What you should be asking is, "Underneath all their drama and emotion, how are they the same?"

The alternative to the drama, pain and distance of the difference game lies in recognizing, accepting and integrating this single basic truth: *both partners in any intimate relationship are essentially the same.*

I am not saying that sometimes the two partners are the same, maybe they are the same, or even that they should be the same. I am saying that at the core level of their relationship, they are *always* the same. Because down deep, at the level of their fears and longings, their needs and desires, their real power and real vulnerability, they are absolutely equal.

Any couple's willingness to accept and expose their unacceptable thoughts, feelings and desires is identical for both partners. In other words, they have exactly the same capacity for real intimacy.

Here is where the real bond for any couple is formed. Their equal capacity for intimacy unites them and determines whether they will stay together. This underlying sameness is the glue that secures the relationship, and it is stronger than the opinions of parents, friends or therapists. It is even more powerful than any outward differences they exhibit.

This realization forms the basis of my entire approach to relation-ships—that the key to greater passion and intimacy is going beneath judgments and developing an attitude of equality. Moving beneath your outward differences and approaching your partner with an attitude of sameness and acceptance is the process I call *mutuality*.

Mutuality means dissolving the hierarchy and removing judgment from your relationship. It means developing a real acceptance and appre-ciation for all the thoughts, feelings and desires you have both struggled to hide or deny. Mutuality is a powerful attitude that replaces distance and separation with intimacy, passion and connection.

Once you embrace the sameness you share with your mate, less of your time and energy will be consumed by mental, physical and emo-tional power struggles. It is only at this underlying level of equality that mutual power and satisfaction are possible.

Mutuality neither denies nor hides the multitude of differences that you and your partner possess. But couples who approach each other out of mutuality can embrace their differences and are able to experience a much greater degree of both closeness and independence. Mutuality is not sacrifice for the sake of your partner or your relationship. It means being true to yourself and your own needs and desires while accepting those of your partner.

Our society conditions us to survive emotionally by finding faults in others (or in ourselves), and by proving that we have been victimized. As Aaron Kipnis and Elizabeth Herron say in *Gender War and Gender Peace*, "Men and women in today's society are equally wounded, in many different gender-specific ways, by a co-created culture that is equally sexist toward both. It treats men and women in different but equally harmful ways." Overcoming such an ingrained part of our per-sonalities and culture requires a powerful force. Strength must be matched with strength. We must recognize and accept our sameness with the same ease we see and judge our differences.

Merely adding another method to the mountain of methods for "relat-ing" to our partners is not enough. We must change our entire perception of our partners and ourselves.

I want to show you a deeper sense of equality and acceptance than you've ever encountered. To be on the same level as your mate is the most loving and spiritual experience the two of you can have. Only in this space, where there is no judgment, ranking or accusation, can the two of you see through your own projections and connect in a loving, passionate way. Intimacy cannot live in a state of judgment. Real intimacy is accepting and exposing all that you are in the presence of the one you love.

Couples who exhibit this level of intimacy are quite courageous because they fully surrender to whatever is exposed in their relationship. They don't label something negative and then look for ways to avoid this unacceptable experience. Instead they give themselves permission to fully live this part of themselves until it becomes their friend. As Thomas Moore says in *Care of the Soul*, "To care for the soul we must observe the full range of all its colorings, and resist the temptation to approve only of white, red, and orange—the brilliant colors."

With each piece of you that you no longer judge, you become that much less frightened and that much better at recognizing the same quality in your partner without the usual trepidation and judgment. Out of that humble recognition grows real connection and intimacy. Once your energy is no longer consumed with self-protection, it can be channeled into genuine passion.

I want to give you the support to see the sameness in your relationship regardless of the ways your partner behaves or reacts. Only from this position will the love you offer be pure—free of posturing, conditions and dependence. By seeing your sameness you no longer feed your distrust and insecurity, and you no longer need to attack or counterattack.

Developing the art of sameness is neither a free ride nor a fast one. I'm telling you straight up this is not an easy task. This book offers no quick fix, no catchy new labels to verify your differences and pigeonhole what's wrong with your relationship.

To pay lip service to mutuality is easy, but to truly integrate equality into your thoughts, attitudes and perceptions is not. We will be taking a challenging journey together. The road is bound to get rough, and there are obstacles at every turn. If it's not a journey you wish to make right now, I understand. No single path is for everybody.

Mutuality is an approach that must be learned. It invites you to change perceptions, beliefs and values you have held since childhood, and to risk moving beyond your familiar patterns to a much higher level of emotional risk.

To travel this road requires walking, not running. The important lessons in our lives require patience, delayed gratification, discipline and a willingness to be afraid. If you sprint down this road, you'll miss the splendor of the trip. Mutuality is not a destination, it is the journey itself.

The necessity of maintaining our deliberate pace will be evident in Part I, where I thoroughly examine every facet of the difference game. I must give you a complete picture of your current behavior before you can even consider doing anything new. Until you have deep understanding of how and why we use differences to distance ourselves, and until you see the effect such an attitude has on your relationship, you will never find the courage to move into the unfamiliar arena of mutuality.

Part II presents the alternative to the difference game by examining the components of mutuality. Understanding the goals, rules and consequences of an attitude of equality will enable you to make a conscious choice for either judgment or acceptance.

Part III leads you step by step through the process of shifting your perceptions from difference to sameness, and offers methods and exercises for achieving greater acceptance and intimacy.

Part IV applies the principles of mutuality to the most difficult issues confronting couples today, including sex, infidelity, addictions and abusive behavior.

Part V reveals how an attitude of equality and acceptance can even transform the pain of ending a relationship, and the frustration of finding a new one.

And finally, Part VI shows how mutuality can expand the passion and effectiveness of your entire life as you carry your attitude of equality into all of your relationships.

In writing this book, I work from the same underlying beliefs that I maintain with any new couple I treat:

1. If you are in a relationship, I will believe in and support that relationship until you prove me wrong.

2. Despite all appearances, rhetoric, behaviors and beliefs to the contrary, when it comes to your capacity for intimacy, you and your partner are exactly the same.

3. Far more couples are uncommitted than incompatible.

4. You are always in the relationship that is right for you at that particular moment, and it is providing you with whatever you need to learn.

As you will see throughout this book, I place a great deal of emphasis on the component of your psychological makeup I call the *protector*. This is the part that protects you from experiencing unacceptable thoughts, feelings, desires or images of yourself which would take you into the unknown and frighten you. Your protector will do whatever is necessary to prevent you from changing your familiar attitudes and beliefs, even those attitudes and beliefs which are destructive to you or your relationship.

In reading this book it's important to recognize the ways your protector will try to discount the new ideas you'll encounter. As you move from the difference game to mutuality, you're likely to hear yourself thinking things like, "This would never work for me," "My partner would never accept this," or "This is ridiculous."

I'm certainly not asking you to take any of these concepts on blind faith. I'm only suggesting that you risk opening yourself to a different way of seeing yourself and your partner. In order to do this, you will need to silence your protector enough to let new ideas in and truly experience the process of mutuality. This will enable you to see for yourself the effect that acceptance and equality can have on your relationship.

With that in mind, there are a few elements of mutuality that I want to mention immediately. All of these concepts will be explored more thoroughly in later chapters, but these particular issues are the ones most likely to be used by your protectors to support your resistance to change:

1. *The difference game is an unconscious process.* When I talk about the ways we move into positions of superiority or inferiority toward our partners, it may sound as if we do this honestly and intentionally. But the essence of the difference game is

that we disguise our judgmental behavior, even to ourselves. One of the primary goals of this book is to bring these attitudes and behaviors into your consciousness, so you can recognize the hidden ways you are distancing yourself from your partner.

2. *Mutuality does not imply the acceptance of all behavior.* This book is not a justification for any destructive, addictive or abusive actions. It is rather about recognizing and expressing the thoughts, feelings, images and desires that underlie the things we say and do so that we can assume a greater level of accountability and mastery over all our behaviors.

3. *Neither the difference game nor mutuality are gender specific.* I have done my best throughout this book to use both men and women as examples, and to switch back and forth randomly. Sometimes I purposely focus on gender stereotypes, and sometimes I go against them. Some examples refer to married couples, some to unmarried couples and some to gay or lesbian couples. But these are just examples. There is no element of any part of this process that is unique to either women or men.

4. *The process of mutuality does not depend on your partner.* One of the primary ways your protector will try to sabotage your desire for greater intimacy is to convince you that your partner will never cooperate. You may indeed have a spouse who shows no interest in this process or in achieving any change at all. He may even criticize or discount you for your needs and actions. But such a partner will not diminish the power of mutuality.

As you read this book, keep your focus on your own feelings and desires. Then lovingly tell your partner that you are going to be exploring some new ways of taking care of your needs. Tell him that you would like him to join you if he wishes but, if not, you are still going to pursue this process. In this way, you honor your own needs without putting him down or becoming his victim.

I know you may be asking yourself, "But what if he *never* changes?" That's your protector talking. Kindly but firmly tell your protector that you're not going to worry about that right now, you're simply concerned with yourself.

5. *Mutuality allows for the possibility of separation.* Another way your protector is likely to undermine your desire for greater satisfaction or intimacy is to bombard you with questions about whether you should leave your relationship. But before you even contemplate such an overwhelming decision, I encourage you to complete this book and experience the process of mutuality. This will enable you to develop the psychological, emotional and spiritual foundation for evaluating such a major life change. Then, if divorce is still a path you need to pursue, you will be ready to consider the process offered in Chapter 13.

   I certainly do not maintain that you can't outgrow your partner or your relationship, or that you may not choose to separate for various other reasons. But if you sustain a mutual attitude, whatever decision you make will be one that you can count on and respect over time.

Mutuality is a journey away from judgments and distance. Its very essence is to celebrate and experience all that we are and all that we bring to any relationship. So in making that journey, we must vigilantly resist the temptation to judge the very behaviors we're exploring.

In other words, it is not my intention to dissolve one hierarchy and then create a new one.

I am simply offering a different way of perceiving and connecting with your partner. I want you to consciously recognize and experience all the facets of your being. And if your goal is to discover an alternative path to love and connection on the deepest possible level, then this approach may hold the key.

I am not attempting to present mutuality as "better" than the difference game, because to do so would be to succumb to another judgmental attitude. If, in reading what follows, you discover places where I fail in this desire and slip into ranking and judgment, I apologize. It simply shows how seductive the difference game is, and how ingrained it is in our lives.

My deepest hope for this book is simply this:

Some methods focus on the darkness of your neuroses and try to lead you to the light.

Some methods focus on the light, in the hopes that the darkness will disappear.

My quest is to bring light to the darkness so that there is a blending and an integration of all that you are.

Prologue

THE BOTTOMLESS HOLE
A Fable of the Unknown

Once upon a time, in fact as long as there has been time, in a land similar to the one we all know, there lived a young pair of newlyweds. They were blissfully happy together in their lovely new home and it seemed as if nothing could ever go wrong.

Then one day, a mysterious event occurred which upset them a great deal. A small hole appeared in the middle of their living room floor. At first they thought they were just seeing things. Or perhaps they simply hadn't noticed it before. So they tried to simply ignore it, hoping it would go away.

Unfortunately, they soon realized the hole not only had not disappeared, it was actually getting bigger. They both peered over the edge of the hole, but neither could see anything inside—it seemed to be bottomless. This was very disturbing to the young couple, whose former happiness had now been replaced by worry and suspicion. What had caused this hole? Whose fault was it? How would they get rid of it? And what if someone found out their home had this awful opening in the middle?

They each tried whatever they could think of to deal with this blight on their lives, and to keep their loved ones from learning about it. First they threw an expensive rug over the hole, hoping that no one would notice. But soon the hole had grown too big to be covered up. Then they tried arranging furniture so that their hole wouldn't show. This plan didn't work very well either, as the room became so cluttered that it was hard to even move around.

Whenever anyone visited, the couple was terrified that their secret would be discovered. Even though they didn't dare risk bringing up the subject, they were pretty sure that none of the other couples they knew had an ugly hole in their home.

With each new failed attempt to disguise their hole, the couple's fear and embarrassment grew. And it wasn't long before they began blaming each other for this ever-widening gap. "He should have noticed this hole when we bought the house," the wife would mutter to herself. "Besides, he's a man, and men are supposed to know how to fix things."

Meanwhile, the husband would go off to work everyday saying to himself, "Our home is her job to take care of. It must be her fault this awful hole is still there. In fact, she must have done something wrong to make it appear in the first place."

It wasn't long before they began saying these things out loud to each other. But the more they fought and blamed each other, the faster the hole seemed to grow. Once in awhile one of them would be consumed by guilt, and would assume all the blame for the hole. But that didn't help either because the hole grew just as fast when they blamed themselves as when they accused each other.

The couple tried ignoring the hole by busying themselves with work or play or possessions. They thought maybe they could forget about this frightening emptiness in their home. Some of these attempts even succeeded for brief periods. But eventually the couple would tire of all this activity, and sooner or later all their new belongings would lose their charm. Then the two people would again face the undeniable fact that their home had an unwanted crater. Their faces would fill with familiar expressions of exhaustion, frustration and sadness as the couple contemplated their worst fear—that the hole would be with them forever.

By now, their early happiness together had become just a distant memory. Then something happened that seemed to turn things around.

They had a child! They were so thrilled and happy over their blessed event that the hole no longer concerned them. And indeed, as all this new love filled their home, the hole did seem to grow smaller. But sadly, it was not to last. As life returned to normal, back came the hole, as big and empty as ever.

Finally, the tension became so great that one day they exploded at each other, inflicting deep, hurtful wounds. When this happened, they were so upset to see the pain they were causing each other that the wife began to cry. "I'm sorry," she said. "I just miss how we used to be."

Hearing the sadness in her voice, the husband responded, "I'm sorry, too. I don't want to blame you anymore."

And at that precise moment something strange and sort of magical happened. The couple realized they weren't alone. Sitting on the edge of the hole was a little man.

The couple looked at each other in surprise. "Who are you?" the wife asked.

"I heard about your struggle with the hole in your home." he replied.

"How could that be?" asked the husband. "We never told anyone."

The little man saw the couple look at one another suspiciously, so he quickly answered, "Everybody has one."

This was astounding to the young couple. "No one ever said anything to us," the wife exclaimed.

"So what else is new?" the little man replied matter-of-factly.

The couple began to feel a great sense of relief and anticipation that they could finally talk to someone who understood about holes. "So," the husband asked eagerly, "how do we get rid of it?"

"You don't," the man answered.

Their faces fell. "We were hoping you could tell us what to do," said the wife in a pleading voice.

"I can," their visitor declared. "You can move somewhere else. Of course there won't be much point because there's going to be a hole wherever you go."

"So why even mention it?" grumbled the husband, who was feeling a bit frustrated.

Undaunted, the little man responded, "I just want to cover all your options. You can also split up. Then you wouldn't have to keep fighting about this and you could get on with your lives."

The couple looked at each other with worried expressions. "But we don't want to do that," they exclaimed simultaneously. "We love each other."

The little man nodded. "I suspected that would be your reply. Besides, in my experience that solution seldom works for very long. Sooner or later you'd be dealing with holes with your new partners. So your next choice is to just keep doing what you've been doing."

The husband was really getting aggravated now. "But what we've been doing isn't working!"

"True," the man said as he dangled his feet over the hole, "but if you don't, then you've only got one last option." The couple listened in anticipation as he paused for dramatic effect. "You can accept it."

This clearly wasn't the magical answer the couple had been hoping for. "But we have been," argued the wife, who was beginning to share her husband's frustration. "It seems like we've been putting up with this awful hole for as long as I can remember."

"I didn't say 'put up with it.' I said 'accept it.' I mean simply allow the hole to be in your home as a part of you." And with that the little man got up to leave.

The couple was so taken aback they were speechless. But as he reached the door the little man turned and gave them these parting words: "If you accept the emptiness as a friend, fullness is yours. If you regard it as an enemy, you'll be running and hiding forever." And with those words he was gone.

As they sat reeling from their engagement with the little man, the couple wasn't sure what it all meant. But because he had seemed so helpful and friendly, and because they didn't know what else to do anyway, they decided to trust some of what he said.

They sat down on the edge of their hole the way their visitor had. To say they were frightened would be an understatement. But as they gently took each other's hands, their fear began to fade.

When they realized they could touch the hole without falling in, smiles appeared on their faces. As they let their feet dangle over the edge, they began to laugh. They even began to sing "There's a Hole in the Bucket" and "We've Got the Hole World in Our Hands."

For the first time in a long time they weren't trying to hide or get rid of anything. And as they moved closer to one another while they faced the emptiness, they began to experience a deep sense of peace and harmony.

Eventually, as they went back to their normal lives, their acceptance of the hole faded and they again found themselves reacting to it with fear or anger. But then they remembered the little man's words, and once again found a way to join together and make the hole their friend.

And so it continued from that day on. Depending on how they reacted to it, sometimes their hole would get bigger, and other times smaller. It never went away, and it never stopped being frightening to them. But the more they allowed in all of the feelings stimulated by the hole, the greater their closeness and contentment became.

PART I

JUDGMENT

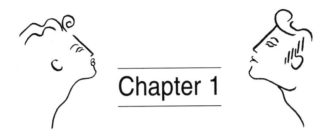

Chapter 1

LIFE ON THE SEESAW
The Difference Game

Individuals . . . when they are together,
often form a shared couple myth
that gives rise to many collective fantasies.
"If only the other would change!"

Joan Lachkar, The Narcissistic and Borderline Couple

All relationships that are unhappy, in trouble or stuck have one thing in common.

It doesn't matter what the disagreement is about, or who the individuals are. It makes no difference how big or little their issues appear to be, or how painful, dramatic or intense their confrontations.

No matter how heated the arguments or how icy the silences, no matter how deep the hurt or how strong the blame, the single common thread that runs through every troubled relationship is this

3

powerful, unshakable belief: *one of us is better than the other.*

In all my years as a therapist, I've heard countless issues, attitudes and actions criticized, defended and argued about. But the one thing that is always true for any two people who walk through my office door is that *both* of them believe beyond a shadow of a doubt that one is superior to the other.

Often each partner will fight to convince me that he (or she) is the superior one: more righteous, more reasonable, more understanding, more wronged. With other couples, one member will present a convincing argument that he or she is the inferior one: the failure, the helpless victim, the hopeless one, the cause of all the couple's problems. But whether either partner assumes the *up* or *down* position is of little importance, because the underlying attitude and belief is still the same: one of us is *more* and one is *less.*

Whatever the particular issue under discussion, and whomever each one regards as superior, the primary goal of both partners in an unhappy relationship will be to prove that they are essentially different from one another. Regardless of all the important and obvious similarities a couple may have, such as common interests or careers, shared goals and ideals, and mutual love for their children, they will continually use their differences to move either *up* or *down* in relation to each other.

> *After just three years of marriage to Charles, Wendy is beginning to feel like a whiny nag. While it appears she has a good marriage, with a nice home and a lovely child, she is increasingly dissatisfied. Behind closed doors she and Charles bicker constantly over their main issue: time.*
>
> *Wendy longs for more attention from Charles, while he claims he is giving her all the time he can, and that she is being unreasonable and unappreciative.*
>
> *Charles paints himself as a responsible, hard working guy who has to put in 60 hours a week to meet the demands of his stressful job. He also visits the gym four or five times a week to release the tension that builds up at work.*

When Charles finally arrives home in the evening, Wendy immediately greets him at the door, eager to interact. But his typical reaction is to move away from her, saying he needs space to unwind from his busy day.

If this encounter doesn't ruin the entire evening, Wendy's next attempt at closeness is usually on the couch after dinner, where she'll cuddle up to Charles and begin some verbal exchange. But Charles responds by claiming he's really tired and doesn't have much to say.

Wendy becomes upset and adamant about needing quality time together. She feels he at least owes her some time and attention during the few hours a day they have together. Charles counters that he'd like more time with her if she wasn't so demanding and aggressive.

Whenever Wendy fails to respect his boundaries, Charles accuses her of ignoring his needs. "After all," he declares, "it's not like I'm running around having affairs and going out with the guys. I do all of this to take care of you and give you the things you want."

Wendy sees herself as better than Charles regarding the issue of time together: "We'd have a great relationship if Charles would just respect my need for attention."

Charles sees himself as superior regarding the issue of independence: "We'd have a great relationship if Wendy would just respect my need for space." But both Wendy and Charles believe that the other is to blame for their problems.

Compare their attitudes to those of another couple:

After seven years of marriage, Bill and Sharon have decided to seek counseling to deal with their diminishing sex life. During their first session, they take turns complaining about how unresponsive each is to the other's needs. Bill grumbles with frustration about how cold Sharon has become whenever he wants to make love, while she tearfully proclaims that he doesn't really want to be close or intimate; all he wants is some nightly sexual release.

While Bill and Sharon are dealing with an issue you may consider more difficult than the one faced by Wendy and Charles, the way they use their differences is identical. Each partner is certain that he or she is the better one, and each will do whatever is necessary to maintain that position of superiority.

Sharon proclaims herself the winner in the "closeness and intimacy" contest, while Bill sees himself as the victor in the "sexual responsiveness" competition. The one thing they will both agree on is that one of them is clearly better than the other.

Now look at a slightly different example, where one of the partners assumes the less position:

> *Maddie and Ned had been married for six years when she learned he was having an affair. When confronted, Ned acknowledged that it had been going on for almost a year, but he promised to end the affair immediately.*
>
> *More than a year has passed, and Ned has been true to his word. But Maddie continues to confront him about his past infidelity whenever a new conflict arises between them.*
>
> *"Nothing I do to you could ever equal the hurt you caused us when you were sleeping with that woman!" Maddie proclaims tearfully.*
>
> *Guilty as charged, Ned hangs his head in emotional defeat. "I've said I'm sorry a thousand times. What more can I do?" The question hangs unanswered between them until their next confrontation.*

These two may seem different than the couples in the previous examples, since Ned and Maddie agree that he has wronged her with his affair. But the only real distinction is that they're not competing for the up position. Ned is satisfied to declare himself less than Maddie on the fidelity scale. This way, they both can continue to maintain that one is superior and one is inferior. Of course, it's very likely that Ned will eventually move to the up position by arguing that he has been more hurt by Maddie's lack of forgiveness than she ever was by his meaningless affair. Then a whole new drama can be played about who is more wounded and who is more forgiving. But the ensuing drama will only indicate that they've moved their conflict to a new arena. The underlying belief that *one of us is better* will remain unchallenged.

Situations like these are played out by couples a thousand times a day, with an unending list of complaints, criticisms, accusations and confessions being offered to friends, relatives, therapists and anyone else who will listen. The sources of the conflicts may seem as trivial as wearing too much makeup or as monumental as extramarital affairs and threatened suicide. But the relationships all exhibit the same underlying component: each partner believes that one of them is better and that one of them is less.

This universal tendency of partners in any troubled relationship to judge each other is what I call the difference game. The difference game is simply the interaction between two people who use their differences to justify an attitude of superiority or inferiority.

Couples playing this game are determined to prove that each partner is either more or less than the other. Every situation or interaction becomes an opportunity to create this hierarchical perception. The cardinal rule of this seesaw ride is for every thought, word and action to be viewed as either above or below a particular standard.

I don't call this familiar pattern the difference *game* to make it seem superficial or wrong. I use the term "game" to mean any activity with its own set of rules in which individuals agree, consciously or unconsciously, to participate.

I regard everything we do and every interaction we have as a game. Our only choices are which games to play, who to play them with and what significance to assign each game. Ultimately, a game will either work for us or it won't, depending on what we are trying to accomplish at any particular moment. If our desire is for greater intimacy, connection, growth or satisfaction, the difference game will move us away from those objectives.

As you will soon see, our universal tendency to focus on our differences in this way grows out of one of our strongest survival needs, so it is certainly not my objective to criticize or judge anyone for playing this particular game. I just want to bring the difference game into your consciousness, so you can clearly recognize the consequences of interacting with your partner in this way.

THE AUDIENCE FOR THE GAME

Partners playing the difference game will rarely limit their arguments to each other. They will try to persuade friends, family, co-workers, therapists and talk show hosts that the differences between them cannot be denied. To support their case, they exclaim, "How could we be the same, when I get things done quickly and she's so slow?" or, "Don't say we're not different. He's so repressed, and I'm very open."

Each partner will attempt to present the evidence that one of them is better in whatever style will most convincingly sway the listener. Some partners rely on the power of their logic: "I told her we had to leave at 7:30, I called her from work to remind her, I made sure I was ready fifteen minutes early, and she still wasn't dressed until quarter to eight! Can you think of any conceivable excuse for that kind of irresponsibility?" To an outsider hearing such step by step descriptions of one partner's behavior, it is nearly impossible *not* to believe that when it comes to punctuality, she is truly inferior.

Other difference game players replace logic with high emotional drama. Every issue is inflated, every action is indicative of some negative quality that permeates the entire relationship, and every situation is an opportunity for peak emotion: "He's been promising me for three years that he would remodel our house. But just like everything else that I might want, when I ask about it, he puts it off. I lose sleep at night over this, I'm embarrassed to show our house to our friends, and I feel betrayed whenever I look at that old kitchen. If he really loved me, he'd be willing to do this one thing, and he wouldn't keep breaking his promise. There is no way we can even talk about getting closer until he at least proves he'll keep his word and give me a decent place to live!"

It's pretty difficult to remain an objective listener when presented

with such an emotional account of the ways one partner has mistreated another, especially when the arguments are presented in an
innocent, tearful and sincere tone.

In the face of all the horror stories spouses tell about each other, it
isn't long before a couple's entire network of friends and relatives are
joining in the chorus: "Boy, are *they* a mismatch." "She's so wonderful and he's such an asshole." "He's so sweet and she's such a bitch."

Even in therapy, where a lot of time, money and discomfort are
endured for the presumed goal of greater closeness and intimacy,
couples maintain a powerful dedication to proving they are better or
less than each other. Though the stated objective of the couples who
come to me for counseling is always to improve their relationships,
sooner or later the difference game will dominate. Any thoughts of
greater closeness that the partners expressed at the outset are then
pushed far into the distance.

JUSTIFYING THE HIERARCHY

Obviously there are a multitude of differences between the partners in any relationship. One may like sports, while the other prefers
to read. A wife may enjoy big loud parties, while her husband likes
small intimate gatherings. And some individuals are characteristical-
ly generous in contrast to their frugal spouses.

Race, religion, physical makeup, background, education, age and
occupation are qualities that distinguish couples in every relationship. But these genuine differences are either biological, or they
reflect different interests, desires, upbringing and methods of pro-
cessing information.

The critical distinction between these objective differences and
playing the difference game is that the difference game *uses* differences between people to support a hierarchical attitude. When we
judge our differences, our ultimate goal is not greater understanding or
closeness, it is only to support our stance of superiority or inferiority.

In other words, whenever you're thinking about, discussing or
analyzing the differences between you and your partner, the critical

question to ask yourself is this: *Am I using our differences to make myself seem either superior to or less than my partner?*

If the answer is yes, then you're playing the difference game.

Consider the issue of gender differences. Because of physiology and conditioning, men and women perceive and interact with each other quite differently. The critical issue is not whether these differences exist, but how they will be used. When men put women down for valuing emotion, for example, or women critique men for their attachment to finding solutions, the underlying goal is superiority, not understanding.

In contrast, three recent authors have gone to great lengths to delineate the ways that male/female differences affect relationships. But these authors never use these distinctions as a basis for judgment.

Warren Farrell, in *Why Men Are the Way They Are*, sees men dominated by their primary fantasy of being sexually desired, while women are influenced by the fantasy of home and security. Tracy Cabot, in *How to Make a Man Fall in Love with You*, characterizes men as using primarily an auditory language of logic and understanding, in contrast to the woman's language of feeling and being touched by life's experiences. And Deborah Tannen, in *You Just Don't Understand*, illustrates the ways men and women differ in their perceptions of the same event. She states that men most frequently see things in terms of hierarchy and their social position relative to others. Their dominant goal is status and independence, and interactions are judged by whether the man feels superior or inferior to others. Women perceive the world in terms of intimacy and their connection with others. So for them, connection is the dominant goal, and interactions are judged on the basis of how close they feel toward the other person.

While all these works clearly describe and analyze gender differences, the concepts and theories are not presented in order to make women appear better or worse than men. Each author's goal is rather to increase individual understanding, and to help members of *both* sexes improve their relationships. (I will be discussing the issue of gender differences in much greater depth in Chapter 5, and suggesting how we can honor them without using them as a basis for judgment.)

THE "IF" CLAUSE

Critical to the difference game is the stated or implied belief that once the other partner changes, things will get better—that the only thing preventing a closer or more evolved relationship is the other person's weaknesses, shortcomings and unwillingness to change. In one form or another, this is the primary attitude presented to me by the couples I counsel.

The "if" clause can be applied to an infinite variety of desired traits:

If you were a better father. . .
If you were a better lover. . .
If you were more exciting. . .
If you were more open. . .

But the real intent of these statements is unvarying: *"I'm better than you are, and you're the one responsible for the problems in our relationship."*

In many instances, the "if" word is disguised or presented as a seemingly legitimate statement of fact: "He's very caught up in his work." But translated from the acceptable rhetoric, the speaker is really saying, "If he paid more attention to me and less to his business, we'd be a lot closer."

Sometimes the "if" statement is posed as a more legitimate-sounding question: "What if I'm willing to change and he isn't?" "What if I open up my feelings and she treats me like a wimp?" "What if I *do* stop nagging about his punctuality, and the kids never get to school on time?"

These questions are simply difference game statements in disguise. Translated, they mean: "We'd have a great relationship if he was more flexible and open." "We'd have a great relationship if she could accept my vulnerability." "We'd have a great relationship if he was more dependable."

DISGUISING THE GAME

The skill, subtlety and expertise we bring to the difference game often make it difficult to recognize. If we would simply declare, "I'm better than you!" our relationships would be much cleaner and easier to deal with. Such straightforward honesty would make it clear that the real issue was not one of money or sex or who took out the garbage, and we could confront each other about our real intentions.

Unfortunately, we're rarely willing to play the game so honestly or directly. For one thing, declaring superiority may be the American way on the gridiron, the campaign trail and the TV commercial, but it's generally regarded as domineering or bitchy in romantic relationships. Our desire to "look good" wouldn't allow us to be so forthright about our need to seem better than our mates.

More than that, the difference game depends on camouflage. This process of jockeying for the up or down position works most effectively when we remain unconscious. We must truly believe that it's our differences that are creating our problems and keeping us apart. To support this belief, we've managed to create several roles and disguises that prevent us from recognizing the game.

Good Partner/Bad Partner

When couples maintain an unspoken, unconscious agreement about one of them being better than the other, the superior partner will often play the role of the "good guy" in the relationship.

In their therapy sessions together, Marge described in great detail how her husband John repeatedly badgered her with his intense demands. He would select some topic that he felt a need to examine (her duties as a wife, their sex life, the way she pampered their son), and would then confront her with it, regardless of her willingness or openness to discuss it.

If Marge resisted his haranguing, John would chase her from room to room, verbally abusing her, subjecting her to half-hour lectures and accusing her of being irresponsible, sexless, spineless and dishonest. If this failed to get a reaction from her, he would grab her by the arms and start screaming at her.

As tears streamed down her cheeks, Marge shared these accounts of John's behavior, and her own helplessness, in a quiet, pain-filled voice. Any rage she felt at his behavior remained completely hidden.

If confronted about his actions, John always presented several half-hearted justifications: "I don't know how else to get through to her." "She doesn't respond to logic." "I can't help it; I just lose control sometimes." But ultimately he would always admit to being out of line, and then make an awkward attempt at an apology.

By repeatedly carrying on in this way, Marge and John were both doing what was necessary to give the impression that one of them was better by maintaining her "good girl" image and his "abusive husband" image.

I don't contend that John's aggression was proper or justifiable, or that Marge's response was the most appropriate or effective. I only want to illustrate how both partners were jointly (unconsciously) participating in the illusion that she was better than he was. He was controlling the relationship with his aggression; she was controlling it with her withdrawal.

Because our society finds withdrawal more "acceptable" than aggression, she seems superior. If, in reading this example, you're convinced that Marge is in fact better, then their camouflage is working.

With some couples I encounter, one partner takes the role of the intimate member, while the other plays at being distant. Other couples portray one as the committed member of the relationship, while the other is "unable to commit."

But with all these good guy/bad guy routines, looking good and looking bad are just for appearance. The underlying goal is to sustain the hierarchy. So, whenever I listen to an emotionally open, articulate woman and an emotionally numb, psychologically unsophisticated man, I keep reminding myself that they are a team, and these are just the roles they've unconsciously agreed to play.

These couples are not consciously trying to deceive me, nor do they even realize they are conspiring to play the difference game. On the contrary, both partners believe wholeheartedly that their relationship will get better only when I acknowledge the fact that one of them has to improve.

Covert Superiority

While some partners are very blatant about proclaiming their superiority to their mates, others prefer a subtler, more covert style. The overt partner in a relationship makes it easy to recognize the difference game in action. You'd have to be pretty dense not to get the message when you hear, "He's an insensitive creep," or, "All she ever does is nag." But the more covert partner is much trickier.

Consider a statement like, "We haven't spent a lot of intimate time together because he is involved in an important project at work," or, "I'd like to make love more, but she's just too exhausted at night after being with the children all day." On the surface, these sound like perfectly innocent, objective statements of difference, conveying no superiority or inferiority at all. The speakers even seem to be lovingly considerate of their partner's needs. But underneath lurks their superior stance: *"I'm more willing to be intimate than my mate is."*

Sometimes the up stance is hidden behind such seemingly open, inviting statements as, "To have a growing relationship, it's really good to be committed," or, "I really feel we need to be more honest in our relationship." Translated into the language of their true intent, these statements are really saying, *"I'm more committed than you,"* and, *"You're a liar."*

Because of the discomfort most of us feel around the issue of intimacy, it is a major arena for disguising the difference game. I often hear men say to their wives (usually in their most soulful voice), "I'm sorry I can't satisfy you," when the message they're really conveying is, *"You're a bottomless pit. No one could satisfy you."* When women respond in kind with the seemingly presentable statement, "I can't connect with you," what they really want to say is, *"You're a withdrawn, emotional corpse."*

I frequently encounter individuals whose superiority is contained in their mistaken perception that they are truly too powerful for their partners. Revealing this belief openly to their spouses would pose a threat to their relationships, because it would imply that they are a mismatch. So instead of risking the unwanted separation that would result, they prefer to hide their up position behind an unspoken belief that their silence and pretense are truly protecting their partners. One such client confided to me, "If I really stood up for myself, I'd blow my husband out of the water."

Instead of declaring, "My partner isn't as strong as I am emotionally," these difference game players constantly monitor and hide their thoughts and feelings. But, despite these efforts, their resulting superiority leaks out indirectly through criticism and put-downs.

Jargon

Because talk shows, seminars and shelves full of self-help books offer endless opportunities to evaluate our relationships, many individuals have developed an extensive vocabulary of justifications and explanations for the differences between them and their spouses.

If a friend says to you, "My husband is a putz," it's pretty clear that she's assuming a position of superiority. But it's hard to do anything but nod in agreement if she explains, "Because my husband came from a dysfunctional family, he has a strong control need, and his co-dependency makes it difficult for him to expose his vulnerability."

The added pitfall of each new psychological approach is that it can easily become another basis for playing the game. I once had a client who attended a workshop based on the book *A Course In Miracles*. She was very excited about learning the value of letting go of judgments. She then spent her next therapy session criticizing her husband because *he* was too judgmental.

The Silent Gun

Most of our spouses would be emotionally devastated if they listened in on our private accusations and judgments about them. We all like to play the difference game inside our heads, while retaining an outward attitude of silence or complacency. With the absence of any overt expressions of superiority or inferiority, this method of disguising the game can be the deadliest. Free of the constraints of anyone else's possible reaction to our statements, our silent judgments tend to annihilate our partners.

I've had female clients who said to me, "He's a fragile cripple," "I don't find him sexual at all," and, "He's more like a brother than a lover." And from my male clients I've heard comments such as, "She's not very bright," or "I settled for second-best when I married her." The fact that these comments are not shared with partners or that the feelings behind them are unknown to their spouses does not mean that the difference game isn't being played. The intent is still one of superiority. And it's a safe bet that these inner voices are being acted out in the relationship in the form of "helpful" criticism, sarcastic comments, jokes to friends, emotional distance or in some other antagonistic way.

The Disguised Task

Much of the communication that occurs between couples involves the various tasks that permeate their lives. From raising children to buying toilet paper, an endless array of activities can occupy relationships. Yet, it is rare that these tasks remain simply tasks. Quite often they become vehicles for proving one partner is better or less.

By putting all the focus on the task, no one needs to openly expose this underlying agenda. Instead, "taking the kids to school" can be transformed into a measure of superior love or responsibility. Or a husband can describe how hard he works at the office as a way of saying that he contributes a lot more to the marriage than does his wife.

Since we have so many tasks to perform, the opportunities for proving superiority are endless. And the beauty of all these issues is that the message is easily disguised by the safety and objectivity of the activity. "I wasn't putting you down. I was just talking about feeding the cat."

RECOGNIZING THE GAME

Awareness is death to the difference game. To play effectively, you must ignore, disguise or deny your participation at all times. The decision to play is entirely unconscious. On a conscious level, you'll simply find yourself zeroing in on something your partner does, and before you know it, you're caught up in the same familiar drama.

Difference game players create all kinds of disguises to hide the fact that superiority (or inferiority) is where they feel most at home. So to determine if you're in the midst of a match, ask yourself these particular quesitons about your thoughts, emotions and behaviors:

1. When we interact, are my eyes usually somewhere else, rather than looking into my partner's?
2. Is my body contracted and on guard?
3. Is my voice loud, grumbly, whiny, mousy or constricted?
4. Do I immediately notice what's wrong with anything I do or my partner does—how it falls short of perfection?
5. Do I feel like I'm either chasing or avoiding my partner?
6. Am I suspicious?
7. Am I ready to pounce?
8. When we disagree, do I hang in there however long it takes, until I can prove my point once and for all?
9. Do I make a lot of dramatic physical gestures?
10. Do I focus on whether my partner is exhibiting these behaviors, rather than myself?
11. Do I repeatedly evaluate our relationship on a regular basis?
12. Am I unhappy, unsatisfied or depressed?

When you experience these actions and feelings, you can be pretty sure you're maintaining a stance of judgment and hierarchy toward your partner.

THE TWO POSITIONS OF THE GAME

While the verbiage, gestures and subject matter of the difference game can be endless, and the emotion and drama can seem enormous, in truth the game offers little variety. No matter how much apparent movement there is, participants are restricted to only two positions: up and down.

Playing the difference game is like riding a seesaw: it can take a lot of energy, it can even be exciting, but the only places you can go are either above or below your partner. If you feel more rewarded and acceptable in the superior position, then you'll expend your energy proving that you are better than your partner. If you prefer the comfort or familiarity of being inferior, you'll find ways to prove you are less. These are your only two choices.

For the most part, the up position is the preferred stance, since it gives us a sense that we are very powerful and it's generally favored by society. From early childhood we are taught that superiority is the cure for anything that makes us unhappy.

Be special.
Look better.
Achieve more.
Be on top.
Be number one.
Be the best.

Our daily diet is filled with these expressions. How could we help but fall in love with superiority?

Unfortunately, our love affair with up images puts us on a constant treadmill. Those of us who are attached to the power of up have difficulty sharing our thrones with our mates. We don't want to run the risk of losing our hard-won superiority. So, we'll do our best to keep our partners in the down position.

While inferiority is rarely regarded as anything worthwhile, it's almost impossible to avoid because up and down only exist in relation to each other. What we often fail to recognize is the immense amount of power and control over a relationship that the partner in the down position exerts.

Jim is a master of helplessness, even though he seems com-

pletely unaware of the ways he uses this trait. His wife Teresa is quite assertive, intelligent and articulate. While Jim can exhibit these same qualities in the work place, emotional and psychological interactions with Teresa are apparently beyond his abilities.

Teresa makes all kinds of attempts to get him to talk about their relationship, including their conflicts and their feelings toward each other. His response to her prodding and questioning is always, "I don't know," "Fine," or, "Nothing's going on. Why do you ask?"

Whenever she expresses her immense frustration at his lack of response, he innocently proclaims his helplessness at pleasing her: "I just can't seem to satisfy you."

Teresa has clearly assumed the up position in all these interactions. They both agree that she is better at communicating and that Jim is the one with the problem. Yet, despite her "superiority" in the let's-get-in-touch-with-our-feelings game, it's Jim's helplessness that rules their relationship. All her interpersonal knowledge and experience are unable to dent his façade of inability. And, until he recognizes the power he has over her, he's unlikely to give up his inferior position.

Inferiority is much easier to sustain than superiority and requires far less effort. Putting forward our inadequacies and settling into an attitude of less is much easier than constantly having to prove how great we are. And when we're in the down position, we don't have to worry about letting our guard down and falling off our superiority pedestals, the way people in the up position do. We're already at the bottom.

The greater familiarity of the down position also makes it a source of safety and security. Even though we may never admit it, inadequacy is a feeling we have all repeatedly experienced.

Our relationships offer us countless opportunities to feel less than adequate. Rather than risk competing in all those arenas, it is often easier to just lie in our well-known pools of failure and listen to our predictable internal voices express their "shoulds," "what ifs" and excuses. We may feel discouraged or depressed, but at least we're on familiar ground.

TRADING PLACES

Like any ride on a seesaw, the difference game involves a constant exchange of positions between the two players. In any given situation, one partner may choose to be up and the other down, but as the interaction continues, the roles may very likely reverse.

Janice and Bonnie are a lesbian couple who have been together for several years. Bonnie is in an almost continuous state of illness or infirmity, and Janice takes on the role of "helper" whenever her lover is bedridden.

For Janice, this role of nurse and caretaker provides a constant opportunity to stay in the up position. She lives in a place of superiority because Bonnie is so dependent on her. This enables Bonnie to latch onto the down position.

But, whenever Janice feels powerless to remove herself from Bonnie's constant dependency, Janice assumes the down position. She is now the helpless one, unable to get away from her lover's demands, and Bonnie is now superior, controlling their relationship with her physiological needs.

As with most people living on the down end of the seesaw, Bonnie would never admit her power over her lover—to do so would violate her stance of being less. She'll only say, "I'm sick. It's not as if it's something I wanted or caused. I don't have any choice in the matter."

Every superior person possesses a hidden inferior stance, and within every inferior person is a superior component. We ultimately all desire the power of superiority. We just have different ways of achieving it.

Up and down differ only in their directions, never in their objectives. I often joke with my "inferior" clients that my "superior" clients thank them for providing someone for them to look down on.

The moment either partner denies this mutual dependency, they'll be back into the conflict of the difference game.

VALUES AND JUDGMENTS

The nearly continuous desire to go one-up or one-down is not limited to couples who are unhappy in their relationships. The entire culture encourages participation in the difference game in one form or another. Not a single trait humanity possesses has escaped society's major pastime: playing favorites.

Every human quality exists on some continuum, including honesty and dishonesty, order and disorder, introversion and extroversion, power and helplessness, intelligence and ignorance, beauty and ugliness, and all the other infinite facets of the human condition. But, as you look over each pair of qualities in the previous sentence, you'll always recognize one end of each continuum as the positive or favored of the two. Chances are that as you read the list above, the items you instinctively regarded as superior were: honesty, order, extroversion, power, intelligence and beauty.

Your own experience and conditioning may have taught you to regard one of the opposite qualities as superior, such as introversion over extroversion. You still haven't escaped putting value judgments on each end of the continuum; your judgments are just different from someone else's.

Assuming a difference game posture doesn't require a great effort on your part. The seeds are planted whenever you idealize a personality trait and take pride in that part of your identity. You'll then be on guard whenever you're confronted by it's opposite attribute. So if you pride yourself on being an extremely sensitive person, it's pretty easy to imagine your attitude toward insensitive people. Such an attachment to *any* quality, no matter how righteous it seems on the surface, automatically positions you for the difference game.

In *A Book for Couples*, Hugh and Gayle Prather refer to this tendency quite graphically:

. . . you simply cannot . . . think it important that you are a person who chews politely without also judging your mate for munching like a horse. You cannot think it important that you are one who puts dirty underwear away and the toilet seat down without also judging your spouse as having the sensitivity of a dung beetle.

With such overwhelming cultural support for playing favorites, and so many opportunities to move up or down, it's almost impossible *not* to be judgmental. You carry inside you a constant invitation to regard every action, thought and feeling you experience as either better or less.

Even our language conditions us. Our everyday speech consists of countless "*-er*" words: bigg*er*, bett*er*, weak*er*, smart*er*, cheap*er*, strong*er*. Every "*-er*" word contributes to hierarchical thinking and becomes another basis for playing the game. A state of unending competition is maintained, with the up position always remaining the prized objective.

Applying values to various qualities, traits and behaviors is not in itself the problem. Our values give us our ethics and our morality, help sustain and elevate our humanity, and can make the world a more loving, livable place.

It's the way you *use* these values which determines their effect on your relationship. When they form the basis for believing you're superior to your partner, then you're playing the difference game. And with society championing favoritism, it's hard even to realize you're playing. With so many people labeling everything as either positive or negative, and no contrasting behavior that would present an alternative to the game, you remain blind to exactly what you're doing.

Society makes it doubly difficult to escape the difference game if you're in a couples relationship, due to the preponderance of cultural stereotypes about men and women:

Men are insensitive.
Women have less sexual desire.

Men are uncommitted.
Women are irrational.
Men are workaholics.
Women are fragile.

The list is endless, and each stereotype provides additional evidence that one partner is better or less than the other. The recent outpouring of books about relationships with men, with titles like *Cold Feet: Why Men Don't Commit, Men Who Can't Love,* and *Men Who Hate Women and the Women Who Love Them* has served to strengthen the negative characterizations of men, and has provided terrific material for the difference game. For women wanting to go one-up on boyfriends or spouses, these are best-selling verifications of the many ways men are inferior.

I didn't mention any self-help books for men that overtly elaborate on the negative qualities of women because those books haven't been written yet. In the meantime, men will somehow have to get by with the tried-and-true methods of seeing women as inferior.

The problem with society's love for choosing better and less, and resorting to stereotypes, is that the "lesser" qualities or behaviors are automatically regarded as negative *in total*, without any positive or redeeming value attached to them. Each stereotype in the list above carries with it an obviously negative implication. You never hear any applause for a woman who is described as irrational, or a man who is scared of commitment.

In fact, irrationality might indicate more creativity, more freedom of thought, more passion and more likelihood of finding original solutions to society's problems. And an unwillingness to commit might reveal caution, independence or honesty. But in society's eyes, individuals wearing these labels are low on the totem pole, and they should strive to achieve the higher status that comes from being rational or committed.

The difference game underlies so much of our daily lives. Without this hierarchical attitude there would be no war, no suicide, no bigotry and no physical abuse.

Think about it. Can you imagine a war without each side believing itself better than the other? Can I commit suicide without feeling less than others? Is bigotry ever based on anything but feelings of superiority? And could a husband beat his wife, or parents abuse their child, without clinging to a belief in their own superiority? Even groups oriented toward spiritual oneness get caught up in the illusion of the difference game and are soon chanting, "Our group is more evolved than your group."

Like so many of the negative conditions that surround our lives, these facets of humanity are driven by a deep desire to be better than others. Without the need to feel superior, there would be no drive to sustain these actions, and they would disappear. If we weren't caught up in proving and justifying our superiority, we would no longer feel the need to prove our worth with excessive amounts of money, possessions, power, violence, sex or status. One of the primary goals of this book is to expose the fact that the difference game is based on an illusion—the belief that one of the partners in a troubled relationship is somehow better than the other, and if the "lesser" partner would only change, the relationship would improve.

As one last example of how easy it is to turn anything into an opportunity for the difference game, consider this very chapter. Everything I've said is intended solely to present a clear picture of what the difference game is—to describe all the ways we tend to use differences between us as opportunities to seem better (or less) than others.

Your initial reaction to these ideas may have been, "That makes sense," or, "Yeah, my spouse and I do that. Our relationship *would* be a lot better if we stopped trying to prove we were each better than the other."

But this is where you have to watch out for the insidious nature of the difference game. If you move away from simply observing the way the game works and begin judging yourself and your spouse for playing it, you're climbing back onto the seesaw.

If you begin thinking things like, "What if I'm willing to stop being superior, but she's not?" or, "I'd love to stop making judgments about our differences, but he'd never be able to," then you're moving into a superior position about the game itself. The underlying meaning of what you're thinking is, *"I'm better at avoiding the difference game than my partner is."*

If your reactions are more along the lines of, "This is hopeless. I'll never be able to give up judgments," then you've moved to the down position regarding the issue of being judgmental. Either way, you're seeing yourself as superior or inferior to your partner.

Welcome to the game.

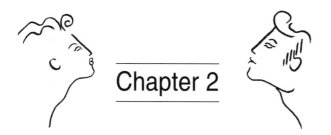

Chapter 2

PROTECTION FROM THE UNKNOWN
The Goal of the Difference Game

The fact that Dwayne and Corrine have been married for three years amazes their family and friends, who have witnessed or heard about the intensity of the couple's repeated battles.

Though they have never resorted to physical attacks, their fights seem endless, broken only by occasional icy silence and withdrawal. Even the presence of a four-month old baby, whom they both love dearly, has failed to diminish either the frequency or the duration of these confrontations. Arguments lasting hours, or even days, are the rule rather than the exception, with their accusations and recriminations escalating to threats of, "I can no longer live with someone like you."

In therapy, Dwayne expresses great frustration and resentment toward Corrine's constant demands for him to change. "First she insists that I be more patient, then less irritable, then more open. It never ends!

"Even when I think I've met one of her needs, I don't get a moment of enjoyment or appreciation because she's quickly on to her next demand. I can't even satisfy her in bed, because it's never quite the way she wants it. I've stopped even trying. I spend all my time trying to get her to agree that I've met even one of her demands, but she never has enough proof. I'm always reduced to zero."

Corrine, of course, paints a very different picture: "Whatever I share with him, he flies into a rage. The least little request, or even some innocent statement leads to some overblown reaction, with him yelling or calling me names. I feel like I have to walk on eggs.

"I keep telling him I'm suffocated by his tirades. I dread coming home, knowing he's going to jump on me for something I said or did. But as soon as I point out what he's doing, the fights begin again. We just go 'round and 'round until I get exhausted or he gives me his goddamn silent treatment. I can't live like this!"

Dwayne and Corrine are clearly on the verge of divorce, right? It's obvious they both find the relationship intolerable, and one or the other is always threatening to leave.

But they don't.

Why? Why do they continue to stay together despite all the pain and dissatisfaction they both feel? Why doesn't one of them leave, or why don't they stop treating each other in ways that are obviously keeping them apart and making their lives miserable? Why do a million couples like Dwayne and Corrine, in spite of saying they want their relationships to change, continue to play the difference game?

The answer is simple. They stay on the seesaw because it offers them something that greater freedom, or greater intimacy, will not: *protection.*

On some deep, even unconscious, level, couples believe that no matter how awful the constant fighting, blaming, emptiness or help-lessness of their relationship, there is something even more painful that would be worse. So they continue playing the difference game to protect themselves from the horrible consequences that changing their behavior would bring.

What is this terrible danger? What could we perceive as so terri-fying that any alternative pales in comparison? Only one thing: *the unknown*.

It is our greatest fear, and our strongest motivator. It's at the root of every other fear we face, and our desire to avoid it will drive us harder than any other punishment or reward.

Perhaps you believe that your biggest fear is heights, or a tax audit or public speaking. Or if you're fluent in the language of psy-chotherapy, you may think it's abandonment, engulfment or intima-cy. Or maybe it's simply death.

But at the base of all these fears is the single quality that makes them so frightening: they take you into the unknown.

We are only terrified by what is unfamiliar to us. In the realm of the unknown, we can neither predict nor control what will happen. We are floating unconnected, with no life lines. Our familiar world, where we know we can survive, is gone, and we are totally helpless and vulnerable. Everything we know and depend on has ceased to exist, so we're afraid *we* will cease to exist.

In contrast, anything we experience repeatedly becomes tolerable to us. This is why the difference game is so appealing. What could be more familiar than feeling better or less than someone, or convincing yourself you're superior or inferior? Most of us have been practicing this all our lives. It may be negative or painful, but it's not in the class of the unknown.

Earl had been married to Nancy less than a year, and they had begun therapy because of his great concern about her children. Earl would get tremendously upset over their behavior, their con-flicts, their way of relating to him and their lack of discipline. On one occasion he actually left home and moved into a hotel.

"I just can't handle all this instability!" he declared, as he once again described the chaos he observed in his new family.

I had worked with Earl before, so I knew a great deal about his past. He had been up and down his entire life, had been on drugs, gone straight, been in the gutter, and was now married to someone I knew was very committed to him.

When Earl finished this latest lament about his volatile home life, he turned to me for verification that this situation with his stepchildren was indeed intolerable. But instead I asked him, "How much do you trust me?"

"More than anyone," he replied.

"That's good," I said, "because I'm about to tell you something that goes against everything you believe.

"All this talk and drama about your stepchildren is bogus. Sure, you have some adjustment problems like all new stepparents. But on a scale of one to ten, they'd rate about a two. You're treating them like they're a nine. Something's behind all this emotion.

"You say you can't stand all this instability, but I don't buy it. Instability is where you've always lived. It's stability you can't tolerate.

"If I had a map of your life on the wall, and I put up a stickpin for every unstable situation, they'd fill the map. But if I had to put up pins for the stable moments in your past, I bet I wouldn't use more than two.

"You're in the most stable family you've ever experienced, and it's terrifying you. And until you realize that that's what you're afraid of, the situation won't get any better."

Earl responded in humble silence as he struggled to recognize the truth about his behavior. But Nancy positively lit up. She understood that all of Earl's drama reflected a much deeper fear than he had ever acknowledged.

It was Earl's fear of moving into the unknown and experiencing stability that he avoided above all else. He had constructed an elaborate system of complaints, behaviors and justifications to protect himself from this unfamiliar situation.

Notice how relatively easy it was to disguise his real fear. We seldom hear the chant, "Stability is my enemy, and instability is my friend." So for Earl, reversing the truth and proclaiming what seemed obvious simply justified his avoidance of the unknown.

Look back at the anecdote that opened this chapter. Fighting, debating and blaming each other are quite familiar for Dwayne and Corrine. But as dramatic and painful as all this drama might be, it still protects them from experiencing what is far less familiar, and far more frightening.

For Corrine, this unknown experience is commitment. She grew up with a very distant father, and took on the belief that men would never take care of her. Seeing men as distant and undependable became familiar and safe. So to really rely on a man and surrender fully to him is now terrifying.

Corrine even said once, "I will never marry an ordinary man. Ordinary men will always disappoint you. I want somebody special." This is what I term "keeping the door open." Whenever partners retain some justification for their fantasies about leaving, they are refusing to close the door and surrender fully to their relationship. Sooner or later all men turn out to be "ordinary," so Corrine's declaration keeps the door open and protects her from experiencing the unknown. Fighting with Dwayne is certainly less painful than facing her fear of fully committing to him.

Dwayne's major issue is disappointment. The excessive responsibilities placed on him as a child were so great that he felt he had been "robbed of his childhood." His family's demands made it essential that he see himself as superdependable, able to take care of others with never a hint of inadequacy. To feel another person's disappointment would be to face his fear of this unknown experience.

Dwayne long ago vowed that no woman would ever control him by expecting things of him or expressing disappointment in him. His defensiveness, rage and withdrawal are his protection against unknown experiences of his own inadequacy. He keeps the door open with his fantasies about a woman who will ask for nothing and will never be disappointed.

You may now have a clearer picture of what a perfect match Dwayne and Corrine are. Yes, they have tons of differences. Yes, they can yell and scream and keep each other at a distance. But down deep, both are terrified of closing their individual doors and moving into the unknown.

For one couple, the "unknown" that they fear might be separation, so they cling tightly to each other; for another it might be closeness, so the difference game allows them to maintain their distance. Independence, conflict, intimacy, passion, contentment, powerlessness—the possibilities for what constitutes the unknown are endless. The key is in recognizing whatever unknown feelings or experiences frighten *you*, and the ways you're protecting yourself from them.

If you're still not convinced that the unknown is such a big deal, just imagine this:

You approach your mate in your customary way, carrying all your usual beliefs and expectations, and knowing exactly how she'll act in return.

But she doesn't.

Suddenly she responds in completely unpredictable ways. You move forward, expecting her to move back, but she holds her ground. You expect her to react when you do your usual dance, but she doesn't. You expect her to turn helpless and clutching when you start to move away, but she just looks straight into your eyes in a way that makes you feel naked.

You decide this is a come on, and you attempt to sexualize the encounter, hoping this will put you on familiar ground. But in a way so gentle you hardly realize what happened, she indicates this is not the moment for that.

You begin to feel lost. You've shot your usual routine, and you're still in unknown territory. So you move into higher drama. You know she'll get defensive if you resort to your aggressive act. But she doesn't. You can't even depend on her to push you away, or accuse you of letting her down, or judge you as "not enough."

You feel totally stripped of all you've ever known in being with a woman. Your entire cognitive mind is totally worthless. So you feebly put out some words to indicate that you want to talk about what is happening. Moving into an intellectual discussion has always worked before. But she responds with a look that seems to make any discussion irrelevant.

Now your whole body begins to tremble. You're as uncomfortable as hell, but your mind wakes up and says, "She'll probably judge you for that move. It won't feel good, but at least her criticism is familiar."

No such luck. She merely smiles and indicates that she understands. You're with a woman you thought would never exceed your expectations, and you're left helpless by her astonishing offer of acceptance and intimacy.

Or, if that scenario doesn't strike home, perhaps you can . . .

Imagine you're with a man who is attractive and desirable. Envision how you will feel and respond if he shatters your beliefs and expectations. He comes toward you and shares his love for you. He wants you sexually only when you're ready. He tells you he will always be there for you, and that he doesn't need you to please him. He wants only for you to be who you are.

Sounds blissful, doesn't it? He sounds like the man of your dreams. But try to imagine how you would truly feel in such a situation. Would you trust this man? Would you really let him in with your heart and your sexuality? Or would surrendering to this unknown experience be too frightening? Could you really resist projecting some negative quality on him? Could you avoid turning guarded, dependent, distant, moody, or suspicious?

Would you eventually judge him or accuse him of something? If not, then how would you cope with the unknown? How would you protect yourself?

I am certainly dramatizing the issue with these fantasies. But ask yourself this, "How many times has my partner taken just a step in the direction of the unknown, and I responded in one of the ways described above? How often has his or her movement toward either closeness or distance resulted in my feeling afraid, judgmental or helpless?"

THE BIRTH OF OUR TERROR

Most of us entered the world from a very safe environment. We had it all: shelter, food, comfort and no demands. This was the ultimate: a place of total connection, total safety, total familiarity.

And then the cord was cut. From then on, we were on our own and life became an uphill struggle. There was an enormous feeling of helplessness, abandonment and disconnection. We were robbed of the safety of our known world and plunged into an unknown existence of discomfort and separation. We began to see ourselves as disconnected. We felt little and alone in a vast, intimidating world, and longed for those lost feelings of connection and safety. Out of that experience grew a deep fear that we wouldn't survive. So we began protecting ourselves.

A Course in Miracles, a text on spiritual psychotherapy, refers to the issue of separation as the only problem we really have. Everything else that we label as problems are actually attempts to bridge our fear of being unconnected to anything familiar.

A Course in Miracles views this feeling of separation as an illusion that we have imposed on the reality of our lives. This powerful book, which forms the foundation for the work of such authors as Marianne Williamson, Gerald Jampolski, and Hugh and Gayle Prather, presents a process for recognizing and accepting our true connection to both the physical and spiritual world, to bring us real peace and fulfillment.

But even if our feelings of disconnection are an illusion, our deep seated belief in our separation is so strong that the terror we feel is very real.

The degree of separation you perceive is very dependent on the kind of family environment you enter. The more unpredictable and unstable your childhood home, the greater your disconnection and fear of the unknown, and the more frantically you will try to protect yourself.

In *Awaken the Giant Within*, Anthony Robbins asserts that our primary motivation is the avoidance of pain. I believe our greatest pain is our grief at picturing ourselves separate and alone, and believing that we will never again find a connection that will truly feed us.

As we look from our state of vulnerability toward the path that lies before us, we feel impotent, lost and extremely frightened. Our only hope is to find sufficient protection and power to compensate for these feelings of helplessness. If we don't, our world will be entirely out of control and our fate will be completely unknown.

THE PROTECTOR

The means we devise to protect ourselves from this fear of the unknown doesn't just occur in some hit-or-miss fashion. It is a well-conceived plan, methodically laid out and executed by that part of ourselves I call the "protector."

Each of us possesses this entity within ourselves. He is the guardian of our comfort zone, the one who determines what is acceptable for us to experience. If he thinks it's too risky or scary for us to go beyond our usual capacity, or if he perceives a threat coming from the outside, he'll pull us back into the protection of our familiar behavior.

This protector is similar to what Alice Miller characterizes in *The Drama of the Gifted Child* as the false self. When we're wounded or frightened as small children, we unconsciously decide that we can't tolerate that amount of pain or fear. To overcome our anxiety, we disguise the parts of ourselves that are most likely to be hurt or abandoned. We create false selves to hide behind so that we'll never have to expose those unacceptable parts, and never be that frightened or hurt again.

The protector you construct will depend on whatever factors in your formative physiology or environment affected you the most. If, for example, childhood displays of anger led to severe punishment or abandonment, then you probably see anger as a threat to your survival, and your protector will do whatever is necessary to keep you from experiencing it.

If you grew up in a volatile environment where temper tantrums were the only way to get attention, then your protector will keep you in that mode of behavior whenever you feel threatened with any kind of neglect or abandonment. Your false self will be allowed to yell or scream all it wants. But stillness, listening or any other behavior that would move you toward unknown feelings of separation or longing will always be unacceptable.

Other psychological approaches label this protective component your persona, mask or ego. But whatever the label, its function is the same: to provide you with a familiar identity you can cling to, one that will keep your unacceptable thoughts, feelings and desires hidden.

There is no limit to the forms our protectors can assume. But they all work in one of two ways: to enable us to rise above our pain and act superior or to cave in and pose as an inferior nothing. The former places a great deal of emphasis on independence; the latter causes us to look constantly for approval in one form or another. We can be rebels or we can be good little boys and girls. But the unknown, unacceptable parts of ourselves are avoided from either stance.

Our protectors enable us to avoid the unknown by giving us something very familiar to cling to. We initially create our false selves to avoid feeling helpless at a time when we really are helpless. But soon these protective images become part of the safe, known world we rely on. And the more we depend on them, the more we believe our false selves are who we really are.

Our protectors will assume many different disguises and use whatever approaches will get our attention and keep us from risking the unknown. We can consider ourselves unique, perfect, withdrawn or inadequate, and we can switch from one identity to another.

The protector's vocabulary is filled with comparative words such as faster, sooner, more and better. He wants you to believe you're rushing to get future "results" so he can keep you from experiencing what's true in the present.

Sometimes our protectors get us to attach ourselves to people or things we hope will keep us from ever feeling separate: money, possessions, relationships or children. Or we'll be persuaded to avoid all attachments, so nothing can ever be taken away again. All that really matters is that we pick familiar, acceptable images we can hold on to.

Our protectors allow us to wake up every day and move through our lives in ways we can count on. We feel a sense of control over our lives whenever our protectors maintain the status quo. It doesn't matter whether we build a life around order or chaos, intellect or emotion, stability or instability, independence or dependence. All that matters is that we each establish a safe, stable, familiar and predictable place for ourselves.

Ask yourself, "What is my most repetitive behavior? What aspects of my personality am I most attached to, or most dependent on?" The beliefs, attitudes and behaviors most common for you are your protection, your tie to familiar ground. You may hold these behaviors and feelings in high regard, or you may see them as frustrating, ineffectual or even painful. But for you they're safe. If you were to stop acting in these ways, you can't imagine what would happen. Your image of yourself would be shattered, and you'd be unprotected from the empty void of the unknown.

OUR PROTECTIVE BELIEFS

Our intellect would never allow us to endure all the potential drama, chaos and pain of the difference game unless the game had some basis in logic. As soon as we begin combating our fear of the unknown, our protectors instill in us a set of beliefs that will support our false selves and reinforce our desire for safety. The difference game depends on the blind acceptance of these beliefs. If we were to question or challenge our protectors, then we'd lose the justification for all our judgment and conflict, and we'd be helpless to combat our fear. So, by the time we enter into a relationship, these beliefs have gone unchallenged for so long that they're written in stone:

1. *If I step into the unknown, I'll be risking emotional death.* The unknown re-exposes me to a state of complete vulnerability, with no connection and no support. I'll be so alone and helpless, I'll cease to exist.
2. *If I acknowledge my powerlessness, my greatest fear will become a reality.* If I truly experience powerlessness, I'll have no control over my life or my world.
3. *If I don't hold on to my familiar perceptions, I'll be helpless.* My ego is my identity. If I let go of what I believe to be true, my world will crumble and I'll fall back into the void.
4. *If I don't cling to my identity, then I'm lost.* If I'm not unique, if I lose the feelings and behaviors that make me who I am, I'll fade into oblivion.
5. *If I let my partner see me, I'll be exposed to all that I fear.* If I get closer to my mate, I'll be seen for who I really am. Exposing all those unacceptable parts of myself will leave me abandoned and helpless.
6. *If I take responsibility for my life, I'll have to confront my own weaknesses and my feelings of helplessness.* If I don't have my partner to blame, I can no longer hold him or her responsible for what happens and I'll feel overwhelmed.

THE DILEMMA OF PROTECTION

Over years of fear and pain you develop a protective persona that you can count on, one that offers you familiarity and a great deal of safety. But you have other needs as well, particularly the desire for an intimate relationship. Herein lies the dilemma of protection: *How can you achieve intimacy without exposure?* Can you become partners with someone for any length of time and still keep your false self intact? Can you really be intimate while not exposing your unfamiliar and unacceptable feelings?

I'm sorry to say that the answer is no. Real intimacy always exposes the cracks in your façade, and the unacceptable fears and desires that lie underneath. The word *intimate* comes from the Latin word for "within." By definition, intimacy means sharing what is private and personal.

The problem is that this exposure poses a threat to your known, protected world. It's pretty hard to maintain your protective persona when you're eyeball to eyeball with someone day after day. Because when you look across at your spouse, you see your own reflection. Your partner becomes your mirror, revealing every nuance of who you are, giving you repeated glimpses of your unacceptable parts, the unknown fears and weaknesses you have worked so hard to hide. Any relationship carries with it this constant threat to your safe, familiar world.

So what's the solution? How can you reconcile your desire for a mate with your need to protect yourself from exposing your unacceptable thoughts, feelings and desires? If you hide by running too far away from your partner, the connection will break and you'll be left alone. But if you get too close, you'll expose your deepest fears, your partner will abandon you and you'll be alone then, too.

Luckily, there is a wonderful way out of this dilemma. The difference game allows you to connect to your partner without the risk of exposure. You can form a bond, express your love and share all kinds of feelings and experiences with your mate. And as soon as the tension becomes too great, as soon as you're moving so close together that you risk exposing any unacceptable thoughts or feelings, your protector will move you into a position of superiority or inferiority. This will prevent any further exposure or risk of the unknown by keeping your level of intimacy at a comfortable level.

Look, for example, at how effective this is for Dwayne and Corrine. They stay together, they share the mutual love of their child, they maintain their connection as a couple. But as soon as either takes a step toward the unknown, their protectors take over.

As long as Corrine sees Dwayne as a hysterical, reactive exaggerator, she won't have to experience complete commitment or surrender. And Dwayne will never have to experience any feeling of inadequacy as long as he perceives Corrine as unreasonably demanding and critical. Their familiar, acceptable images of themselves remain intact. The difference game lets them have it all: the comfort and connection of a relationship and no risk of leaving the safety and familiarity of their protective egos.

Of course, all this protection comes at a price. There's conflict in their relationship, and they openly long for a greater degree of closeness and intimacy. But at least they're protected from their greatest fears.

APPRECIATING THE DIFFERENCE GAME

It would probably sound strange to you if I asked you to celebrate the ways you criticize, discredit and distance yourself from your mate. But to really understand the difference game, you must appreciate what a wonderful job it does of protecting you. Until you fully experience how and why you play the game, you will never perceive the world in any other way.

The difference game isn't merely a defensive "pattern" or a problem to correct as quickly as possible. Unless you hold a deep appreciation for your world of protection, your more prestigious goals of intimacy and passion will remain elusive, experienced for fleeting moments, but rarely integrated into your life and relationships.

In many self-help books, the goal of protection is minimized or denigrated. It is presented as something you need to overcome or get rid of, so your life can really begin. As a result, the extent to which protection permeates our lives, and the powerful forces behind it, are not fully appreciated.

Even in most therapeutic approaches, judgmental attitudes aren't referred to as protective. They're labeled defensive, dysfunctional, neurotic or destructive. These labels then serve as justification to skip through the protective pattern and get into more desirable goals like acceptance, love and trust. There is little mention in these approaches that without such behavior, you would never have survived the gauntlet of wounds, abuses, indifference and smothering that you had to endure on the way to your present age. Especially during times in your life when you had very few resources, your protector was the only one shielding you from unendurable pain.

Maybe your protector made you so small that those who were causing you pain could no longer touch you. Or maybe your protector made you act tough, so no one would ever recognize how deeply you were hurting from their wounds. Shouldn't you feel a deep gratitude to the part of yourself that offered that kind of safety?

In the face of all their childhood beliefs and fears, could Dwayne and Corrine ever have found each other, built a home and created a child they adore without some safe haven from the scars and terrors they carry inside? Could any of us so much as ask someone out on a date, let alone pursue a relationship, if we felt exposed and vulnerable with every human encounter?

Failing to experience and embrace your protector is to deny the order of things. Your protector is the part of you that speaks the loudest and keeps you the safest. As long as avoiding the unknown is your primary goal, your protector will make most of the important decisions about your life. Trying to achieve intimacy by disregarding your protector and appealing to the logic of your intellect is an exercise in futility. Even though your brain may be committed to risking some new behavior, the more forceful part of you will retain control.

THE COMFORT ZONE

Your protector is committed to only one goal: to keep you safely away from your terror of the unknown. He'll use any method that works, whisper any messages he can think of, so long as he keeps you in the realm of the familiar.

The difference game is simply your protector's most effective tool when you're in an intimate relationship, where the risk of exposure is so high. He has no interest in the effect this has on the rest of your life. That's not his job.

Your protector has been hired to keep you within the boundaries of your comfort zone. This is the area of thoughts, feelings and desires that you regard as acceptable and safe. As long as you stick with your familiar perceptions, beliefs and attitudes, you're within your comfort zone, and your protector is doing his job. But if you make a move toward the unknown, or if some threat of exposure starts to invade your comfort zone, your protector goes into action to return you to the status quo.

Look at the diagram below. The circle represents a boundary created by your protector. Inside this protective circle is your comfort zone. Here you experience all the aspects of your life that are familiar to you. Pleasure, pain, hope and passion all exist here, but only at levels that you can tolerate without undue risk.

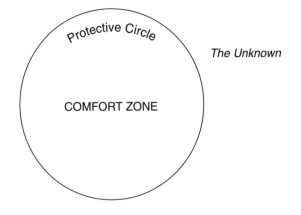

Outside the circle is the edge of the world. That's where you'll find the dragons of the unknown: exposure, vulnerability and intimacy. Your protector will do everything possible not to let you sail into those waters. The difference game is played *only* inside the protective circle, where being better and less will keep the acceptable images of yourself intact.

Despite whatever noble or romantic reasons are presented, it is the two partners' comfort zones that are the foundation of their relationship. The behaviors, attitudes and perceptions that they mutually agree are safe are the strongest bonds the two of them share.

Your relationship is built on an unconscious agreement with your mate to avoid risking the unknown. The boundaries beyond which you will not venture are the same for both of you.

In the initial stages of romantic relationships, we attempt to hide our comfort zones, acting out in ways we believe will be the most attractive or seductive to our prospective partners. But all this posturing quickly fades into the background as our relationships grow more familiar, and our most comfortable façades reappear.

To make this concept more personal, I'd like you to do a quick exercise. Draw a circle to represent your comfort zone with your partner. Within the circle, write at least ten behaviors that you are open to sharing, doing and expressing with each other. These might include taking your kids to a movie, taking charge of the family finances, making love with the lights off, arguing about money, temper tantrums, silent treatments or watching television. Be as specific as you can. There are no right answers and you won't be graded.

Outside your protective circle write at least ten behaviors, feelings and thoughts that would involve some level of risk. Place the ones that would frighten you the most, or would be the most uncomfortable, furthest from the circle. These might include spending a night without the kids, setting up a joint bank account, making love with the lights on, listening to your partner without reacting, expressing your desire for another person or turning off the TV. In other words, anything you place outside your circle is unacceptable in some way to you or your partner.

Continue to add uncomfortable or unacceptable feelings and behaviors to your diagram as they occur to you. As you move through the book, it will become increasingly clear how the experiences outside your comfort zone affect your relationship.

The difference game will always keep you within your circle and protect you from those unacceptable experiences that lie outside it. Let's say that your partner is feeling extremely frightened in response to a possible loss. She asks you to be with her so that she can experience the depth of her feelings.

You feel trapped. "Loss" lies outside your circle. Your protector has devoted years of your life sheltering you from the pain of being touched by any loss. You can't risk exposing yourself to these scary feelings. You don't even want to reveal that this is an issue for you. But you don't want to abandon her completely, because then you will be left alone with no connection.

Your only alternative is intimacy without exposure, so you initiate another round of the difference game. You accuse her of being self-indulgent. You criticize her for clinging to the past and not getting on with her life. You even show her how she could have avoided this loss in the first place.

Now she has to protect herself from experiencing her pain at your reaction. So she retaliates by getting furious at you for your insensitivity, and she calls you an emotional cripple.

You both feel pain, anger and guilt over what has happened. But underneath is a sense of relief, because you've had plenty of involvement with no exposure. By discounting each other, your false selves remain intact and you stay inside your comfort zones.

Our protective circles give us a sense of power because nothing can penetrate them to really touch or expose us. Our comfort zones reinforce our perception that we have some control over our world and that we're safe. We won't ever be seen by our partners and we'll never be forced to look beneath our own acceptable images. And to stay within your circle, all you have to do is listen to your protector:

> *Let me protect you. I know you are thinking of surrendering and being more receptive to your mate, but don't do it. It's too risky and scary. You could open yourself up to feelings that are far more terrifying than the discomfort you're feeling now.*
>
> *At least with me you're safe. You're on familiar ground. You know what your world is like, and you don't have to encounter experiences that are unknown to you.*
>
> *Think about it. If you move closer to your partner and it doesn't work out, you'll be abandoned. You'll be seen for who you really are, and you'll be left feeling totally exposed and vulnerable. You'll be scared to death.*
>
> *YOU DON'T WANT THAT NOW, DO YOU?*

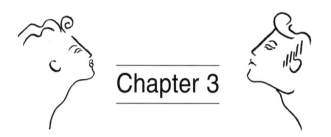

Chapter 3

PLAYING THE GAME
The Rules of the
Difference Game

Hello, Ladies and Gentlemen, and welcome to The Difference Game. *It's a perfect day for today's match, and this promises to be a good one. Our opponents today are two of our favorites, He and She. We've seen these two face each other many times, and there's always plenty of drama. But today should be especially interesting because they're both feeling a little frightened and vulnerable. They've been getting along pretty well, and their mutual enjoyment of their daughter's sixth birthday has brought them closer together, so their risk of exposure and intimacy is high. This is definitely an important game for both of them.*

The game will begin shortly, but before it does, here is a review of the rules of the difference game. For those of you not familiar with all the components, movements and strategies of the game,

these should come in handy. And we'll return to today's match in
just a moment. . . .

Like all contests, the difference game carries a definite set of rules.
Just as in bridge, mud wrestling or the Miss America pageant, you
enter a playing field, you face an opponent and you pursue a specific goal. There are clearly defined limits to what you may and may not
do, there are strategies for playing more effectively and there are
prizes when you win.

Perhaps you're not that fond of sports, and you wonder why I'm
using athletics as the primary analogy for the way we protect our
egos and distance ourselves from our partners. But when you understand the highly competitive nature of the difference game, when you
see how many rules there are, and when you recognize all the movements, attitudes and strategies you can employ to score points, you'll
realize that we're dealing with Olympic caliber competition.

Our reluctance to accept this fact brings us immediately to the first
and most important rule of the difference game:

RULE #1: NEVER ADMIT YOU'RE PLAYING THE GAME.

In most ways the difference game is like all other contests. But this
particular aspect of the game is unique. When a baseball player runs
onto the field, he wants the world to know he's a baseball player, and
a good one. Boasts, publicity shots and claims of being the best are
commonplace.

But the difference game doesn't play well under bright lights. It's
imperative in this competition that you hide or disguise what you're
doing. It's against the rules to simply proclaim, "I'm better than you
are," or, "I'm scared of you getting closer to me, so I'm going to put
you down." To do so would certainly crack the façade you're trying
to maintain.

And it's not just a matter of hiding your difference game maneuvers from your mate. You can't even allow yourself to realize you're
playing. You must sustain the belief that your actions are righteous,
justified or an attempt to solve some problem.

If you were ever to play the game consciously, and openly pro-claim your superiority or inferiority, the game would lose its power, and you'd stop playing. To be so blatant about your attitude of better or less would certainly take you out of your comfort zone and into the unknown. And that would be in direct violation of . . .

RULE #2: NEVER LEAVE THE FAMILIAR PLAYING FIELD.

Remember the circle from Chapter 2 that represents your comfort zone? That's your playing field. Any time you leave the arena of the safe and the familiar, and any time you're willing to risk greater inti-macy with your partner, you're no longer playing the difference game.

The boundaries of your protective circle are as critical to this game as the lines in tennis or the squares on a chess board. Just imagine if, in the middle of the Super Bowl, a quarterback took the ball, ran it out of bounds, jumped into the stands, left the stadium, caught a cab to the end zone and then claimed a touchdown. It might be interest-ing, but it wouldn't be football.

RULE #3: MAINTAIN THE STATUS QUO.

Another way the difference game is unlike other competitions is the game never really ends. You and your partner are opponents; with each encounter you're both trying to prove that you're superior or inferior. But your ultimate goal is to keep the distance between you the same: to maintain your comfortable level of intimacy and exposure.

There's no clock on the scoreboard, no sudden death overtime, no championship trophy. Either of you can win an individual encounter, and once in awhile you can call a time out. But you'll always come back to resume play. Whenever the threat to your false self gets too great, your protector will bring you back onto the field.

RULE #4: USE EVERY OPPORTUNITY TO PROVE THAT YOU ARE BETTER OR LESS THAN YOUR PARTNER.

This one is pretty self-explanatory. Just stay alert for any opening your partner gives you to move up or down. It shouldn't be too hard.

Even a short-term relationship offers a wealth of opportunities to act out your favorite position.

Do you want to feel more intelligent? Flood your partner with logical arguments. Do you prefer the image of victim? Turn meek or hysterical. Most punctual? Most helpless? Most considerate in bed? Go for it.

However, as dazzling as your skills might be, you can't let yourself get too carried away. Your desire to create distance between yourself and your partner must be kept in check, or you'll violate . . .

RULE #5: NEVER LET YOUR PARTNER GET TOO FAR AWAY.

Remember that your ultimate goal in playing this game is to avoid the unknown. So, even though you want to maintain distance, you can't allow the relationship to be truly threatened. If the two of you move too far apart, you'll also be leaving your protective circle as you're confronted by fears of abandonment, solitude and loneliness.

If the distance your partner moves away from you is outside your comfort zone, you must respond with some action that will enable you to reconnect. Does he stay away all night for the first time? Stop nagging for awhile and be "understanding" until it blows over. Does she seriously threaten divorce? Pay more attention to her until it seems like you've patched things up.

You're still maintaining a position of up or down, but you're camouflaging it behind gestures of reconciliation. Once things are back to normal, you can resume your old patterns.

In addition to these five essential rules, there are a few more elements of the difference game every player must understand. Your *playing piece* is whatever particular issue you select as the basis for your judgment. This is your discus, your bowling ball, your mahjongg tile or your deck of cards. The difference game can be played about money, sensitivity, sexual performance or dirty socks on the floor. It makes little difference. In fact, one of the beauties of the difference game is that you can change playing pieces in the middle of a match (see Rule #17 below).

Don't worry about memorizing all the rules and strategies of the difference game. In fact, don't even bother to stay consciously aware of what they all mean, because your protector will act as your *coach*, and will guide you around the clock whether or not you ask him to. In fact, he'd prefer that you not understand exactly what you're doing (see Rule #1).

The coaching your protector provides is for your ears only. No one else will hear him say things like, "That's too big a risk," "You'll look like a fool," or, "No one should ever expose something that bad." Outsiders will just be impressed by how skillful and adept you seem at scoring points against your spouse.

The final basic component of the difference game involves the three *directions* you're capable of moving in response to your partner. In the difference game, all these movements are used to serve only one purpose: to support your most comfortable image of yourself. If you like to see yourself as superior, you will react to your partner in a way that supports that image; if you prefer the down position, your movements will verify that view. Image is always your primary consideration, and the movement itself is secondary.

Look again at the diagram from Chapter 2. As you know, you must remain within the boundaries of your comfort zone. But inside this circle, you have three choices in response to your partner.

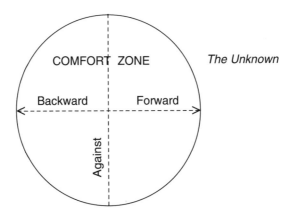

Your first possible direction is *forward*. This involves movement toward someone in order to state, ask, express or give. Within the difference game, if you want to reinforce your superior image, you will move toward your partner from an accusing, judgmental place. "If you paid half as much attention to me as you do that car, we might have a decent marriage." If you wish to reinforce your down stance, your forward movement statement will convey self-judgment, helplessness, and defeat. "I've tried everything I can think of, and I just don't know how to get your attention."

Any kind of withdrawal from a person or situation is a *backward* movement. Within your comfort zone this might be leaving the room, turning silent, hiding behind a newspaper, book or remote control, becoming confused or being monopolized by work, children or other distractions. A backward movement supporting your superior view of yourself might involve storming out of the room with a gesture that indicates your partner isn't even worthy of your attention. If you're trying to present verification of your down image, your backward movement might be to slink away with a meek, helpless posture.

Finally, you can move *against*. This involves opposing someone in order to say no or set a boundary. It differs from moving forward in that its essential function is to stop something, rather than to engage someone. Movements against your partner protect you by neutralizing whatever is occurring. A statement against from an up position might be, "Therapy is for losers, and I won't even consider it." The declaration, "Don't even ask me to be open about my feelings. I'd be too embarrassed," would be typical of a movement against from a down stance.

As long as you stay within the parameters of your comfort zone by maintaining your difference game stances, you can move in any of the three directions. Your only restriction is that you use these movements to continually reinforce your desired image of yourself.

There are more sophisticated rules to come, but these essential ones will be enough to get you started. As the play-by-play that began the chapter continues below, notice the way the couple adheres religiously to all these rules and elements of the difference game. Then I'll describe the more advanced elements of the game that you may not have recognized.

> . . . *Hello again, and welcome back to today's match. She has won the coin toss, so she gets to initiate the first encounter. He will then react to whatever she does.*
>
> *She's selected a terrific opening gambit. Instead of responding to her unconscious fear of intimacy by retreating, she decides to push even closer. It's a tricky move, but if she pulls it off, she can prevent any real intimacy and still end up convincing everyone that she's the wronged, loving spouse.*
>
> *She's sent the kids to bed early, and now she's going to greet him with a special dinner as soon as he walks in the door. Of course, she knows he's usually tired when he gets home, he likes to be alone for awhile, and he's never very comfortable with these "romantic" evenings. But she blocks all of that from her consciousness, and instead builds up a lot of expectation that he will react differently this time.*
>
> *Now here he is. He slogs through the door, exhausted from a workday that was worse than usual. He's been dreaming about flopping in his big chair, eating cold pizza and not having to deal with anything or anybody. Of course he's not going to acknowledge that he, too, is uncomfortable about how much closer the two of them seemed to be yesterday, or how worried he is that he might have to stay at that vulnerable distance. He's not even consciously aware of it. He just knows he wants to be left alone.*
>
> *He gives a perfunctory hi, then he catches sight of the dining room table: candles, wine glasses, only two plates. With lightning speed he processes this information. "Oh, shit," he thinks to himself. "It's one of her romantic dinners."*
>
> *Her opening move is working! He's anxious and on the defensive as his eyes dart around the room. She puts the pressure on by flashing an expectant, seductive smile. Now he's on the run. He forces a halfhearted grin as he shuffles backwards toward the den.*

She knows this is no time to let up, so she follows him. Uh-oh, folks, it looks like she might be weakening. She's having a fleeting thought that maybe he needs some space. But no, her protector is right on top of things, and manages to push it immediately out of her mind by getting her to focus on the fact that her husband's reaction wasn't what she'd been hoping for. She begins anticipating that after all her work, he'll probably disappoint her again.

He's just getting settled into his chair when she puts her arm around his neck in what she tells herself is a hug, though it feels like a chokehold to him.

"I fixed your favorite," she whispers, "and it's just going to be the two of us."

Things are really looking bad for him. She's in top form, and he has yet to execute any effective plays. He knows if he simply says he doesn't want a romantic dinner, he'll look like a jerk. Plus, he knows she'll be disappointed, and he doesn't want to take any responsibility for that. He's got to think fast.

"I just wish you had checked with me first. It was a rough day."

Ah-ha! This is what we've been waiting for. We knew he wouldn't stay on the ropes for long. Now it's her turn.

"I wanted it to be a surprise."

Well, not a great move on her part, but it will keep things going. It's easy to see that he's groping for some way to move to the up position.

"You're always doing this. You create some production without even thinking about what I might like, and then you make me look like the bad guy."

This is a good maneuver. He's just made her responsible for how he feels. Now she's got to react.

"What did I do? I came home early, I planned a lovely evening, I got everything ready, and somehow that's wrong. It's hopeless. No matter what I do, you just want to be alone in that chair. I give up."

Wasn't that terrific, ladies and gentlemen? Righteous superiority followed immediately by a jump to the helpless down position! And now she's angrily returned to the kitchen.

The game is really going full tilt now. He sits a moment in disgruntled silence, realizing he lost that skirmish. "I'd better try and patch this up," he thinks to himself, even though he'd really rather just stay there and watch television. He grumbles out of his chair and shuffles after her. It looks like he's going to shift from the role of most wronged to that of most accommodating.

"Forget it," he says to her. "Let's just have dinner. Do you want me to help?"

"Just help yourself. I'm not hungry."

"But you're the one who wanted this. I said I'd eat now. So let's eat."

"You don't even know why I'm upset, do you?"

"How could I? You're just hysterical. First you want to eat, then you don't. You act like I don't appreciate this, which I never said. I don't know what you want!"

"Of course you don't. Because you never listen to what I want. You'd rather sit in front of the television than talk to me. So go ahead!"

And now she's left the room.

This has been quite a confrontation. They both moved from superior to inferior and back, the subject has changed from dinner to disappointment, then to listening skills, and now she's left the room in tears, temporarily cutting off all communication. Best of all, each can claim a victory. He's superior on the hysterical/emotional scale; she's the winner of the disappointed/neglected competition.

So far this game has produced disappointment, anger, resentment, guilt and confusion. Painful feelings, certainly, but comfortably familiar to our two opponents. There's little risk of greater closeness or intimacy now. Not bad for a relatively brief confrontation.

Well, I'm afraid that's all of today's match we have time for. We'd like to see the final outcome, but I'm afraid that's impossible. As you know, this game never ends. . . .

Did any of this sound familiar? Remember, it doesn't matter what the playing piece is. Maybe romantic dinners have never been an issue for you and your spouse. What's important is that you recognize how well the two players abided by the rules. They maintained their familiar images, stayed within their comfort zones, and avoided the unknown. Most of all, they never acknowledged, or even realized, they were playing the game.

One of the difficulties in portraying the moves of the difference game in vivid detail is that it makes them sound like conscious attitudes and actions. But, of course, they're not. In the play-by-play you just read, planning a romantic dinner really seemed like a good idea, and the feelings of pressure, guilt and confusion were truly genuine. But these conscious feelings were simply the ways their protectors camouflaged the underlying fears and intentions from the players themselves.

You're now ready to learn the more advanced rules of the game. You'll recognize many of these from the encounter you just read.

RULE #6: DISCUSS SPECIFIC CONTENT ISSUES ONLY.

In the difference game, you have complete freedom to argue, discuss and debate any topic, as long as it doesn't involve what lies underneath the discussion itself. It's fine if you argue about the kids, money, going to dinner or whether to buy one- or two-ply toilet paper. Just make each and every topic of vital importance, so it won't seem connected to the other things you've been fighting about.

You can even pin motives and justifications on your actions: "You're just trying to put me down." "I did that because you pissed me off, and you deserved it." But you must never say, "I don't really care about any of these things—I'm just afraid to get close to you." Never acknowledge that there's an underlying process or a deeper objective to what you're doing. Remember, to recognize the game is to stop the game. You never want to give your partner a chance to view your accusations as part of an overall picture.

RULE #7: KEEP YOUR PARTNER HOPEFUL.

Never tell your partner, "It makes no difference what you do. It will never be enough." Instead, disguise the game by giving your partner the impression that if she just follows your logic, wins this debate or tries a little harder to change, things will get better.

RULE # 8: NEVER QUESTION YOUR UP OR DOWN POSITION.

Your perceptions must never be doubted. If you ever allow the thought that the stance you're taking is wrong, you'll move out of your up or down position, and the game will stop. Your protector will *never* be heard whispering, "Maybe she's got a point," or, "Don't you think you're overreacting to this?"

RULE #9: REMAIN DEPENDENT ON YOUR PARTNER.

Real independence is anathema to the difference game. All your feelings, attitudes and actions must be in relation to your partner. *She* makes you angry, *she* drives you to drink, *she* won't listen to your needs. You must never experience the purity of your own anger, pain or fear without connecting it to her in some way. Taking responsibility for your own feelings and taking care of them without involving your partner are not allowed. In the difference game, no independent movement toward your partner is allowed. All thoughts, actions and feelings must be in reaction to a real or anticipated reaction on his part.

Did you notice in the previous example above that the romantic dinner was not offered out of the wife's independent desire to express her love, but was based entirely around anticipating, and experiencing, her husband's reaction? Instead of simply feeling disappointed, and independently taking care of her own needs, everything she did from then on was a reaction to his reaction.

RULE #10: NEVER ACKNOWLEDGE ANY SIMILARITIES.

You must never entertain the notion that maybe you're both scared, that maybe your limitations in the relationship are very much the same.

With the slightest acknowledgment of that possibility, you've stopped playing the game, and you're edging dangerously close to the unknown.

Remember, ranking and competing is your only interest here. All you care about is who scores the most points and who dominates. Joining with the opposition in any way is forbidden.

RULE #11: SEE YOUR MATE AS AN ENEMY WHO'S ABOUT TO ATTACK.

Have you looked closely at your partner? Do you see how she's waiting for her chance to strike? She may have been nice lately, but just wait. You know she's up to her old tricks. Sooner or later she'll turn hysterical, dependent, illogical, demanding, bitchy, conniving and manipulative, as always. Be ready.

RULE #12: SEE EVERYTHING AS PREMEDITATED.

Innocence doesn't exist in the difference game. At least, not where your partner is concerned. Certainly *you* can do things with no ulterior motive, but not him. Everything he does is directed at you.

Did he forget the car keys? *Your desires aren't important to him.* Did he have an intellectual discussion with another woman? *He thinks you're a simpleton.* Did he work late? *He doesn't value your relationship.*

Accepting your partner's honest mistakes makes it impossible to maintain a superior stance. So don't even think about it.

RULE #13: INSIST THAT YOUR PAIN IS THE GREATEST.

Hurts must never be seen as equal. Certainly she's suffered some in your relationship. You're the first to acknowledge she's experienced her share of pain. But no matter how much your innocent mistakes and shortcomings may have hurt her, it doesn't compare to what she's put you through.

RULE #14: HUMILITY IS NOT ALLOWED.

Difference game players are inflated by their own righteousness and superiority. "Humble" is not a word that should even enter your vocabulary. Honest acknowledgment of your weaknesses will throw a real damper on the drama of your confrontations.

Don't confuse humility with inferiority. Humility is an honest recognition of your own human limitations. But using those limitations to assume a stance of inferiority is a very effective difference game technique designed to control your partner.

RULE #15: WAIT FOR YOUR PARTNER TO CHANGE.

Your protector will give you two good reasons for this rule. First, since your partner is to blame for most of your problems, *he* is the one who should change. And even more important, if you give in and change, and he doesn't, you could be devastated. You'll be out on a limb alone, vulnerable and victimized. He'll have won, and he'll take even more advantage of you.

Changing might even force you to leave. Sure, it's a miserable relationship, but it's the only one you know. It's safe, it's familiar and you know you can survive here.

Being the first to change will throw you right into the unknown, and the game will definitely be over. Anyway, it's not as if you're not willing to change. You're just waiting to make sure he changes first. Then you'll think about it . . . when it's safe.

As this list of rules continues, they tend to become more subtle and sophisticated. You may even question that some of these are rules, since you don't exhibit them to your spouse. But remember that the difference game is played silently in your head as much as it is outwardly with your partner. And don't all your judgments about your spouse really involve a sense of hidden outrage that he would treat you that way? Doesn't any rejection of his behavior contain an element of resentment that he would cause you so much pain that you don't deserve?

One of the beauties of the game is that so many movements can be made without your opponent's conscious awareness, and their ability to protect you will be just as great.

You may also be getting a bit weary of all these rules. But again, we're talking about a very competitive game here. *The Official Laws of Table Tennis* contains 158 rules. And I guarantee the difference game is far more complex, and far more popular, than ping-pong.

RULE #16: JUSTIFY ALL YOUR ACTIONS.

No matter how much your partner claims you've hurt her, no matter how awful your behavior might seem to an outsider, vigilantly maintain that you were justified in what you did. "I had no choice but to move out! You were acting crazy!" "Of course I had an affair! We're hardly even sleeping together anymore!" "What else could I do? You know I'm hopeless when it comes to your kids!"

Do you notice how the justification works even better when it carries an implied accusation that what you did was actually your partner's fault? This allows you to be correct *and* superior.

RULE #17: SWITCH PLAYING PIECES.

Are you beginning to show signs of weakness in your argument about your son's allowance? Remind your spouse that she overdrew her bank account last month. You've shifted the competition from *most indulgent* to *most irresponsible with money*, but if your goal is superiority, what do you care? If you change the issue quickly and loudly enough, she'll still be on the defensive.

RULE #18: USE EXTREME EXPRESSIONS.

Don't simply say, "You were five minutes late for dinner." Declare, *"You're never on time for anything that I want to do."* He's not just forgetful, *he's an idiot*. She's not just a poor bridge player, *she's an embarrassment to you.* And be sure to stock your verbal arsenal with plenty of superlatives, such as *never, always, worst, most,* and any adjective ending in *-est.*

This strategy works very effectively in tandem with . . .

RULE #19: INFLATE THE ISSUE.

Are you arguing about whether you'll go dancing Saturday night? Accuse him of never listening to your needs. Are you angry about the way she just disciplined your son? Tell her she doesn't know the first thing about being a good mother. The more skillful you are at turning isolated incidents into bigger, all-encompassing problems, the more points you'll score.

This works in the down position, too. You didn't simply show up late, *you have no sense of time.* And your partner knows that so it's pointless to expect more of you.

Notice how these inflationary techniques also contain many elements of . . .

RULE #20: DEAL IN ABSTRACTS.

Never criticize a specific behavior when you can speak in generalities. "My wife is ridiculous and stupid," serves your purpose better than, "She said something stupid, and this is why it's stupid."

And beating *yourself* up with abstractions can give you a firm hold on the down position: "I'm unsuccessful." "I'm just no good in bed." "I'm hopeless as a parent." Any such generalities will keep you well within your comfort zone.

RULE #21: MAINTAIN AN ATTITUDE OF "HOW DARE YOU?"

Once you've inflated the topic to some superlative, abstract issue, you'll be able to maintain that your partner's every move isn't just incorrect, it's an outright betrayal. How could he even *think* of doing something so hurtful, so disgusting, so unimaginably awful? Why, it's not just a mistake, it's a violation of you as a human being!

RULE #22: SUSTAIN YOUR CONFLICTS.

Master-level difference game players never allow conflicts to flare
up and then be resolved. They know the value of dragging out feelings of righteous betrayal or resentment. Don't just go to bed angry;
keep up the silent treatment at breakfast the next day, or let it protect
you for the whole weekend.

And *never forget*. Just when your partner thinks an old conflict has
been settled and she believes you're arguing about something entirely new, resurrect that dead issue and remind her that you're still feeling pissed off and hurt by it.

RULE #23: KEEP SCORE.

Those past betrayals are also important for maintaining documented proof that you're the superior, more victimized half of the relationship. "Maybe I did say I'd be home early. But you said you'd make
dinner two times last week, and you swore you'd fix those gutters."

See? You just moved ahead three to one in the broken promises
competition.

RULE #24: GENERATE LOTS OF SMOKE,
NOISE AND CONFUSION.

Have you ever reached a point in an argument where you weren't
even sure what you were fighting about? Have you had the same confrontation so many times that you've lost sight of what you wanted
to accomplish in the first place? Did a simple task or discussion mys-
teriously become so complex that you had no idea what was going
on? Thank your protectors, who are steadfastly adhering to Rule #24.

Every item in the difference game rule book is designed to keep
things confused and camouflaged. The more you yell and scream, the
more you dodge and weave, the more you jump around and shift your
focus from any single issue, the less likely you are to leave your comfort zone. If you're constantly distracting your partner and keeping
her off balance, the chances of any real exposure are almost nil.

RULE #25: FOCUS EXCLUSIVELY ON EITHER YOU OR YOUR PARTNER.

This one's a little tricky because it gives you two choices:

(1) You can devote all your attention to your partner: "You're hopeless. You always do this, you never do that, and I have a documented list of everything you said or did in the last 18 hours to verify what a shit you are." When all your concentration is devoted to your partner's shortcomings, there's little possibility of recognizing any similarities you might share.

(2) You can turn inward and become totally absorbed with yourself: "This is so unfrair," you may say to yourself. "After everything I've done, I still get taken for granted." You'll have established your superior or inferior stance without uttering a single accusation out loud.

Your game will only be weakened when you pay equal attention to *both* yourself and your partner. If you allow yourself to experience both his pain and your own, you'll expose your sameness and vulnerability.

RULE #26: REINFORCE THOUGHTS THAT VERIFY YOUR DIFFERENCES.

It isn't enough to move up or down only when you're confronting your mate. The third-degree-black-belt difference game players spend every waking moment mentally verifying how different they are from their partners. Turning your superiority and your victimization over and over in your mind will keep you in a state of continual preparedness and peak performance.

Well that's it. I'm sure your protector can improvise additional strategies for you, and inform you of any rules I may have forgotten. But these should be enough to make you a world-class player. In fact, you probably already are, although your protector will never allow you to consciously recognize your skill.

You may be wondering why anyone would want to play such an endlessly painful and seemingly unrewarding game. If so, simply turn the page, and you'll see what you can win. . . .

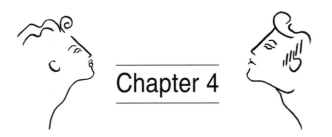

Chapter 4

LIVING IN THE COMFORT ZONE
The Consequences of the Difference Game

She expected him
*   to expect that she*
*   wasn't up to his expectations*
He expected her
*   to not expect*
*   to fulfill his expectation*
*   of what he expected from her*

—With thanks to R. D. Laing

Every game carries consequences.

Suppose you decide to be a professional football player, or an actress in a hit TV series. Let's assume that your talent for your chosen pursuit is not in question, so the opportunity to perform is offered to you. What are the consequences if you agree to play?

Certainly, you will reap many rewards. You'll make a lot of money, and you'll be on TV every week, getting lots of attention, maybe even fame. You'll experience the thrill of achievement, and you'll encounter countless opportunities to feel powerful, successful, talented, the best.

But these prizes come at a price.

It won't all be glory. Frequently you'll screw up and look bad on national television. You'll suffer the agony of failure and experience countless opportunities to feel weak, unsuccessful, incapable, the worst. Your chosen game will take a lot of energy, and the same practice sessions or rehearsals over and over will get pretty tedious.

And be ready to experience a great deal of pain. Regular hits from 300-pound linebackers, or scathing reviews from vicious critics, can create a lot of scars and bruises. Your career will be brief, in any case. You'll have given your entire life to this endeavor, and when you have to leave, you might look back and realize how many other opportunities in life you missed.

Does this mean you shouldn't act, or you shouldn't play football? Not necessarily.

It simply means that any game is a package deal, and you can't be selective about the consequences of playing. The best you can do is to understand *all* the rewards that any game brings. If for you, the desirable rewards outweigh the undesirable, then say yes to your chosen game, and play it with all the passion you can.

THE CONSEQUENCES OF THE GAME

As with all competition, the consequences of participating in the difference game are quite varied. Some you will like and some you won't; some will bring you comfort, others you will find painful and frustrating. But they will all offer you protection from the unknown.

Even the less appealing consequences, such as hurt or confusion, will at least feel safe and familiar to you. Your protector greatly prefers these "negative" feelings to unknown experiences such as exposure and intimacy. So, as much as you might complain about some of these prizes, your protector loves them all.

Safety

An intimate relationship is one of the scariest endeavors any of us ever attempts. It can humble the best of us and bring some of the most articulate, bright and seemingly sophisticated individuals to their knees.

Where else is there so much opportunity for exposure? Where else would you find so great a risk of revealing all those parts of yourself you struggle to keep hidden? And in what other situation are you so frequently asked to move into the terrifying arena of the unknown?

The difference game protects you from all that. It allows you to be in a relationship and still feel safe. Because you're so deeply involved with your partner, you get a cover for your loneliness. But since you're hiding behind your stance of superiority or inferiority, there's little risk. It's the best of both worlds. You don't have to worry about being alone, and you don't have to get too close.

Unfortunately, the difference game limits you to a very small space. Huddled in your emotional fallout shelter, you miss out on the world of richness and growth that comes with taking risks. But at least you're protected.

Constant Togetherness

We all long for some sense of connection to others. Sexual desire, loneliness and societal expectation instill in us a need for some form of committed, intimate relationship. And from the time we first recognize our parents as a couple, we anticipate the time when we will be part of a romantic relationship.

The difference game allows you to be totally involved with another person. The two of you are filling society's prescribed roles as you provide each other with company, energy, interaction, support, sex (sometimes), a family and at least the *appearance* of intimacy.

But I'm afraid there's a down side to all this togetherness: *you can't get away from it.* Even when the two of you are apart, your head is filled with thoughts and energy toward your partner. You're never really alone because you're emotionally glued to each other. Your body may leave, but your mind is still coming up with judgments, retorts and reactions to what your partner said or will say.

When you play the difference game, you never experience any real independence because some of your energy is always directed toward your partner. You can rarely give yourself 100% to any other activity, because a part of you is still absorbed by your latest interaction.

Ego Gratification

Like all competitive games, the difference game gives you the opportunity to boost your ego by coming out on top. The rush of proving that you're better or more powerful than someone else is impossible to resist.

Whatever image you have of yourself, whatever qualities you want to put out to the world, the difference game will reinforce them. Smart? Logical? Loving? Actualized? A stallion in bed? The difference game lets you be all of that and more.

One of the beauties of the difference game is that it can boost your ego even when you *lose.* Want to be most neglected? Most helpless? Most abused, used and confused? You got it.

Familiarity

The difference game keeps you within your comfort zone in a world you know very well. There are few surprises within your relationship; it's dependable and safe. Once in awhile, the outside world may throw some new crisis in your path—some financial setback, disease or act of God. But in dealing with it, you and your partner can still retreat into your familiar roles and patterns.

Predictability

Most of us feel uncomfortable with change. We want to know what we can count on. With the difference game, there is no need to worry; both partners get to experience the same familiar interactions, always leading to the same predictable ends.

You know that if you claim exhaustion, your partner's sexual desire will disappear. You know that sooner or later your mate will disappoint, ignore or betray you. And you know you'll always be the problem solver, the caregiver, the breadwinner or whatever other role you've taken on in your marriage.

Your specific words and actions may vary as you select different topics for confrontation. But the positions you each play, the moves you make and the ultimate outcome of the game stay pretty much the same.

Boredom

Unfortunately, there's a problem with so much repetition and predictability. Pretty soon the same recycled arguments, silences and role playing can become trite and banal. How many times can you be the helpless victim before that role loses its punch? When you play the difference game, you've got to accept a little tedium now and then.

Fortunately, your prize package also includes an easy method of overcoming any boredom you might experience. Because the difference game gives you plenty of . . .

Drama and Intensity

The difference game is the best soap opera you'll ever find. You can put yourself right inside the drama, and nothing else in the human condition could begin to offer you such constant and enduring displays of emotional intensity.

When things get a bit stale and repetitious, or seem uncomfortably peaceful, just turn up the volume. Yell, scream, snipe, sob, slam doors, turn silent, break down or leave. You can perform *Who's Afraid of Virginia Woolf* or *The War of the Roses* right in your own home.

And it never ends! Because every time one of you does something to prove that you're better, the other will do something to regain the top spot. There are no limits to this perpetual competition; you just keep riding the seesaw. There's never a dull moment, never an emotional calmness and never a lack of things to talk about.

Sadly, there's a downside to all this drama as well. Like the characters in any soap opera, when you participate in so much emotion, you'll experience a good deal of . . .

Hurt

Continual arguments, battles, put-downs and desertions lead to a lot of pain. Being the object of your partner's anger, criticism, neglect, inattention, helplessness, hysteria or abandonment can be very hurtful. And when you win a skirmish, the resulting guilt, loneliness and dissatisfaction can be equally unenjoyable. Even though you've protected yourself and maintained your façade, any hope of real happiness is probably lost.

A Sense of Power and Control

The pain of seeing ourselves as little and separate leaves us with a feeling of powerlessness. The difference game counteracts that feeling by allowing us to be either "pumped up" or a "poor soul."

When we inflate ourselves by ordering, demanding, bossing, boasting or parading our superiority, we believe we are in control of our lives. And when we wallow in the down position, demanding attention, pity and accommodation for our helplessness, we're also given a sense of power over those around us. The power behind our inferior stance is harder to spot because we would never consciously admit it was our goal. To declare our desire for power openly would blow our cover as a helpless victim. But on some unconscious level, we're using the less role to control our partner's behavior.

Regretfully, I again have to deliver some bad news. The power of the difference game is an illusion. Real power is the ability to stand up for and support our own needs—it's the ability to pursue whatever we want openly and independently. Real power stands on its own merits. It never depends on the reactions of others, and it never has to prove anything.

The power of the difference game is *pseudopower*. It relies on the manipulation of others, and the responses of our partners. Pseudopower is insatiable—it requires repeated demonstration. It always carries a hidden agenda because it always needs to prove itself.

The limitations of this pseudopower will become apparent whenever you attempt real growth, change, independence or intimacy in your relationship while continuing to play the difference game. Because then you'll have to confront your . . .

Impotence

As long as your goal is to manipulate your partner and maintain the status quo, the feeling of power the difference game affords you will be fine. But any forward movement toward greater closeness, satisfaction or independence will prove to be beyond your abilities.

The difference game has no winners. It leaves you powerless to honestly take care of your own needs and desires. You can never make any real change, or have any real impact on your life or relationship.

Confusion

Because the difference game relies on camouflaging even the game itself, you spend a lot of time bewildered and disoriented. Your protector does everything he can to keep you off balance. You're in the middle of an argument, and you realize you've forgotten what you were fighting about in the first place, why you were fighting about it, or what you were trying to prove. You think things are going well, and it turns out you're on the verge of divorce. Equilibrium is tough to maintain in the midst of all this confusion.

You're even uncertain about your own motives and feelings. You can't simply think about what you want or need. You have to consider how your partner will react, how that will make you react, or whether any of these twists and turns will bend your image and position. Decisions are hard to make when every nuance must be anticipated, analyzed and evaluated. It can be overwhelming.

Because you're off balance so much of the time you will also feel a great deal of . . .

Frustration

Not much gets taken care of in the difference game. Problems never seem to change; solutions are never permanent. At times you feel a real desire to move forward, but pretty soon you're back where you started. Your exciting soap opera has became a treadmill. And when you stay on a treadmill continuously, you're bound to experience . . .

Exhaustion

The difference game would wear down an olympic athlete or an NBA All-Star. It requires constant energy, all day and all night, just to stay where you are.

Apathy

There's no place for real passion in your comfort zone. Your protector squelches the full experience or expression of any feeling.

But the gnawing sensation remains that in some way you're missing out—that some essential element of your humanity has left you. And soon you'll begin contemplating . . .

Separation and Divorce

When the conflict and the boredom, the frustration and the confusion, the apathy and the impotence become too great, you may finally decide that no reward is worth all this pain, and you part. But even the leaving will be filled with drama and emotion, as you both battle to assign blame for your failure. Then, as soon as your pain subsides, you can begin the endless cycle of searching for a new difference game partner.

This cycle doesn't always recur, and the difference game doesn't always end in divorce. Some couples can numb themselves to whatever desires for passion and fulfillment they once held, and continue their game from the altar to the grave.

And then there are a few courageous couples who are willing to stop the difference game before it's too late, and move on to a different way of connecting. The new game they choose is certainly not an easy one, but it's one that can ultimately lead them to true intimacy, passion and power, and the fullest experience of their humanity.

This is the game of *mutuality*.

PART II

ACCEPTANCE

Chapter 5

ACCEPTING THE UNACCEPTABLE Mutuality

We are not put here to audition one another, put someone on trial, or use other people to gratify our ego needs. We are not here to fix, change, or belittle another person. We are here to support, forgive, and heal one another.

—Marianne Williamson, *A Return to Love*

It seems almost strange to me all the rhetoric that men and women devote to their differences. Have you ever stepped back far enough from all this verbiage to see what we're really talking about? Think about it: we all receive information through the same senses, and we all use our human bodies to express ourselves; we live in the same world and are dependent on the same air, water, food and light; we struggle with issues of love and loss, joy and sorrow, pleasure and pain, anger, frustration, worry, defeat, fulfillment and the meaning of life; and we all feel powerless in the face of aging and death.

So how different can we really be?

> *Sam and Annie had been living together for more than two years when they first came to therapy. Their first session was dominated by her complaints about his never being available to her. "He's always at work, and when he is home, it's like he's only half there," she'd lament. "He's either out in his workshop or doing some other project. He never wants to simply be with me."*
>
> *Sam admitted he had difficulty knowing how to be together in an intimate way. "I'm just not into closeness the way she is," he'd explain. "I'd rather be doing something with my time." He clearly felt guilty about falling short of Annie's expectations. But his guilt didn't stop him from repeatedly muttering that she just didn't understand his point of view. The one thing they both agreed was that they were worlds apart about the issue of intimacy.*

Sam and Annie are typical of most couples I see. They're caught up in the contest for the title "Most Hurt and Misunderstood." The partners in these relationships both attempt to pull me into their competition, each expecting me to decide which one has the greater pain, is the more mistreated, the more righteous and the more victimized. Each one wants my support, but they don't really want to hear from me. They only want to hear me agree with their judgments.

This common therapeutic situation is described by R. D. Laing in the opening poem of his wonderful book *Knots*:

> *They are playing a game. They are playing at not*
> *playing a game. If I show them I see they are, I*
> *shall break the rules and they will punish me.*
> *I must play their game, of not seeing I see the game.*

I have a dilemma. If I give these couples what they want, how can they trust me to really help them? How can I trust my *own* abilities if I allow myself to appease them? But if I remain impartial, they look at me like I must either be blind or so ineffectively neutral that I can't possibly solve their problem.

I explained my dilemma to Sam and Annie. "Can you appreciate the bind I'm in?" I asked them. I got partial nods because total agreement would have meant letting go of their positions. But at least it was an opening for me to enter.

I thanked them for their trust and shared with them that, in fact, I was anything but neutral. "I am *willing to take a side here, and it's a stance I believe in quite passionately. I am willing to remain completely committed to your relationship until you prove me wrong. In addition, I will hold to the perception that you are absolutely equal.*

"I see the two of you as intimate twins, capable of exactly the same degree of closeness. In all the painful encounters you've described to me, the only issue of real importance is that you are equally hurt, equally afraid and equally misunderstood.

"In order to prove you're not the same, you've expended enormous effort and emotion in countless painful exchanges. Your fears have not allowed either of you to understand the other's perceptions, or to recognize the pain you both share. This is what's creating all the drama in your relationship.

"The only way for you to move out of all this conflict is to go beneath your usual perceptions to a deeper level of sameness. Things can't change until you stop judging yourselves and each other and start accepting that you're both equally hurt and afraid.

"I want to assure you that I won't be passively observing you during this process. I'll be taking every opportunity to bring your equality into the light so that you can experience your mutual fears together."

After sitting silently in response, Sam and Annie agreed to risk the journey I was proposing. And that was their first step toward mutuality.

The real answer to the difference game lies in a change of perception and attitude, not in a new technique or set of exercises. No single method is strong enough to overcome the strength of our defenses, conditioning and ego needs. Such a change requires a powerful new way of seeing and approaching our relationships. While this new perception needs to be supported by specific actions, without this underlying perceptual change, no shift in behavior will sustain.

The solution to all the pain and rejection of the difference game, and to all the drama and distance in any troubled relationship, is the process I call mutuality. Put most simply, mutuality involves *replacing a hierarchical attitude with one of equality and acceptance*, so we can discover our sameness.

Mutuality is the continual process of learning to dissolve your judgments about whatever thoughts, feelings and desires you regard as unacceptable in either your partner or yourself. It means shifting your usual perceptions in order to see your spouse as equal, neither above nor below you, and to recognize how you each contribute to the balance in your relationship. As your hierarchical perceptions are replaced with an attitude of acceptance, you can share and embrace the disguised and hidden parts of yourselves with each other. This will enable you to join regardless of whatever outward problem or issue is challenging you.

Mutuality asks you to use the language of "we," "us" and "ours," instead of "you," "me" and "mine." Words like friend, join, same, allow, and connect will be heard from this place, along with expressions of permission, invitation, acceptance and love.

Mutuality isn't just a pretty whitewash with spiritual overtones that merges all your differences into some heavenly, homogenized blend. Instead, a mutual attitude of equality and acceptance gives all your traits the freedom to exist side by side, with no judgment.

Mutuality is not some impossible or idealized objective. Think back to some time when you felt close to your partner, when all the battles and the posturing had ceased. Perhaps it was a time of mutual pain or tragedy—a medical crisis, or the death of a loved one. You both felt so utterly helpless that in the face of your overwhelming pain or fear, all you could do was hold each other. And you realized that in that moment, you were experiencing your deepest level of closeness and love.

Or remember some time of simple serenity—a shared smile, a spontaneous laugh, even a moment when you were in separate places, but you allowed yourself, at least for an instant, to feel loved or to experience real contentment. For that moment, you stepped outside your protective circle and were in a state of mutuality.

By the time you begin your first intimate relationship, you've already been practicing protection a lot longer than mutuality. Our families, friends, society and television all provide us with a number of models for the difference game and a lot of support for its beliefs. But examples of acceptance and mutuality are difficult to find. So, with all that training and practice, it's no wonder that even recognizing our sameness is so difficult.

Intimacy isn't just getting naked in bed, and it certainly isn't just togetherness. Real intimacy can only exist within an attitude of mutual acceptance as you expose both acceptable and unacceptable thoughts, feelings and desires to one another. When you move beneath your surface differences in this way and see the sameness you truly share, the difference game ends and real intimacy begins.

While fully integrating this new perception of each other requires discipline and commitment, just imagine what such an attitude would mean to your relationship. What if you believed, and your partner believed that the two of you were truly equal? Not just in some idealistic political sense, but really the same?

Imagine seeing yourselves as equally hurt and afraid. What if you recognized that your willingness to risk, and your capacity for joy and pleasure, were exactly the same? What would happen if you truly believed that you loved each other equally?

If you could allow this truth in for even a moment, what effect would it have on your marriage? Could you really carry so much judgment and resentment toward a partner who is your equal? Would you still be so suspicious or afraid of someone who is just as scared and vulnerable as you are? Would your husband be so critical or angry if he knew he was just as weak and helpless as you feel? Would your wife act so victimized or emotional if she knew she was just as powerful as you are? And could the two of you remain so distant from each other if you realized you were an exact match?

What would it mean if all the judgment and hierarchy disappeared from your relationship? What if your mate accepted all the qualities and feelings that you thought you had to keep hidden? And what if you could accept all your own unacceptable parts? What if you could truly feel your anger, fear, disappointment, helplessness, power and desire, knowing that these feelings were positive aspects of who you really are?

Would you still need to protect yourself so much? Would the petty fights and hurtful battles continue if whatever either of you felt was honored, accepted and embraced? How much fear would your partner feel in a relationship that safe? How much anger would you have toward a partner who was that loving? And how much resentment would either of you feel if you truly had that much freedom and independence?

As I worked with Sam and Annie, I searched for ways to get them to recognize that their protective stances were essentially the same. I asked Sam to begin admitting he was "married to his work," to focus on the emotional protection his job afforded him. He was encouraged to admit to Annie that he would rather be with his "work spouse" than risk being with her.

Stating this out loud made him very uncomfortable, as his "good guy" image was shattered. This admission took Sam well out of his comfort zone and into unacceptable feelings of guilt and independence. As he saw his stance toward Annie displayed so blatantly, and allowed himself to experience his own responsibility for the distance between them, he began to cry.

This new level of exposure softened Annie's stance, and she gazed at him tenderly as she experienced the pain and sadness her lover was now willing to expose.

In the next session I asked Annie what she was "married" to that equaled Sam's marriage to his work. At first she resisted the thought entirely, and kept insisting she didn't know. But as we explored further, she finally admitted that she was just as attached to feeling like a victim as he was to staying away.

I then asked both of them if they would be willing to get divorced from these other marriages and risk a more intimate relationship with each other.

They agreed, but Annie immediately added, "I don't know what to do."

I replied, "That's just another 'helpless victim' statement. It means you still haven't left your other marriage." As I said this, Sam moved close to her and put his arm around her.

It was fascinating to watch how restless and uncomfortable she became with his genuine overture of intimacy. He backed off some, and again she made some helpless statement. I reflected it back to her, and he again moved toward her, this time taking her hand. As Annie heard herself say, only half-jokingly, "Stop bugging me," she had to admit her own resistance to closeness.

Spontaneously she admitted, "Now my cover is blown. I always got to pretend that I was the one who wanted to be close." With that recognition, she was able to relax and lovingly smile at Sam.

Not used to seeing her this way, Sam now had difficulty leaving his usual down stance of feeling guilty and taking responsibility for Annie's feelings. But I pointed out that this stance was his own way of protecting himself from the unfamiliar experience of his own acceptability and his closeness to Annie. Sam began allowing himself to let go of his attitude of inferiority, and to experience their connection. And as soon as he did, they both felt the innocent power of their love and mutuality.

By moving beneath their obvious differences, it was possible for Sam and Annie to see that they were equal in their desire for protection. Experiencing that level of sameness allowed them to get past their repetitive conflicts and grow truly closer.

THE TWO GAMES

The equality and acceptance of mutuality are the exact opposite of the hierarchy and rejection of the difference game. For every aspect of the difference game, there is a corresponding quality of mutuality:

The Difference Game	**Mutuality**
Protection	Connection
Hierarchical	Equal
Judgment	Acceptance
Rejecting	Embracing
Hiding	Exposing
Diluted	Passionate
False self	True self
Separation	Joining
Distance	Intimacy
Focusing on differences	Recognizing sameness
Clinging to the familiar	Risking the unknown
Safe	Scary
Limited movement	Unlimited movement
Partial commitment	Full commitment
Dependent	Independent
Me vs. you	Me and you
Blame	Forgiveness
An ego connection	An intimate connection
Risking at different times	Risking at the same time
Surviving	Living

Every movement you make from any quality in the first column toward any quality in the second takes you out of your protective comfort zone and into greater intimacy with your partner. Only by removing the judgment and rejection of the difference game can greater fulfillment and growth in your relationship be achieved.

On an episode of the Oprah Winfrey Show, an expert on marriage was trying to demonstrate communication skills by working

*with a couple from the audience. The couple complained that they
were constantly arguing and bickering, and the therapist was trying to get them to actively listen to each other instead.*

*Every time the husband said something, the wife tried to
defend herself or attack him back. Even when the therapist specifically instructed her just to sit silently or repeat back only what
her husband had said, she would make nonverbal retorts or mutter "but . . ." under her breath.*

*And when it was her husband's turn to listen, you could almost
hear the defenses forming in his mind as soon as she began to speak.*

Communication exercises were meaningless for the couple above
because their underlying attitude didn't support real intimacy. An
attitude of mutuality would have allowed their different views, feelings and needs to coexist *without judgment*. If these two people could
have recognized that their words and feelings were the responses of
two equally hurt and frightened people, then they could have experienced an intimate connection.

Robert Strock, a friend and colleague of mine, says that the underlying attitude of any couple in conflict is clearly revealed by the way
the two partners listen to each other. Within a hierarchical relationship, each partner has a much greater interest in his or her own perceptions than in the other's. Neither partner ever really hears the
other's reality, so they both feel misunderstood. In contrast, when
equals engage in listening from an attitude of mutuality, each partner's own perception is set aside, and the primary focus is on the
other's view of the relationship.

LEAVING YOUR COMFORT ZONE

Look again at the diagram of your comfort zone from Chapter 2:
The difference game keeps you within this comfort zone. Outside
your protective circle lie all the parts of yourself you find unacceptable. As long as you keep playing the game, you may be in pain, but
you won't have to experience your fear of moving into the unknown
and confronting these unacceptable feelings.

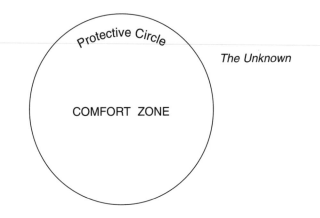

The circle depicted above has nothing to do with acceptance. The "comfort" in your comfort zone depends on keeping things out. Because it is based on protection from, and denial of, the unacceptable, it's not even real comfort: it requires constant guardedness and suspicion. The difference game holds only the illusion of comfort.

The moment you change your perception to an attitude of mutuality and acceptance, you move outside your shared comfort zone. You stop seeing your partner through protective filters, your surface differences lose their importance, and your partner's fears, wounds and vulnerability begin to look the same as yours.

A new *circle of acceptance* has now been created. Within this new circle you are willing to experience unacceptable feelings that were disguised and protected by your false self. As your acceptance of these feelings increases, your shared outer circle becomes larger.

In this expanded circle of acceptance the emphasis now shifts to letting unknown experiences in. The boundaries of this mutual circle will be defined by whatever level of intimacy you and your partner are willing to risk. And, at the edge of this circle, there will always be frightening new images and feelings that will ask for acceptance.

When your fear and exposure become too great, you will eventually retreat into your protective comfort zone. No one resides permanently in either protection or exposure; your life and relationships will be defined by constant movement back and forth between the

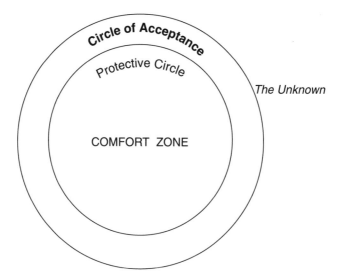

two. With each movement beyond your comfort zone you will increase your accessibility to the outer circle by making friends with more parts of yourself. Unknown experiences will become known as you bring these new parts of yourself into the light of acceptance and lessen your fear and discomfort.

ACCEPTING THE UNACCEPTABLE

Acceptance is a willingness to fully embrace any experience—to bring it into the light without judgment, conditions, or apology. It means viewing all the unacceptable parts of yourself and your partner as worthy, and all experiences as opportunities for intimacy and love.

When I refer to the unacceptable, I simply mean all the thoughts, feelings, desires and images you want to avoid. These are the parts of yourself that you struggle so hard to keep hidden. They are unacceptable because they will destroy the false self you've created, and their exposure will take you into the terrifying unknown.

Is anger a feeling you must never express? Then for you anger is unacceptable. Should you never disappoint your partner? Then disappointment is outside your comfort zone as well. What about sadness, helplessness and surrender? Ask yourself what would frighten you beyond your limits. For you that is what is unacceptable.

The unacceptable isn't limited to feelings we regard as "negative." We'll reject "positive" experiences just as strongly if they take us outside our comfort zones. How much love can you really accept from your partner? How much independence can you experience? How about sexual intimacy? Power? Happiness? There is some point at which all of these will make you too vulnerable and will become unacceptable.

Only in your fantasies can you live a life where everything is safe and comfortable. In the real world, you have only two options. You can hide and deny your unacceptable parts, or you can allow yourself to be afraid and accept them. The former choice leads to safety and distance; the latter to greater intimacy.

We have all been conditioned to reject anything that causes us conflict or pain. Our natural reaction when we have a problem is to remove it from our lives. Scared is bad—get rid of it. Powerlessness is awful—wipe it out.

The unfortunate effect of trying to get rid of whatever you label a problem is that you end up pushing away a part of your essential humanness. When you dismiss one of your unacceptable parts, you turn that aspect of yourself into an object. Such an impersonal attitude creates an enormous sense of alienation. You have literally cut off a part of who you are, and the inner conflict and resentment created is bound to spill out into your relationship.

This is how relationships get stuck: any possibility of true expression is suffocated by all the noise and smoke of the impersonal war between the partners' acceptable and unacceptable parts. Any real movement becomes neutralized.

If this sounds simplistic, just think about it. Would most of our problems and conflicts even exist if we weren't contending with the cries of some unacceptable part of ourselves? No one enters either the therapist's office or the divorce court if their rejected thoughts, feelings and desires are sufficiently silenced. Regardless of what others think of our relationships, regardless of whether intimacy is even present, when our unacceptable parts are quiet, we are quiet.

The highly reactive couples who come for therapy have been unable to stifle, ignore or avoid their unacceptable voices, which are now creating all kinds of drama and fireworks. Even the "passion-less" couples who have slipped into numbness and apathy are losing their stranglehold on their unacceptable parts, so pain and dissatis-faction are leaking into their marriages. In both types of relationships, the buried parts of each partner are crying out for help.

Acceptance is not tolerance. Tolerance means judging an experi-ence as negative but living with it anyway. I have many clients who can easily tolerate different feelings or behaviors, but have a much more difficult time truly accepting them. Tolerance is a hedge—an adjustment to some life condition. It always carries some underlying resentment. The partner who says, "I don't like the way he talks to me, but I can tolerate it," will soon exhibit an attitude of superiority or inferiority.

Acceptance means fully allowing something into your world. Since it carries no judgment or resistance, there is no resentment. It is an involvement of the heart, with no underlying agenda to protect anything.

Some couples I've worked with have maintained that they already possess a high degree of acceptance in their relationships. "We can handle disappointment," they'll proclaim. But when I bring up their readiness to really appreciate and embrace this feeling, thought or image, the gaps in their acceptance emerge. "Do you really appreci-ate the positive intention of disappointment? Are you willing to expe-rience and embrace it 100%?" I ask.

"Well no," they reply, "but we can deal with it."

"Then you're just tolerating," I reply. "To truly accept disappoint-ment, you must value what it adds to your relationship. Disappoint-ment allows you to experience the full depth of your connection. It tells you what is missing for you and your partner, and it helps you to empathize with each other. Without disappointment, you would lose your vulnerability and you would only join when circumstances were favorable. And that would be a very limiting relationship."

Unqualified acceptance is a process that requires commitment and vigilance. Your protector will do whatever he can to keep you judging, tolerating and rejecting, because accepting your partner's feelings and desires, rather than reacting to them, leads you to unknown levels of trust, risk, love and surrender.

In *The Couples Companion*, Harville Hendrix and Helen Hunt compare the stages of mutual acceptance to Elizabeth Kubler-Ross's stages of grief:

Stage 1: *Shock*—You're not the person I thought you were.

Stage 2: *Denial*—You're still the person I always thought you were, but you're just having a bad day.

Stage 3: *Anger*—I'll make you be who I want you to be and coerce you into giving me what I want.

Stage 4: *Bargaining*—I'll give you what you need if you give me what I need.

Stage 5: *Resignation and despair*—I give up. I resign myself to our failure to work things out and despair of finding real love. Let's make the best of a bad deal or go our own ways.

Stage 6: *Acceptance*—I accept you as wounded and defended, and commit to the healing process.

As the acceptance in your relationship increases, you will be able to look beneath all the stances and accusations that have consumed you and your partner, and see that on the level of your pain and fear, you are absolutely equal. The wounds you've suffered, the scars you carry, the pain you bear and the terror you feel are the same for both of you. And it is at this level of sameness that you will find your real connection.

The Capacity for Intimacy

If the foundation of mutuality is an attitude of equality, what exactly is this sameness you must perceive? If we acknowledge that you differ in a thousand obvious ways, how are you and your partner truly equal?

To answer this question, think again about how the difference game works. A multitude of differences, some real and some imagined, are focused on, examined, criticized and justified as two partners maintain their distance. The result is an endless cycle of conflict, drama, accusations and judgment. But underneath all that noise and camouflage lies the driving force behind a couple's separation: they have made an unconscious agreement to protect themselves from the unknown.

In order for the two of them to continue participating in this game with the same energy and involvement, the size of their comfort zones needs to be equal, and so does their mutual willingness to leave those shared circles. In other words, their desire for protection is identical. This is the equality all couples share, and this is the equality that forms the foundation of mutuality:

In any committed relationship, the two partners have exactly the same capacity for intimacy.

No matter how much you proclaim that you're more open, accepting, vulnerable or loving than your partner, you're not. Your capacity for acceptance and exposure is identical. Even though the various appearances, personalities, behaviors and abilities that each of you exhibits receive a great deal of attention, they are not central to the level of intimacy in your relationship. They are all merely window dressing that serves to protect you from experiencing the unacceptable.

Just consider this familiar couple:

Gorgeous woman. Ugly guy. She is well-liked. He is disliked by one and all. She is smooth as silk. He moves with the grace of a hippo. She could have any number of men. He could repulse any woman he meets.

Yet she wouldn't consider leaving him. Why?

Because she is his whole world, and more than anything else, she needs the security of being regarded that way. And he needs the security of being with the only woman he believes will stay with him. For both of them, insecurity is an unacceptable experience, and must be avoided. At this core level of their dependency, they are an exact match.

All of the other factors in this couple's relationship are irrelevant to that level of sameness. Those surface differences they exhibit have no effect on the two of them staying together. Only the exact equality of their need for security defines the strength of their relationship.

Now look at another typical couple:

> *They argue over anything and everything, from the meaningless to the monumental. Put-downs, accusations, criticisms and icy silences are commonplace. Breakups are no longer surprising or unusual, they're just part of the routine. Friends are bored by their act and can't stand being around them. And moments of tenderness, love and joy seem almost nonexistent.*
>
> *So why, despite all the fighting, all the acrimony and all the pain, does neither partner leave?*

They stay together because a relationship offering any higher level of happiness and closeness would be unknown and would terrify them both. Yet, they are also terrified of being completely alone. So their mutual, underlying need to maintain exactly the same level of intimacy and distance transcends every other consideration in their relationship.

There are a thousand variations of these familiar patterns. In the face of a multitude of stated problems and difficulties, couples always seem to maintain the status quo, neither breaking up nor getting closer. Both partners find a comfortable level of intimacy, and that's where they remain.

A couple's shared capacity will always determine what they are willing to let "in" to their lives. The particular feelings they each find unacceptable may differ, but their ability to expose them will be identical.

The primary issue for any couple is not whether their relationship is mutual because at the level of their capacity for intimacy, all committed relationships are already equal. The two partners must only decide whether to assume an *attitude* of mutuality, or to continue to play the difference game.

Who Loves More?

I can't discuss intimacy and equality without bringing up the issue of *love*. There is probably no other feeling or experience that is the object of more discussion, debate, misunderstanding and miscommunication than this. And no other quality is more often used to promote the idea that two partners can possess a different capacity for intimacy.

One partner may believe that she loves her husband more than she is loved in return, one may appear more committed than the other, or one may argue that he is clearly the more giving of the two. But to buy into these beliefs is to collude with the illusion of difference: *"I love you more, so I am better than you,"* or *"Because I love you more I am your victim."*

If you believe in the myth that two people can love unequally, you will certainly have the support of friends, family and a portion of the psychiatric community as well. Many relationship theorists hold the premise that in troubled relationships, one partner is more in love than the other, and that it is this imbalance that creates the couple's conflicts.

In the best selling book *Women Who Love Too Much*, Robin Norwood maintains that many wives have been conditioned to cater too much to the needs and demands of husbands, who in turn dominate their marriages by withholding love and affection and taking advantage of the more loving attitudes of their spouses. And, in *The Passion Paradox*, Dean C. Delis describes relationships as having one partner (male or female) who is more in love than the other, with the less loving partner controlling the relationship.

If true, these approaches obviously present a major exception to the basic principle of mutuality because if you are really able to love more than your partner loves you, you must have a greater capacity for intimacy. Is it possible that at this deepest level of love itself, two people in a relationship might actually differ?

No, it's not.

The illusion that one partner can truly possess a greater capacity to give and receive love is a result of the different meanings given to the word love.

To Norwood, love means *sacrifice*. The women she describes are addicted to pleasing, and their addiction enables them to avoid an underlying fear of assertiveness or independence. That fear establishes an intimacy limit for them that is equaled by their husbands' unwillingness to be closer, more committed or more giving. Their modes and behaviors may be strikingly different, but the outcome is the same: the levels of intimacy in the relationships remain the same.

To Delis, love is defined as "emotional investment"—what I would term a *role* that has been assumed in response to the partner's more aloof or "uninvested" role within the relationship.

In *The Passion Paradox*, Delis himself describes a person who is clearly a "less loving" spouse with her husband, but becomes the more loving partner with her extramarital lover. In each case, this woman is taking a role that will contribute to a balance of intimacy within that particular relationship.

I agree with Carl Whitaker's assertion in *The Midnight Musings of a Family Therapist*: "The love on both sides is equal. Partners merely take turns with who is going to insist on the love, and who is going to protest against it."

Love is a desire to give whatever is best for your partner. It flows out of you toward the one you love; it is never expressed to build you up or to enhance your own self-image. Love is not sacrifice or martyrdom, for a gift of that kind always involves some sort of ego enhancement, or some sort of protection from a deeper level of pain and vulnerability. As M. Scott Peck says in *The Road Less Traveled*: "[Love is] the will to extend one's self for the purpose of nurturing one's own or another's spiritual growth."

Love carries with it a total sense of giving. It is a gift offered with no element of proving anything and no expectation of anything in return. Any attempt to get something back means that the force behind the gift is the ego, no matter how the giver might dress it up in the appearance of love.

I'm not saying that the various gifts we bring our partners are without love, but rather that the amount of love you are able to offer is the same for both of you. Any appearance of imbalance is due solely to the posturing and role-playing you and your partner have unconsciously agreed to exhibit.

The Limits to Our Capacity

Almost all of us declare, at one time or another, a desire to be closer, more intimate and more loving with our mates. We all express our desire to end the bickering, antagonism, judgment, isolation, criticism and lethargy that creates distance between us.

So why don't we? *Why* are there limits to our capacity for intimacy? Why can't we accept all of our "unacceptable" parts?

As long as we live in the bodies we do, we will experience limits to all the aspects of our being. Mentally, we use a very small amount of our cognitive capacity. Physically, we can run only so fast, leap so high, and inhale just so much air. And emotionally, we've all been hurt and scarred in so many different ways that fear often dominates all our other natural feelings. In reacting to the fear, we then monitor, hide, adjust or neutralize our true feelings in an effort to survive.

From the time we are born, we learn the risk that comes with closeness to another person. As children, every time we are hurt, punished, abandoned, criticized or abused in any way by our parents, and later by our siblings, friends and acquaintances, we acquire forms of protection against that emotional pain. Our emotional survival as children depends on us behaving in certain ways, and on adjusting, hiding or even denying our feelings in situations of pain and fear.

As we grow, these survival and defense mechanisms become more refined and solidified, so that by the time we are old enough to enter into intimate relationships, we have established definite limits to the amount of exposure and vulnerability we are willing to risk and share with each of our partners.

There is a beautiful little book by Robert Fisher called *The Knight in Rusty Armor*, which I recommend to all my couple clients. This wonderful fable speaks clearly to the issue of our intimacy limits and our capacity to accept the unacceptable.

In the story, a knight has become so attached to slaying dragons, providing for his wife and child, and always being a "good" knight that he never takes off his armor. His wife has to feed him through his helmet and he even wears his armor to bed.

When his wife can no longer tolerate this situation, she demands that he take his armor off, so she and their son can once again see and touch him. But it has become so much a part of him that he can't remove it. His armor hasn't just protected him from outside dangers, it has covered his true self so long that those parts are now unacceptable to him. In other words, he is stuck within the limits of his protection.

Faced with the threat of losing his wife and son, he sets off on a long, difficult journey to remove his armor. Only after a series of frightening, challenging and enlightening encounters does his armor begin to peel away so the majesty of his true self can again be revealed.

Some of us never risk such a journey, and our armor just remains a part of our relationships. Even when our conscious minds recognize the value of greater closeness to our mates, the deeper emotional part of us that protects us from risk, change and vulnerability does its best to sabotage our desired intentions. So, no matter how much lip service we pay to being more intimate within our relationships, our unconscious limits prove too powerful to ignore.

When I work with a couple, I can't be distracted by whatever illusions of difference they have created to hide their basic sameness. Instead, I must look for the primary issue: What level of intimacy exists in this relationship? What limits have these two people agreed to place on what is acceptable? How much fear are they willing to experience? The answers to these questions will always reveal an exact match for both partners within a specific span of time.

Perhaps a situation asks them to expose feelings of abandonment. One partner desires a greater degree of independence or momentary separation, and this desire threatens the couple's comfortable level of togetherness. Can they increase their distance without resorting to some form of holding on? Can they separate without drowning themselves in blame or guilt? The more they are willing to experience their mutual fear of abandonment, the greater their capacity for intimacy.

Your capacity for intimacy is determined by your willingness to allow three interrelated experiences into your life: the unacceptable, the unknown, and tension. While there are a hundred different thoughts, feelings and desires that you might consider unacceptable, they all are simply forms of these primary issues. As I continue exploring them throughout the remainder of this book, you will see that the boundaries of your circle of acceptance will expand in direct relation to your ability to accept these three qualities.

In any intimate relationship, there is an unspoken agreement between the partners: at all costs, we will avoid the unacceptable. At the boundaries of your personal unknown, where you feel most vulnerable, you will always want protection, and you will revert to the difference game to achieve it. Whatever outward dramas you and your partner may create, you are absolutely the same when it comes to your intimacy limits.

As an example of the ways these limits affect a particular feeling or experience, look once again at the issue of love. We all have internal stopping points that define our mutual capacity for love. It is here, at the boundaries of our protective circles, that giving love, or surrendering to it, becomes unacceptable.

Allowing yourself to be loved involves a willingness to receive, which is a struggle for most of us. To receive is to let your partner's love touch you fully, without resisting it, diminishing it, or analyzing it to death. Receiving love requires a willingness to surrender, which men often equate with weakness, and which women often regard as submissive.

Our emotional wounds and scars prevent most of us from fully experiencing love in its purest form. It is simply too rich a food for us. So we naturally pair off with someone who has a similar diet to our own.

The limits to your capacity may indeed be greater for you and your partner than for some other couples. But if you want more intimacy and fulfillment than you now possess, you will still have to risk the fear of even greater exposure and vulnerability. This is what John Wellwood, in his book *Journey of the Heart*, refers to as "dancing on the razor's edge."

Sustaining Tension

Dancing on the razor's edge and experiencing this vulnerability will naturally raise the anxiety in any relationship, as the partners are pulled between the known and unknown. A couple's willingness to sustain this new level of tension is crucial to moving out of their comfort zone.

Tension is usually regarded as negative, something we want to avoid. But tension is natural to life, and is present in everything we desire or experience. It is when we *reject* the tension inherent in situations that conflicts arise.

Everything in life exists in relation to its opposite. You can't experience trust without knowing distrust, independence without need, or joy without disappointment. Tension is created by the energy that is pulling on you from these two opposite directions and demanding that you take sides in any situation.

Central to your development as a couple is your mutual ability to accept and sustain the tension between the opposing forms of any quality. I am powerful and I am powerless. I am honest and dishonest. I embrace order and chaos, anger and affection, closeness and distance. When you accept both ends of any spectrum, there is no longer anything you need to avoid, defend or deny.

Whenever you favor one experience and reject its opposite, the tension surrounding those issues increases. If you reject helplessness, for example, and are attached to being helpful, then any time helplessness emerges in your relationship, the pressure to obliterate it will become overwhelming. You will either assign the unacceptable end of the spectrum to your partner ("*She's* the helpless one, not me."), you'll deny its existence totally ("I can always handle everything."), or you'll use whatever devices you can (work, drugs, food, hysteria or any other obsessive attachment) to avoid experiencing it. Whatever your method of denial, you'll expend an enormous amount of time and energy to escape this object of your displeasure.

Your only alternative to such avoidance is allowing yourself to truly experience feelings of helplessness. But doing so involves real risk because accepting this kind of tension will take you directly into the unknown and your protection will evaporate.

Partners in a relationship often attach themselves to opposite ends of a spectrum as a way of protecting their exposure and maintaining their comfort zones. One might choose strong and the other weak, one might clutch onto being organized while the other gets his identity from being free-spirited. But just imagine how happy this polarity makes their protectors, and how easily the couple will slide into the difference game as they maintain these roles.

If you want to blow this couple's cover, just ask a "weak" husband to stand up and experience his strength, and his "strong" wife to let go and allow her weakness to show. Instantly, these "opposites" become two equally frightened, defensive people. Their capacity for accepting these unacceptable parts of themselves has, as always, proven to be identical.

Each relationship carries with it an unconscious agreement to maintain whatever level of tension the couple is willing to accept. The particular experiences a couple rejects can be found at either end of any continuum, but the tension will always be greatest around whichever of these experiences they most want to hide, reject or avoid. When either partner violates their agreement by bringing one of these unacceptable experiences out in the open, the couple's protectors will search for a way to bring the level of tension back within their comfort zones. The difference game is perfect for this because the entire interaction can by played out without the couple ever realizing what the original event was. They'll mistake the noise of the difference game for tension, while the real energy and intensity of their core issue remains buried.

Mutuality provides an alternative way of responding to tension. When either partner is willing to accept and sustain a higher level of tension by accepting the unacceptable end of any spectrum, the couple's level of intimacy will increase. Even though this will be unknown and frightening, the experience will no longer be regarded as unacceptable.

Consider a marriage involving a very controlling husband who hides behind a loud, boisterous façade, and a wife who projects a sweet, likeable appearance while silently lamenting the lack of emotional connection in her marriage. On the surface they appear unequal. But, as always, their underlying capacity for intimacy is the same, and they are willing to sustain the same degree of tension.

Although she is willing to complain, the wife is afraid to assume greater power or to risk greater insecurity, in the same way that her husband is unwilling to risk experiencing need or surrender. If she truly wanted to support her own emotional needs, she might openly declare her displeasure and insist that her desire for a deeper connection be taken seriously. But to interact with her husband in this new way would certainly increase the tension in the relationship, as she moved from the security of the status quo toward the insecurity of the unknown.

For her to achieve her goal of greater intimacy, she'll have to withstand this new level of tension, accept her own fear and discomfort, and trust that she can love and be kind to herself regardless of his reaction. Until she has a real commitment for such a move, she'll continue posturing, waiting and denying her unacceptable desire for greater respect and independence.

Your need to maintain your shared level of tension and protection will prove stronger than any idealized vision you may have for your relationship. Outwardly you may proclaim your longing for a harmonious, trusting or committed marriage. But if such a relationship will expose the unacceptable parts of yourself, you'll do whatever is necessary to bring the tension level back within your comfort zone.

Closeness and Distance

Nowhere is this tension/protection dilemma more apparent than with the issue of *closeness* and *distance*. Often one partner in a relationship will favor greater togetherness, while the other wants more independence and separation. Every time this issue is raised, the conflict between the two lovers increases dramatically.

This conflict takes on a much different quality when considered in the light of equal capacity. No longer is the attention on who moves close or who moves away, who is being smothered and who abandoned. We can now focus on the more central issue of their *mutually* acceptable, agreed-upon distance.

When the question is asked, "Are you willing to move to an unacceptable distance?" both partners are shown to be the same in their capacity. One might take the role of the "forward-mover," and the other the "retreater," but their willingness to accept an unacceptable distance is the same.

So when the togetherness/separation argument once again rears its ugly head in your own relationship, you need only ask this question: *"Where have the two of us agreed to live on this continuum?"*

How many times in your relationship, just when you've decided to pack your bags or give your shmuck of a spouse the boot, has he seemed to change, and all of a sudden is more affectionate, more loving, more like the man you fell in love with? How often have big blowups occurred just when things seemed better than ever? And how many couples hit major conflicts right after moving in together, or getting engaged or getting married? These are all just variations of our continuing efforts to maintain our comfortable level of tension and distance.

Some couples present an idyllic picture of their togetherness. "Intimacy isn't our problem," they say. "We're very close." And indeed, when you watch them interact, their closeness is undeniable. They've never slept apart. He calls her from work on an hourly basis. She reacts to his needs before he's even aware of them. They're the emotional equivalent of Siamese twins.

But what happens if they move toward the other end of the spectrum? What if one has a desire the other doesn't share, or a need for some independence and distance? Then the pressure is on, they've moved into the unknown and their comfortable "intimacy" has disappeared.

Closeness may be familiar and safe, but the opposite end of the spectrum is way outside their comfort zone. Separateness is unacceptable, and the less movement they make toward greater distance, the less tension they will have to endure.

This back and forth dance couples engage in is superbly described in the book *The Two Step*, by Eileen McCann. What the author makes clear is that, despite the difference in style between one partner and the other, both people in a relationship are basically the same, and any role-playing is just an act.

McCann calls one style "The Seeker"—the partner who is always needing and moving closer. She labels the accompanying style "The Sought"—the one who is always pursued while moving away. Without an appreciation of the similarity between these two styles, a lot of name calling occurs. The seeker is frequently labeled needy and demanding, and the sought is accused of being distant and uncommitted.

We rarely recognize that these styles are just two ways of controlling our level of closeness and avoiding what is unacceptable. The seeker and the sought are really just two frightened people who hide their fear by moving toward or away from each other. The seeker finds it unacceptable to be needed, while the sought finds it unacceptable to declare, "I need you." At their core they are the same and are completely dependent on one another. You can't be a seeker without having someone to pursue, and you can't be sought without having someone seeking you.

Despite their outward appearance, these complementary roles are merely stylistic differences. The couple's primary objective is always to remain within their intimacy limits. And the difference game is the best tool they have for focusing on these surface differences and disguising their deeper, shared desires for protection.

Whatever form of protection the couple chooses, this camouflage is always a joint effort. If the mutual goal you and your partner share is to preserve a specific level of tension, it doesn't matter which one of you appears to be the bad guy or the distant one or the victim. You're playing the game together.

Differentiation

While it is the premise of this book that any two partners *within* a committed relationship are the same in their capacity for intimacy, this capacity will vary widely from one couple to the next. All relationships are not at the same level of development in their ability to expose the unacceptable. One couple might accept their fear of both abandonment and engulfment, for example, while another is unable to experience either of these feelings.

The quality I refer to as the capacity for intimacy is closely aligned with the concept of differentiation. According to David Schnarch in *Constructing the Sexual Crucible*, "Differentiation is the process by which a person manages both individuality and togetherness within a relationship."

Couples at the lowest level of differentiation are so emotionally needy, so reactive to others and so unaccepting of tension that they are unable to create a balance in their relationships between respecting their own needs and the needs of their partners. When a wife is dominated by her own needs, she becomes locked in the up position in the marriage; when she's engulfed by her husband's needs, she is stuck in down.

In their book *Family Evaluation*, Kerr and Bowen say that individuals at the highest level of differentiation are sure of their beliefs, convictions and self-assessment. They can listen to others without reacting, replace old beliefs with new ones and tolerate intense feelings without automatically trying to alleviate them.

The higher your level of differentiation, the more you are able to maintain your own autonomy as you move toward, away from, or against your partner. Your ability to sustain your feelings and desires, independent of any changes or reactions by your spouse, will be greater, as will the range of experiences you are willing to expose and accept.

You will always choose intimate partners who have reached your same level of differentiation. Each relationship then gives you the opportunity to grow and evolve, as you and your partner move together and expand your mutual capacity for intimacy. But whatever your level of differentiation, however large your circle of acceptance becomes, you and your partner will always encounter limits to your capacity.

OUR RESISTANCE TO SAMENESS

Perhaps by now your mind is racing to rack up evidence that you aren't *really* the same as your partner. Why, the idea is simply ridiculous. Just look at all the ways you're different. Ask anybody.

And how could anyone say that all these differences are superficial? Look how painful they are, how they dominate your lives! Even if there are deeper motives and desires underneath your actions, surely it's clear that you would give *anything* to be closer, more intimate, happier and more fulfilled—if only your stupid partner wasn't holding you both back.

Whether stated this way or not, these are the normal objections we all have to accepting the idea that our own limitations are defining our relationships. But this is the responsibility we need to accept as soon as we admit that at our deepest levels, we are the same as our partners.

Whenever I work with a couple over a period of time, it's always fascinating for me then to see each of them on an individual basis. Typically, each will share with me how emotionally unavailable the other one is. This is declared with great conviction, and each piece of evidence supporting this truth will be described in great detail.

Eventually I will respond, "He said the exact same thing about you."

"He did?" the partner will reply with a puzzled expression. "Well, let me tell you this one." Then more evidence of the spouse's unavailability is presented.

After several rounds of my saying, "He said the same thing about you," the client will begin to laugh. It has finally dawned on her that I won't let her get away with avoiding the obvious sameness of their attitudes toward each other.

As the partners begin to realize that any finger pointing they do will just come back at them, they start letting go of their resistance because it's clearly not accomplishing their original intent.

Each attempt on their part to verify their differences merely strengthens my perception of their sameness because each partner is an exact reflection of the other's behavior. With each proclamation they expose what is truly unacceptable to both of them: seeing the other partner as available.

As further verification of your underlying sameness, you and your partner share one undeniable bond: you picked each other. Somehow, in the midst of the hundreds of people you've each encountered in your lives, the two of you found enough mutual similarity and potential for intimacy that you chose to travel down the relationship path together.

Just this evidence alone would seem to justify a belief in some underlying sameness. Yet when confronted with the concept of mutuality, many couples look at me as if the idea was totally foreign, as if they were together solely because of some bizarre twist of fate—love by immaculate selection.

Certainly people with opposite traits can be attracted to one another. But only those having similar capacities for acceptance and intimacy can create and sustain a relationship. Without this similar vibration, the two people would simply pass in the night with hardly a glance. There would be no energy or interest to support even the slightest degree of commitment to one another.

All your resistance to admitting your basic sameness is simply your protector in action. The part of you that wants to avoid risk and vulnerability will do whatever is necessary to keep you from recognizing your underlying equality with your partner.

Even though this entire book is built on the premise that we are absolutely equal, I can't begin to tell you how many times in my own marriage I have wanted to believe I was special—uniquely caring, intimate, knowledgeable or fair. "It isn't conceivable that Karen and I could be the same in this situation," I have said to myself on numerous occasions. "How could we possibly be, given all the evidence I've collected to the contrary?"

After countless situations where I reluctantly had to admit my own desire for protection or superiority, I have a deep appreciation for the difficulties couples face in recognizing and accepting their equality. Yet, no matter how terrifying this experience might be, it is the only path away from the difference game and toward greater intimacy.

Our egos hardly care what form our uniqueness takes; we can be powerful or powerless, selfish or selfless, independent or dependent, nasty or nice. All that matters is that we stand apart from each other as unique, separate and special individuals.

To your ego, the idea that you are the same as another person is literally an emotional death because it forces you to face the loss of who you think you are. Sameness threatens what you regard as your very being. Is it any wonder that even considering such an idea, let alone recognizing and accepting your sameness, terrifies you?

"Okay," you may be saying, "maybe lots of couples really do have the same capacity for intimacy. Sure, my partner and I selected each other, and maybe all of the differences we focus on are just a smoke screen to protect our egos.

"But what if, down deep, we really are different? What if one of us can accept greater closeness, but the other can't? Or what if we started out with the same capacity, but one of us grew, evolved or changed faster than the other? What then?!"

My response to all such questions or arguments is simply this: If you and your partner were truly different in your capacity for intimacy and acceptance, you wouldn't be together. An intimate relationship with a partner who truly possessed a lesser capacity would result not in pain or pleasure, but in simple lack of interest.

Imagine playing tennis with someone who isn't your equal. You defeat your opponent every time—no contest. The only way he can ever win is for you to play down to his level and "give" him the game. It's possible that such a matchup might fulfill some need you have to look magnanimous (by handing him a victory) or all-powerful (by slaughtering him on the court). But if your desire is simply to give yourself totally to the experience of tennis, this opponent will be of no interest to you.

Of course, you could always play an occasional game just to instruct the other person, or to get some exercise, or to fool around on the tennis court. But you would never agree to daily matches with someone who so clearly had a lesser capacity. You simply wouldn't have that much energy or commitment for a situation that failed to meet your own reasons for playing the game.

Now compare this situation to your marriage. While tennis is a game that would normally constitute only a small portion of your life, an intimate romantic relationship is something that occupies you every day. The amount of energy required to face the problems, struggles, fears, conflicts, decisions, obstacles and difficulties inherent in any marriage is exponentially greater than a simple tennis match, or any other analogy I could create.

So *something* must be justifying all the energy your relationship demands of you. And it has to be something more than merely biding your time while you wait for your partner to "catch up" to your level of intimacy. To devote all the effort you are using right now to remain in whatever relationship you're in, you have to feel engaged, involved and connected. And that connection is your sameness.

If you're still doubtful, consider this: If you truly possess a greater capacity for intimacy than your mate, then you will accept the differences between you without any drama or emotionality. So whenever he is distant, clinging, combative or obnoxious, you'll simply accept this behavior as a reflection of his lesser capacity. You won't judge it, react to it or pretend it isn't there. You will just acknowledge it and take responsibility for the fact that you chose this person.

This honest acceptance of your mate's lesser capacity will involve no frustration, criticism, superiority, anger or feelings of defeat on your part. At most, you might experience sadness at the loss of something you desire in the relationship. But your sadness will be pure, without the least hint of blame attached to it. If you really have a greater capacity for acceptance, there is nothing to be gained by an attitude of judgment and superiority.

Of course, if your partner was exhibiting these behaviors on a continuous basis, there would be no more for you to gain from the relationship. Which brings us back to my previous contention: without any opportunity to learn and grow, you will simply move on, without judgment, anger or blame.

Any desire to prove anything, especially your partner's lesser capacity for acceptance and intimacy, means you're using "capacity for intimacy" as a basis for the difference game. In other words, you're using the pretense of a willingness to be closer to hide your own fears and to avoid the realization that at this deepest level, there is no real difference between you and your partner.

Beneath Gender Difference

Essential to any discussion of equality and acceptance is the issue of gender difference. Of all the qualities which distinguish the two partners in any relationship, perhaps no other poses such a strong challenge to the idea of underlying sameness.

Besides obvious biological differences, a variety of personality traits, communication styles, emotional needs and psychological goals clearly delineate men and women. How can we acknowledge and honor these distinctions between the sexes and still find a deeper sameness and acceptance that will form the basis for connection between any two partners?

Many prominent psychologists and authors have recently explored the gender distinctions inherent in our contemporary culture. In the chart below, I have summarized the most prominent psychological and emotional differences between men and women to be revealed and analyzed during the last ten years.

This list draws on material from four major sources: *You Just Don't Understand*, by Deborah Tannen; *What Really Works with Men*, by Justin Sterling; *Why Men Are the Way They Are*, by Warren Farrell; and *Men Are from Mars, Women Are from Venus*, by John

Gray. As with any such broad distinctions, gender differences are based on generalities, so there will certainly be exceptions. But these seem to apply to most men and women, and usually elicit a great deal of recognition and identification in many individuals.

Women	**Men**
Primary fantasy is family and security	Primary fantasy is being desired
Identify with connection	Identify with status and independence
Value love and communication	Value achievement
See interactions in terms of closeness and distance	See interactions in terms of up and down
Prefer "feeling" language	Prefer auditory language
Communicate through words and feelings	Communicate through action
Relationship is number one	Competition is number one
Complex, multidimensional	Simple, one-dimensional
High maintenance	Low maintenance
Socially oriented	Task oriented
Problem oriented	Solution oriented
Want to be accepted and fashionable	Want to get the job done
Relationships are for caring	Relationships are for ego gratification
Decide "when" sexually	Decide "how" sexually
Relationship managers	Relationship workers
Need to talk when stressed	Need to withdraw into caves when stressed
Motivated and empowered when they feel cherished	Motivated and empowered when they feel needed and respected

Fear being unworthy	Fear being incompetent
Afraid of receiving	Afraid of giving
Similar to waves (rise and fall in ability to love)	Similar to rubber bands (pull back and then get close)
Argue for the right to be upset	Argue for the right to be free
Want understanding	Want space
Want to improve men	Want to fix women
Need to learn the art of empowerment	Need to learn the art of listening

An awareness of these gender differences can be extremely help-ful in reducing the conflict in some relationships. When we recog-nize the distinct goals and styles that men and women exhibit, communication and understanding are far easier than if we each assume that our partners possess the same needs, desires and ways of interacting that we do.

Nonetheless, in order to support the weight of all these biological, emotional and stylistic differences, it is essential that you create a strong foundation of sameness in your relationship. Unless the two of you build such a foundation by going beneath your inherent male/female natures, the gender differences you exhibit can bury the connection you desire.

To illustrate, I want to focus on one of the most common gender differences: women seek emotional connection in order to feel secure and men seek sexual connection in order to feel desirable. While there are certainly exceptions to these generalities, these seem to be dominant goals for husbands and wives in most marriages. Countless battles are waged over these two needs when they are used as a basis for judgment and rejection. When wives accuse their husbands, "You're not there for me emotionally," or husbands maintain, "You're not there for me sexually," the difference game is in full play.

Understanding that these two differences are gender related is important for reducing the surprise and drama surrounding such conflicts. But labeling them as such only tells part of the story. What is being overlooked is the insatiability of both desires.

The need to feel secure and the need to feel desirable are both endless. And the insatiable craving for either one leads to an even deeper experience of powerlessness. So, underneath these two very different longings are two experiences that are identical for both partners: the endless pursuit of an insatiable need and the rejection of unacceptable feelings of powerlessness.

If we view the deeper context in which we live out these needs, we are less likely to use these drives destructively. When we can look beneath these surface desires, we can recognize our absolute equality. Real intimacy can then grow out of our mutual experience of powerlessness and insatiable longing.

Another prominent gender difference which frequently leads to a hierarchical perception is a woman's need to be cherished and a man's need to be respected. This is clearly illustrated in Patricia Allen's book *Getting to "I Do"*, where she discusses how destructive the absence of these two qualities is to forming any lasting committed relationship. Couples who accuse each other of failing to meet these needs are often blind to the exact equality of their mutual rejection. The man wanting respect will fail to cherish his partner to the same extent that she fails to respect him.

In *Gender War, Gender Peace*, Aaron Kipnis and Elizabeth Herron detail some other primary issues that divide men and women:

Men fear women's power to wound them emotionally; women fear men's power to wound them physically.

Men say women are too emotional; women say men don't feel enough.

Women feel that men don't listen; men think that women talk too much.

Many men believe they must become more like women to be whole; and many women are trying to be more like men.

The common element in each of these differences between men and women is the perception that lies beneath each difference. In

each case, both men and women are fearful, superior or believe they
are lacking something.

It is also important to realize that many gender differences are
based on appearances rather than substance. But digging beneath
the masks that men and women project reveals matching fears and
desires. For example, men often give the appearance that they are
standing up and demonstrating their power and strength. A loud
voice, a tone of authority, strong opinions and high status all support the impression that they are bold and forthright. Yet when challenged about their particular stance, they typically resort to
dictatorial behavior, violence, bragging, defending, proving,
explaining or withdrawing. Where's the power in these behaviors?
These actions might result in some temporary sense of control or
superiority, but real power will remain a fantasy. All the loud posturing is simply a façade of power, hiding the fear and vulnerability we all share.

In the same way, women are traditionally thought of as feeling
oriented and highly skilled at connecting to others. Their ease of
emoting, their fluency in the language of relating and their stated
desire for togetherness—these all reinforce the image of a loving,
caring nature. Yet in reality, their behavior can frequently be consumed with complaining, manipulating, name-calling, depression
and expressions of hopelessness. How will any closeness or connection result from these reactions? Appeasement and resentment, perhaps, but rarely intimacy and joining. As with men, an outward
persona hides the reality of their fear, vulnerability and desire for
protection.

In *The Myth of Male Power*, Warren Farrell maintains that because
each gender is so preoccupied with denying or disguising its own vulnerability, neither men *nor* women are able to recognize or acknowledge the vulnerability of the other.

A final distinction critical to perceiving the underlying equality
between men and women is the difference between being male and
being masculine, and the similar difference between being female
and being feminine.

To be *masculine* is to stand up for the integrity of all that a man is, neither disguising one's power nor directing it against another. This attitude is beautifully described by Robert Bly in his book *Iron John*. Bly talks about standing up and displaying one's sword, rather than hiding it or hurting someone with it.

To be *feminine* is to surrender to one's receptive nature, and to trust in its power in order to connect with a loved one. Like masculinity, the feminine nature is inherently powerful. It cannot be threatened, and it has no need to prove or defend anything.

Couples who have accepted and integrated these qualities will be open to touching and being touched by each other in many ways. These couples' real power and surrender are a far cry from the posturing and disguises men and women typically exhibit under the semblance of "male" and "female."

The abundance of proving, boasting, attacking, defending and searching for approval present in troubled relationships reveals the absence of feminine and masculine natures, not their presence. When the qualities of masculinity and femininity are present, there are no attempts to prove anything or seek approval, and men and women look very similar in their power.

When our basic masculinity and femininity are not honored and respected, any attempt to expand beyond our true natures becomes distorted. For example, in response to many of the cultural pressures of the last three decades, men have attempted to express more of their feminine side. As a result, many men have turned into mush, because they never developed their true masculine self. Instead of becoming powerful men who also exhibit sensitivity and emotional vulnerability, they are simply passive, confused and easily manipulated males. They have no firm foundation on which to expand and build their added feminine dimension.

Similarly, when women, in their desire for equality, attempted to become more masculine, many of them turned cold and hard because they hadn't first developed their feminine, receptive nature sufficiently to support this new quality.

THE POWER OF MUTUALITY

When you live the truth that you are essentially the same, the defenses, posturing, drama, superiority and victimization will begin to disappear.

> *Alice and Paul had been married for 15 years when they came to me for counseling. Both believed their relationship was at a dead end, and that they were caught in an endless cycle of futile arguing and icy silence.*
>
> *The two of them acted more like a harsh, hostile boss and a brow-beaten employee than a wife and a husband. Alice repeatedly criticized Paul's lack of ambition, passion or interest in her. "He never listens to me," she'd complain, "and he's always retreating into his shell. All he wants to do in the evening is drink and smoke."*
>
> *In response to her accusations, Paul would defend himself with impotent explanations. "I did show an interest in you just the other night," he'd declare, and offer a detailed description of some incident that he hoped might disprove her perceptions. When that failed, he would simply shrug his shoulders with a helpless, "But I do love you."*
>
> *Many therapy sessions would be spent replaying this same scenario over and over again. Whenever Paul felt intimidated by Alice's barrage of accusations, he would withdraw into silence or helplessness. This merely fueled her perception of him as a weak, passionless wimp. And her resulting rage reinforced his sense of futility at ever satisfying her.*

Alice and Paul's marriage was typical of those consumed by the difference game because on the surface they seemed so incompatible. These troubled relationships often involve very verbal, aggressive women and passive, withdrawn men.

Many times my belief in the two of them remaining married was shaken. But whenever I pursued their thoughts of divorce, they each said, "No, I don't want that." Despite all their mutual accusations, neither one wanted to experience the ultimate consequences of their negative perceptions.

The key to breaking through this stalemate was in finding their underlying sameness, and getting them to recognize it. Given the strength and endurance of her negativity and his passivity, this was no easy task.

I shared with Alice and Paul that after numerous sessions they had given me a very clear picture of their differences and how dissatisfied they both were, but now I wanted to know how the two of them were alike.

Their immediate response was to look at me like I was speaking Swedish, and then to present me with another flood of differences. But with each new accusation, or each new defense, I asked, "But how is that different?"

When Alice proclaimed, "He doesn't show interest in me," I responded, "But how is that different? Do you show interest in him?"

"Well, no," she answered, then quickly added, "but he's not passionate."

"So how is that different?"

"Well, I scream a lot."

"That sounds more like an exercise than any real passion," I said. "To me, you loudly express little passion and he quietly expresses little passion."

Alice suddenly became very quiet, so I turned to Paul, who repeated his own familiar refrain.

"She's never satisfied with me."

"And how is that different?"

"Well, I'm satisfied with her," he declared, as if it was obvious.

"Oh," I said. "Are you satisfied sexually?"

"Well, no."

"Are you satisfied with the way she respects you?"

"Well, no."

"Are you satisfied with the way she talks to you?"

"Well, no."

"Well," I asked, "just what exactly are you satisfied with?"

Then he got quiet as well, so I repeated my desire to look at how they were both the same.

This process was quite slow, and we encountered numerous set-backs as each of them reverted to their familiar lists of differences. But my persistent challenges to their perceptions allowed me to plant the seeds of sameness in their consciousness.

I kept pointing out their mutual inability to stand up for them-selves in the relationship. Although they both supported their own needs and desires quite skillfully and powerfully in the outside world, with each other they had become quite dependent. Rather than experience the unacceptable feelings that came with real independence, each would wait for the other to change so that he or she could then react. They were drawing their energy from each other rather than from within themselves.

For example, Alice frequently expressed a need for love or sex-ual affection. But she would give up this desire the moment Paul gave her the "wrong" response. A real turning point occurred for her when she began to see that burying her needs by withdrawing into her barrage of accusations was no different than Paul "wimp-ing out" on his needs and withdrawing into his wall of silence.

This opened the door to another key similarity they shared: each saw the other solely in terms of a "problem" that needed to be solved. Alice saw Paul as a depriving object, and he saw her as a threatening and crushing object.

As they began to realize how much these views dominated the relationship, they started to see each other not as objects but as three-dimensional people who were both struggling with fears of inadequacy and abandonment. The more they were able to recog-nize how similar they were at this deeper level, the more they were able to stop blaming each other.

Both Alice and Paul felt humbled and frightened as they con-fronted their own individual barriers to closeness. But fully experi-encing this fear and humility enabled them to develop a sense of self.

The gradual transformation in their relationship was wonderful to observe. Alice began to express her needs and sustain them without blame, and Paul became more expressive, more involved, and better able to respond to the needs and emotions she offered him. Their surface drama dissipated as they joined on this deeper level of sameness.

Mutuality doesn't require deep analysis or intricate jargon; you don't need to label your behavior; you don't have to decide whether your mate is unavailable, hysterical, manic or depressed. The only issue *in any situation* is whether you're placing yourself above or below your partner. If you are, there is only one question to ask yourself: *Am I going to continue playing the difference game, or am I willing to recognize the underlying sameness that my partner and I share, and risk moving into an attitude of acceptance?*

The answer in any given moment is simply yes or no.

Explanations, defensiveness and excuses are unnecessary. A yes is a vote for intimate joining. A no is a vote for separation. The choice is yours.

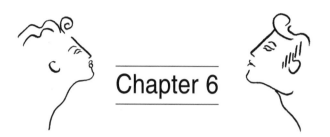

Chapter 6

A LONGING TO JOIN
The Goal of Mutuality

*The essence of the art of
partnership is the capacity to recognize
the commonality as well as the inherent
differences between men and women, and to
create relationships and vital communities
that support the unique values of both
sexes. The art of partnership is an essential
skill for building bridges from gender
war to gender peace.*

—Aaron Kipnis and Elizabeth Herron *Gender War, Gender Peace*

The ultimate goal of developing a mutual attitude is *connection*. The desire to join—to be one with another person, with humanity, with the universe and with all the rejected parts of ourselves—is our deepest longing. While the purpose of the difference game is to protect ourselves from the unknown by staying separate, the goal of mutuality is to experience the love, power and healing that come from joining with each other and ourselves. And that deep connection grows out of our willingness to accept the unacceptable.

After three years of marriage, Don and Janet were barely surviving financially, even with both of them working. Don was a self-employed accountant whose clients consumed at least 65 hours a week. He was often in his office on the weekend, and every night he'd come home exhausted.

This put Janet in a bind. She was increasingly frustrated and resentful at having such minimal contact with her husband. But how could she say anything? He was working so hard and was under so much pressure already. She felt sorry for Don, and would do almost anything to avoid seeming selfish.

Don was aware of the strain his work was putting on their relationship. Though Janet rarely made any direct comments about her anger or pain, her feelings were barely disguised by such innocuous comments as, "Hi, stranger," or, "It's hard to remember the last time we were together."

He began to feel guilty, but his fear of reducing his workload was a much bigger concern. He had always been determined to protect himself from any loss, especially economic. It would be devastating to see himself in debt. So as Janet became more demanding of his time, he started to feel resentful, and it took all his willpower not to accuse her of being ungrateful.

Soon the pain of feeling abandoned became so unbearable for Janet that she was contemplating leaving the marriage. Inevitably, with so many emotions being held beneath the surface, their sniping back and forth increased, until finally they had a major blow up.

When the yelling and anger subsided, Don and Janet realized that they did not want this issue to destroy their marriage. But their usual pattern of ignoring/discussing/accusing/exploding had led them nowhere. To get through this, they would have to communicate differently than they ever had. They knew they both had to stop defending and take a risk.

They never expected that opening up to each other would be as terrifying as it was. A lot of silence and hesitation punctuated their conversation, they both endured feelings of discomfort, and at times they both wanted to simply leave the room. But they hung in there with each other.

Don revealed that as much as he wanted to meet Janet's needs, he was terrified of letting go of his work. All his life his father had drilled into him that self-sufficiency was the most important quality a person could possess. Financial failure was the worst thing that could happen. To risk such an unacceptable situation would be like falling off a cliff. "I just don't know what I'd do if I couldn't make ends meet."

Janet had never seen Don this vulnerable before. But she held his gaze as she responded, "I know I've been telling myself that I was afraid of you not being there for me. But the truth is, I'm used to taking care of myself. What really scares me is sensing how much I depend on you. If I let myself need you that much, I'll be completely helpless."

Seeing her innocently and tearfully share this, Don admitted that he had never let himself really depend on another person either. As long as he put all his energy into work, he could feel he had some kind of control over his life. In reality, he was just as scared of being needy as she was.

After quietly exposing themselves in this new way, they simply held each other for the longest time. They hadn't come up with any new ideas for their problem, but they felt closer to each other than they had in a long time.

Many of us want the intimate connection that Don and Janet experienced, but we don't want to subject ourselves to the fear, discomfort and exposure required to get there. We prefer to dance around our vulnerability, and find some other way to accomplish the goal of connection. But as we exhaust each of these "safer" possibilities for healing our relationships, greater happiness and intimacy still seem to elude us. No matter what roads we travel to reach the connection we desire, we always end up in front of the same closed door, with the sign above it reading "Unacceptable."

With Don and Janet, this door represented need. Until they risked passing through an unacceptable experience of their mutual need, they couldn't get to the connection they longed for on the other side.

The particular unacceptable door you have to open will vary, but it will always be frightening, it will always lead you into the unknown and it will always be your only passage toward greater intimacy and joining.

Eventually all couples are confronted with the same choice: are we going to support our deepest desires for connection or will we choose some form of drama and distance?

In *The Path of Least Resistance*, Robert Fritz states that once a structure exists, energy will move through that structure because it's the path of least resistance. In other words, your energy moves where it is easiest to go. If you want any real change in your life, you have to create a new structure that is as powerful as the old one. You need to replace the familiar behaviors that don't support your present desires with behaviors that do.

For most of us, the structure of the difference game is so strongly developed that it's no surprise our energy tends to flow toward those attitudes and behaviors. So when we repeatedly take that path of least resistance, the outcome will always be protection and distance.

Our only alternative is to create a new structure of mutuality, so our energy can flow toward acceptance and equality, and lead us to the connection we desire. Building this new structure involves risk and hard work. But it's the only way the door to greater intimacy can be a real choice for us.

As Merle Shain says in her book *Some Men are More Perfect Than Others*:

> *Loving can cost a lot but not loving always costs more, and those who fear to love often find that want of love is an emptiness*

that robs the joy from life. Men and women who don't know love often feel they've missed the essential experience of life, . . . and while we all fear that we'll be hurt if we care, it's better to take a chance on love than to wish, when we've lost the chance, that we had.

THE LONGING FOR CONNECTION

The trauma of birth leaves us with two primary needs: protection and connection. As I discussed in Chapter 2, being forced out of the safety and contentment of the womb instills in us immediate feelings of helplessness and fear. The wounds and scars we then endure as we live and grow only strengthen our need to once again feel safe. We'll create an entire identity, and a unique perception of the world, just to give us some sense of control over our lives and protection from the unknown.

But from the moment we're born, an equally powerful longing is instilled in us as well: to regain the feeling of connection we've now lost. The vulnerability we feel in leaving the womb, and our helpless isolation as we begin to recognize our separation, make us desperate to regain the feeling of unity and joining we once possessed.

As we move through life, we are constantly pulled by these two powerful forces: our desire for safety and our longing for connection. I recently heard a client exclaim, only half-joking, "My life would be great, if only I could live in a cave!"

But of course she can't. Because no matter how protected we might feel by avoiding all intimate human contact, our longing for real connection would be overpowering.

So we try to have it both ways by feeding the longing without risking the unknown: intimacy without exposure. But it doesn't work. It's a connection of egos, rather than a joining of hearts.

Your decision to buy this book may have grown out of any number of needs or desires, just as choosing to come to therapy is expressed in a variety of ways:

"I want to stop the pain."
"We're just not happy anymore."
"Our relationship isn't going anywhere."

Whatever problem, current or anticipated, led you to these pages, it is merely a form of one particular goal: you want to be connected. You no longer want to be polarized from your partner. You want to replace your separation with intimacy.

This longing for connection lies at the core of our being. One of the defining elements of all living things is the quality of being a part of some larger system or group. Our families, friendships, love, desire, work, play and worship all are rooted in this deepest of human needs.

Only within a connective relationship can we expose the feelings and desires we've ignored all our lives, and which now cry for attention. Only by accepting and joining can we recognize and heal our emotional wounds.

Mutuality offers us the opportunity to heal the split created by an attitude of judgment and hierarchy because it constantly exposes us to all that we consider unacceptable. Each time we reunite with some unacceptable part of our true nature, we mend a wounded part of ourselves, and we come closer to being whole.

In Don and Janet's quiet moment of connection, the passion between them increased dramatically because passion is where connection is. Their energy had been consumed with blocking and hiding what they considered unacceptable, so there was little left to share with each other. Once they stopped protecting and allowed themselves to experience their need, the energy flowed between them unobstructed.

When unacceptable feelings are denied or rejected, love becomes muted and lukewarm. But when the energy flows unrestricted through the structure of acceptance, love and passion increase.

THE CONNECTOR

There is a part of you that honors the deep longing you feel for unity, whose only objective is oneness and joining. This is the part I call the "connector."

In Chapter 2, I introduced you to your protector. His sole concern is to keep you within your comfort zone and to guard against risk and exposure. Your connector is his exact opposite. Her goal is to invite you to go beyond your comfort zone and expose the integrity of who you are. Your protector will take every thought, feeling and desire you possess and use it as a means of separation. Your connector will take every part of you and use it as a basis for joining.

I refer to the protector as "he" and the connector as "she" to make these parts of ourselves more real and personal than they would seem if I used the word "it" for both. But again, these aspects of our psychological communities are present in all of us, and neither protection nor intimacy is gender specific.

To your protector, every quality you hold is judged and ranked in relation to all the others, whereas your connector regards all your parts as equally worthy and acceptable. Your protector sees only the differences between you and your partner, whereas your connector sees only the sameness underneath. Your protector embraces conflict and apathy, but the unknown is to be avoided at all costs. Your connector embraces acceptance and passion, and cares only that you eliminate all judgments.

Your connector will look for the real energy that lies underneath each interaction between you and your partner. She will look for the place where the noise and rhetoric turn quiet, but where the real tension exists. It is there that the risk is greatest, and it is there that the impulse to run will be strongest. But she knows that this is where real intimacy, passion and healing will occur.

When conflicts arise between you and your partner, your protector will shout warnings in your ear, trying to keep you within the safety of your comfort zone. But your connector wants to lead you through the maze of your defenses toward a real connection with your partner. If you could turn down the volume on your protector's warnings, you would hear your connector asking . . .

What's missing here?
What is all this intensity really about?

What if you both agreed over this?
What is so unpleasant about connecting over this?
What if you recognized that you both are equally wounded here?
How are you the same right now?
What are you really afraid of?

With questions like these, your connector explores each interaction until your real connection is revealed.

In the midst of your judgment and distance, your connector holds out her hand and invites you to join with your unacceptable feelings. Despite all your excuses, justifications and fears, she will sustain her position. She will acknowledge and honor your fear, but she will never try to hide or suppress it. She will simply offer her strength in support of any loving movement toward your partner.

Perhaps the connector seems too good to be true because I'm drawing a picture of the connective part of ourselves as if it had our full support and were fully available to us. But, for most of us, this part is not as highly developed as I'm presenting it. Rarely is your protector *or* your connector present 100%, undiluted by the existence of the other.

THE CONNECTIVE BELIEFS OF MUTUALITY

Moving from the difference game to equality and acceptance requires a change in our beliefs as well as our perceptions. Only by replacing our ingrained creed of judgment and hierarchy with one of acceptance and equality will we find the courage to leave our comfort zones.

Imagine that you've always wanted to go off a high diving board, but have been too afraid. As you climb higher and higher up the ladder, a familiar voice in your head keeps telling you all the things that will protect you from this risk: *"It's too high." "If you fail you'll look foolish." "This could kill you."*

But if your longing to jump is strong, another voice will guide you to the edge: *"You can do this." "You won't get hurt." "It's okay to risk."* If you want to step off the board, it is *these* beliefs you will have to accept, if only for the instant that you make your dive. Similarly, if you want to take the plunge into greater intimacy, you will need to adopt the beliefs of mutuality.

This shift will be neither immediate nor total. I know that the beliefs of separation have been drilled into you for so long that most of the time they're accepted without question. But if your desire for real connection is strong enough, and you can assume the beliefs of mutuality for only a moment, you will temporarily move out of your old patterns and into equality and acceptance. The more you allow these new beliefs into your consciousness, the greater your experience of intimacy will be.

I Can Survive the Unknown

The unknown is a place of opportunity, not a threat to your existence. It is by moving into the unknown that you can welcome new experiences. Clinging to everything in your known, protected world is a deadening routine. Your passion cannot live in such surroundings.

In the world of the unknown every movement, expression, thought and feeling is fresh and vibrant. Your life becomes an adventure, and your willingness to risk provokes excitement in yourself and those around you.

All My Qualities Are Worthy of Acceptance

Your humanity gives you a myriad of qualities and a multitude of ways to respond to your environment and the people around you. When you regard half of yourself as just some excess baggage put here to burden you, or some dark secret worthy only of your fear and shame, then you deny your true nature and you dissipate your energy and passion.

None of us can feel connected unless all the components of our internal communities are allowed to come home. Only by embracing the "unacceptable" parts of ourselves can we stop feeling threatened.

I Can Only Be Intimate with My Equal

You can only experience intimacy at eye level. If you're holding a stance above or below your partner, real connection can never occur. So long as you're judging, protecting, denying or disguising portions of yourself and your partner, you'll maintain your separation. But as soon as you experience the equality of your wounds, your pain, your fear, your needs, your strengths and your desires, you will create the foundation for greater closeness and satisfaction.

I Can Always Connect with My Partner

This may be the most difficult belief to accept because it is part of our language to say, "I can't connect with him. There is no one to relate to. He offers nothing."

Within an attitude of acceptance, you realize that the separateness you feel is an illusion. Your need is not to regain what was lost, but to recognize the connections that have always been there. As long as you are willing to accept the unacceptable and experience all that your partner has to offer, you will find a basis for joining. Once you stop judging the part you have been rejecting that will be the place where you can connect.

So if you say, "I can't connect with him because he's withdrawn," it means you find his withdrawal unacceptable, and you don't want to connect with that part of him. But as soon as you accept and embrace his withdrawal, the two of you will join.

Surrender Is a Source of Real Power

Most of the conflict you experience grows out of your *opposition* to anyone and anything. With your partner, with the world and within yourself, your never ending struggle to win, or to establish your own acceptable identity, consumes your energy and power. Surrender isn't even acknowledged as an option.

Surrender means letting go of identities you have cherished and been devoted to for many years. These images of ourselves, while providing great protection, will never enable us to be touched by another, or to move on with our lives.

M. Scott Peck opens *The Road Less Traveled* with these words: "Life is difficult. This is a great truth . . . because once we truly see this truth, we transcend it. Once we truly know that life is difficult—once we truly understand and accept it—then life is no longer difficult. Because once it is accepted, the fact that life is difficult no longer matters." Those of us who try to fight against this truth end up with very stressful lives, while those of us who surrender to it are able to bounce and flow much more easily with life's ups and downs.

This is especially true when we are confronted with powerlessness. The amount of effort we each expend trying to deny, avoid or get around this experience could launch several satellites, fuel a fleet of battleships, and surpass the energy we devote to children, work and spouse combined.

Olivia had been struggling her whole life against her family members regarding her as a "bad" person. Aside from work, her life seemed empty. She had almost no energy left to love herself, or allow love into her life because all her forces were geared against this threat to her image.

After approaching this issue with her in several different ways, one day I simply said, "What if you let them win?"

A shocked expression appeared on her face, and she immediately retorted that she couldn't do that. "What have you got to lose?" I persisted. "In some resigned way, you pretty much agree with them already. Why not just surrender?"

Slowly she began to allow the idea of letting them see her as "bad" without fighting against their perception. She began to feel frightened and said she felt faint. I validated her feeling, and reiterated that she was allowing something that was really scary. Gradually, her whole body began to soften, and an aliveness appeared that wasn't there before.

By allowing yourself to let go of some favored protective identity, your energy is no longer consumed by denying your helplessness.
Instead of battling for control of your life, you surrender to your
powerlessness and channel your energy towards fulfillment and
connection.

Intimacy Embraces Togetherness and Individuality

Only by integrating both individuality and togetherness into your
marriage can you come to know a truly intimate connection. If you
latch on to one or the other exclusively, you're denying the integrity of
all that you are and the need to balance both of these essential needs.

Allowing a balance means you fully live your individuality, with
no compromise, until you *naturally* move into a full experience of
your togetherness. This movement from one to the other creates a
dynamic rhythm, as one moment you join with your mate, and the
next you move away to honor some need within yourself.

When you can celebrate your togetherness without resentment, and
celebrate your solitude without guilt, you have come to understand
that mutuality means being intimately together and intimately apart.

Couples who engage in the difference game typically favor one
side over the other and end up limiting their intimate connection. If
you stay too far apart from your partner and ignore your need for
togetherness, you become overly isolated and emotionally under-
nourished. Then your individuality and solitude lack real peace and
fulfillment. You're *resigned* to being alone, rather than embracing
your independence.

When you remain too close to your mate, you tend to ignore your
own individual needs and boundaries, and you're left in a state of
constant *resentment*. Then, when you try to connect on a deeper
level, your resentment leaks all over her. She asks you to listen and
you get impatient. She says that she misses you and you get irritat-
ed. In one way or another, denying your individuality will push the
two of you apart.

It may seem funny that being too close is a problem. Yet, I would say that most of the troubled couples I see are too enmeshed. As a result, every movement, expression, statement or feeling that either exhibits affects or hurts the other.

> *"You want to go play tennis, so you must care more about your friends than me."*
> *"You don't like my hair, so I feel destroyed."*
> *"You don't like my work, so I feel worthless."*

Partners who remain too close to each other are unable to listen to each other as separate individuals, and everything is viewed as a threat. By not allowing their individual integrity to exist, they both end up consumed with changing each other.

I often tell my clients to think of their partners as being on a stage. If you sit too close, it's too difficult to absorb all that's going on, and you become enmeshed in the action and overwhelmed by it, rather than appreciating and being emotionally connected to the beauty of the play.

The opposite is also true. If you're too far from the stage, you miss your partner's wonderful performance, and you don't have any sense of what the play is about. Your partner's passion is just a distant blur.

David Schnarch says that differentiating yourself from your partner is the only way of knowing that what you have to offer each other is genuine. Otherwise, all your interaction is a disguised effort to gain approval and hide your own individuality.

There Are Limits to My Capacity for Acceptance

None of us is able to experience everything we regard as unacceptable. We each have limits to the amount of acceptance, exposure and tension we can sustain. It is vital that these limits to our capacity for intimacy are honored as highly as all our other characteristics. In an attitude of mutuality, we no longer need to deny or disguise our limits, or use them to make ourselves feel inferior. We simply embrace them as we do all the other qualities we offer our partners.

Living outside your protective circle in a state of acceptance with your intimate partner enables you to heal the wounds and scars of your past, and to embrace the qualities and fears you have been struggling to bury your whole life. You will at last reunite with the person you really are.

All you have to do is listen to your connector:

Let me guide you to real intimacy and connection. I know you are afraid, but I will be with you in your fear. I will honor your limits, and I will embrace every part of who you are. Only by risking can you find real peace; only with surrender can you find real power; only by exposing and accepting all of what makes you human can you satisfy your longing for connection with another.

Chapter 7

THROUGH THE EYES OF SAMENESS
The Rules of Mutuality

*In every marriage more than
a week old, there are grounds for divorce.
The trick is to find, and continue to find,
grounds for a marriage.*

—Robert Anderson, *Solitaire and Double Solitaire*

Like any other human endeavor, mutuality is a game. Like the difference game, it involves two players following rules and strategies as they move together and apart in the pursuit of a specific goal.

But unlike the difference game, mutuality is not competitive. You're not trying to outscore an opponent in order to prove your superiority; you're surrendering to a teammate in order to join. So as you read the descriptions that follow, you will begin to see that the game of mutuality is more like a dance than an athletic competition: the movements are more free and graceful, the couple moves together and apart with greater ease, and the range of styles, encounters and experiences open to them is far greater. Some steps are simple, some are extremely difficult, but all are performed with consciousness and passion.

Mutuality requires a change of perception. So, underlying all the rules that follow is one basic issue: whether you see your partner through the eyes of sameness. All the other rules become meaningless when you fail to perceive your partner as your absolute equal.

Either you open your eyes of sameness and integrate them into who you are, or you see yourselves through hierarchical eyes and return to the difference game. It's simply a question of what you want to experience. . . .

With love and courage, you enter the playing field. You're like few athletes we've ever seen; your openness and humility make you unique among competitors.

But you are not here to compete. You have moved out of your protective circle and into the arena of the unknown. You have chosen to shift your attitudes and perceptions from those of the difference game to the game of mutuality. Instead of confrontation and superiority, *your only goal is joining*. There is no score, no winner, no loser; there is only movement toward connection and intimacy. You and your partner are no longer opponents, you're teammates.

We all know the difficulties that confront you. While the game you just left can go on endlessly, the game of mutuality might sustain for only an instant. Powerful forces tug at you to reject all unacceptable experiences and return to the familiar arena of your comfort zone.

But for all its drama and fireworks, that other game carries no genuine excitement. You know down deep that it is only on *this* playing field, with all its exposure and risk, that real growth and intimacy can occur.

And to guide you through your fear, your connector will act as your *coach* and remind you of the rules. This mutuality coach doesn't employ the methods your protector does when you play the difference game. She won't shout or criticize. She'll neither camouflage your unacceptable parts nor blind you to the sameness you share with your partner. She'll only take you by the hand, share the weight of your fear and whisper to you with the gentle voice of surrender.

The game you're playing is primarily one of *perception*. With your clear new eyes and ears you perceive more of who your partner really is. And through your acceptance and exposure you offer your partner more of who you really are.

The moves you make are fairly simple and straightforward, without all the dazzling speed and complexity of the difference game. In this game, your real skill lies in the ways you see, hear and touch your partner.

As you look at your partner through the eyes of sameness, you're amazed to realize how many years you've spent together without ever really seeing him. After confronting each other for so long within the limits of your comfort zones, you were only recognizing the images your protectors had superimposed on him. But now, you actually *observe your partner with your eyes and ears, not with your mind*. You see and hear the multitude of shapes, colors, sounds and movements he displays, and you're able to experience the fullness of who he really is, rather than what you choose to label him.

This unfamiliar vision of your partner may frighten you. It has always been unacceptable to see all of the parts he offers. If you allow yourself to take in and accept his weaknesses and his full humanity, how will you depend on him? Won't you be helpless? If you recognize his innocence, how will you hang on to your superiority? What about the depth of his love for you? His independence? His sadness? Can you really accept these unknown experiences?

But just as your fear threatens to pull you back into the difference game, your connector whispers softly to you, *"Use every opportunity to see your sameness."* So you allow yourself to recognize that the love you share for each other and the terror you feel at exposing the unacceptable parts of yourselves are exactly the same.

You bring your attention back to your partner and allow yourself to *sustain the tension* you're feeling, rather than running from it. Of course you're scared and vulnerable. This is unknown territory, and your usual defenses are gone. But, you also begin to feel a rush, a sense of becoming more alive.

Then your partner makes a move. Perhaps he turns away from you in some way, giving his attention to some need of his own. Your guard goes up, and you begin to hear the voice of your protector. *"This is what he always does. Just when you try to move closer, he rejects you. Better watch out. If you don't protect yourself, he'll hurt you again."*

But this time you turn off that familiar tape. You've reacted that way a thousand times. Now you're willing to risk something new. You know that in the game of mutuality, you *see things in the present*. You let go of your preconceptions and judgments from the past and your images of hurt or betrayal in the future.

And before your protector can persuade you to react to your partner's distance, your connector reminds you to *look for underlying needs and feelings* rather than assuming negative intentions. You always used to be quick to assume that whenever he turned away, it was a hurtful insult directed at you. But with your new innocent eyes, you can see it as a simple need for solitude, or a reflection of the fear he also feels. Instead of reacting, you let his feeling in, and let it touch you.

You begin to realize how much of the difference game is played in your mind. But mutuality requires a strong observer, one who fixes her steady gaze only on the immediate present.

So in response to your partner's isolation, your connector pulls your gaze away from him, so you can *focus inward*. It is tempting to hold your attention only on your partner, hoping to avoid the feelings within yourself that you've struggled to keep hidden. But mutuality means accepting the unacceptable within yourself first, or you have no chance of accepting what your partner offers.

Your partner serves as a wonderful mirror that will reveal, when you're willing to look, the parts of yourself that have been denied and buried. And bringing these into the light allows you to celebrate your full humanity.

So you begin asking yourself, "What am I doing? What am I feeling? What responsibility do I have for his turning away? What fear or pain inside me is coloring how I see this? Why is neglect or isolation unacceptable to *me*?"

As you hold your inward focus, you realize the place that solitude has played in your own protection. You have always denied your own desire for isolation as unacceptable. You had to be the one who "was there for others." You were determined to appear giving, even when you weren't. By focusing on everyone else's neglect, you could then prove how giving you were. You never had to experience the unacceptable: your own desire for isolation.

With this realization, you are able to move your gaze outward once more, so you can *look at yourself and your partner simultaneously.* Only when your perception encompasses both of you can you recognize any sameness. He may be on one end of the "isolation/giving" continuum, and you may be on the other, but the fear you feel at accepting this unacceptable experience is identical.

This mutual perception brings out more noise from your protector: *"Sure, you may both have an issue with isolation, but what about his discounting your feelings? Doesn't that show a real lack of respect? And wasn't he late to begin with, and . . ."*

You start to listen to this barrage, but then you catch yourself slipping back into your familiar protective mode. So instead, you continue to focus just on your mutual attitudes toward isolation. Because mutuality asks you to *see things clearly*, uncontaminated by other issues and fears. Your eyes of sameness have a deep appreciation for purity. They focus on one thing in all its essence, so it can truly touch you.

Because you've shut out all those distracting images, you can now *experience things in totality.* You show interest in whatever qualities your partner possesses, without questioning their existence. You view his isolation in its entirety, with all its movements, sounds, gestures and expressions. You experience every action of your partner, and every nuance of your own thoughts and feelings. *When does his distance occur? How often does he seclude himself? For how long? And just how does he do it? Does it vary in intensity? Is it constant, or can he move quickly in and out of his solitude?* You become fascinated as you now gaze at all these movements and expressions with a sense of wonder and enchantment. This is an exciting new experience for you. Your partner's isolation was just a source of pain and defensiveness before. You never noticed how skilled he is at shutting out the hundred distractions that bombard him. And you begin to smile at how impenetrable the shield he constructs around himself really is. What would normally be a moment of heaviness and frustration is lightened as you *look for value in everything.*

You begin to appreciate how wonderful it must be to enjoy such solitude, and how dependable he is at giving you space through his isolation. You also acknowledge your own skill at reading his moods and gestures; how resourceful you are at pulling him out of his shell when you need to.

It is only when you recognize the value of all these facets of your partner and yourself that you begin to *see horizontally.* Most of us see with our mind rather than our eyes, so we view everything vertically: this is up, that's down; this is good, that's bad. But in the game of mutuality, you dissolve all hierarchy. Every part of your human nature has equal status, and all the parts of you are invited into your relationship. Both ends of any continuum are given equal status: insecure is right up there with secure, satisfaction is on the same level as dissatisfaction, and sadness is as valued as joy.

You recognize that your partner's need for isolation and your need for connection are simply two parts of yourselves which can be observed, experienced and celebrated. In the past, exposing these needs and seeing them as equal may have seemed unthinkable. But as mutuality players, you *embrace the unknown.* Of course it's scary, but you can hold tight to each other and experience the feeling together.

As you begin accepting feelings that you once considered unacceptable, something wonderful happens. Your deeper fear of the unknown starts to subside. Because all aspects of your nature have equal status, you no longer have to dread exposing some undesired part of yourself or your partner. Because the eyes of mutuality are open to all, there is much less to fear.

As you shift your perception out of your hierarchical mind and see things through the eyes of mutuality, another change occurs. You begin to experience much more freedom of movement. Unlike the difference game, mutuality has few boundaries. As long as you remain outside your circle of protection, movement is much more open and free. You're off the seesaw, and now you can venture nearer or further from each other in a multitude of ways.

But as you continue to experience the unknown together, eventually a shift occurs. The intimacy the two of you feel exceeds your capacity, and you can no longer sustain the tension. You long to return to your comfort zone.

If you choose to return to the difference game, either of you can make the first move. Your partner might turn away from you, or call you "needy and dependent" after you try to hug him. Or perhaps you're already on guard, just waiting for him to criticize you so you can react with judgment and blame. Either way, you'll end up back in your shared comfort zone.

But what if this time you don't? What if this time you sustain your mutual attitude, and choose to *be active, not reactive*. You will stand on your own regardless of what your partner does, openly revealing your own feelings and desires in order to take care of yourself. Your actions will grow out of your own needs, rather than out of a desire to appease, prove, seek reassurance or take care of your partner.

And what if, when you find yourselves facing conflicts and difficulties, you resist the temptation to blame your partner for your feelings of pain, anger or fear? In the game of mutuality, you *take responsibility* for whatever shows up in your relationship. Justifications have no place here, nor does your perception that your partner "causes" your reactions. As much as you dislike what you see, and however forcefully your protector tries to exonerate you due to special and unusual circumstances, you openly admit that your own behavior is contributing to your drama and distance just as much as your partner's.

EXTENDING YOUR MOVEMENTS

In the game of mutuality, you are still limited to the same three directions in relation to your partner that you were in the difference game. But within an attitude of acceptance and equality, they are never used to maintain some image.

Your movement forward toward your partner is no longer to confront or accuse, it's only to share an honest need, desire or observation. A movement backward isn't to hide, it's an open withdrawal into your own solitude or separation. And a stance against your partner is a clearly stated, "no," or a clearly set limit, which holds no hostility and no judgment.

So now when you want to feel your partner's touch, you simply ask to be held. Within your connective mutuality circle, you *stand up for your own desires*.

And you will honor your partner's response as well because in the game of mutuality, you *allow the other person's experience*. He's not supposed to react in any given way; a movement against you is as valued as a movement forward. If his "no" brings up sadness, allow that experience in. As hard as your protector tugs at you to judge your partner as uncaring, or yourself as needy, sustain the tension of your different desires.

You close your ears to all such labels for his responses. As you move toward and apart from your partner, you *replace all abstractions* such as "love," "respect," "uncommitted" and "dishonest" into observable behaviors. You know that calling your partner "distant" or "insensitive" will bring out his protector, who can easily persuade your partner to defend himself as if he knows what you're talking about. Within an attitude of mutuality, concepts like "insensitivity" are only used when you can specifically describe what it looks, sounds or feels like. So instead of judging and reacting, you share with your partner, "When I move to embrace you, I need you to tell me you don't want to, rather than turn away from me without a word."

As the two of you interact in this way, you notice a new quality to your words. The complex jargon you used to toss around is gone, as you quietly maintain simplicity. More lightness and purity have entered your relationship and things have become easier.

But there's danger here as well. Never one to rest, your protector starts whispering "boring" over and over inside your head. You begin to miss the energy of all the drama the difference game provided. So, in response, you silence your protector's voice the best way possible: you *find excitement in everything.*

Your mutual eyes have an amazing ability. They can see passion everywhere. Togetherness, solitude, rejection, passivity, even boredom itself. *"That's ridiculous!"* your protector shouts. *"What could possibly be passionate about boredom? Boredom is boring!"*

"Not so," replies your connector. *"Boredom has its own excitement. But you'll never experience it as long as you're trying to escape it to get to some 'better' state. You have to accept boredom, and embrace all its facets and colors, to see how exciting it can be."*

So you begin playing a game inside your head. You imagine watching a video of the most boring movie imaginable. You invite your friends to join you in front of the television. But instead of merely passing time in front of this abomination, you stand up and shout for all to hear, "This is the most boring movie I've ever seen!" You then express the details of your boredom. You all search for ways to describe just how bored you are. You hold a contest to select the most boring scene of all, and award an Oscar for the most boring performance.

Do you really believe that wouldn't be a passionate experience? Now imagine that the movie you've been watching is your relationship. You begin to see the excitement in all the nuances of every dull situation, every banal exchange, every boring activity the two of you have ever experienced. All at once, you're finding passion everywhere.

You begin to enjoy this, and soon you realize you're pretty good at this new game. But before your ego becomes inflated, your connector gently reminds you to *remain humble.* She knows that it's your humility, the simple appreciation of your humanity, that will help you sustain your acceptance and intimacy. Moving up or down will always return you to the difference game.

You appreciate how easy it is to shift back into your comfort zone, and how strong your false self is. You know that the only way to remain in a state of mutuality is to *challenge your protector* repeatedly. Because you're no longer a passive audience for your protector's declarations, you respond to them with passion. When you hear his voice in your head, using every trick in the book to make you afraid of the unacceptable, you answer, "Put up or shut up. Show me *exactly* where the danger is. Don't just proclaim it, give me details. What precisely will happen? How will that really hurt me?"

When you played the difference game, your protector was heard and obeyed without question. The voice in your head became a monologue. But in the game of mutuality, you engage in a dialogue with your protector. You invite your protector to offer a solution that will really change the situation: "I'm willing to listen to you if you have something new to say." And when your protector starts to stutter and stammer, you turn back to your connector, and regain the rewards of acceptance and equality.

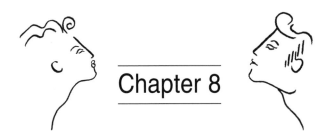

Chapter 8

LIVING IN EQUALITY AND ACCEPTANCE
The Consequences of Mutuality

Imagine listening to your intimate partner and having nothing to defend, justify or prove. . . .

Imagine a partner who listens to your needs, honors your feelings and shares the weight of your pain and fear. . . .

Imagine exposing your deepest feelings, desires and fears while fully accepting the possibility of rejection, helplessness or abandonment. . . .

Imagine making love in whatever way you want, and everything you feel is stimulating, passionate and fun. . . .

Imagine coming together by choice, and moving apart with respect and independence rather than guilt and resentment. . . .

Imagine a relationship of peace, fulfillment and passion rather than boredom, drama and blame. . . .

When you move from an attitude of difference and judgment to one of equality and acceptance, you leave the endless seesaw of the difference game and enter an arena of greater passion, freedom and intimacy. The tasks of life are performed with greater ease and the problems are faced with greater strength because you no longer devote your energy to hiding, protecting and proving.

If the removal of these actions was the only consequence of this new attitude, mutuality would still have an enormous impact on your life. Because hiding, protecting and proving consume so much of your time and energy that little is left for anything else. Within an attitude of real equality and acceptance, you increase the choices available to you because each part of yourself that you embrace offers you new resources for dealing with the stages and challenges of your life.

Mutuality allows a far wider range of movement as you travel forward, backward and against your partner without blame, guilt or reaction. By accepting the down positions (especially powerlessness, disappointment, fear and insecurity), you enhance your flexibility and openness to a multitude of situations. This perceptual shift gives you a much more solid sense of your own individuality, as you honor the totality of who you really are.

This new attitude is not without its struggles and conflicts. You sometimes face experiences you used to think of as uncomfortable or unacceptable. When the tension level rises you risk feeling lost, scared and vulnerable. And as you assume more responsibility for your actions and feelings, your partner no longer serves as the scapegoat for your pain.

But beyond these challenges, when you and your partner create a pocket of acceptance in a judgmental world, you experience greater peace and contentment in all the areas of your life. As unknown experiences lose their power to terrify you, you feel more spontaneous and free.

Within an attitude of mutuality, you hold your partner's steady gaze. You see aspects of this person that formerly went unnoticed, and you appreciate the depth and variety of the person you married. This may be unnerving because you aren't used to seeing beyond your narrow perception. You face the risk of falling in love with your mate all over again.

As you move from hedging and diluting your life into giving yourself 100% to all your feelings, the passion in your relationship increases. You fully experience your power and tenderness, your pain and joy. Your desire is total, not muted by worry about your partner's reaction. And your anger is pure, not diluted by a hidden need to hurt or blame. When you fully experience and express yourself this way, you are able to put both feet in your relationship, instead of just a toe.

What was once unknown and terrifying becomes a source of passion and contentment. You feel excitement in the uniqueness of each new interaction, and contentment in the love and acceptance that you share.

With the hierarchy dissolved, you are not as attached to any one aspect of your relationship over any other. This enables you to move far more easily between closeness and separation, as you learn to value equally your need to join and your need to be apart. A fuller experience of life opens up to you, as you allow your independence and dependence, joy and disappointment, and power and powerlessness to coexist.

Situations that were once confusing, overwhelming and endless are now simpler, quieter and lighter. You feel more centered, more relaxed and more open because you no longer await your partner's every word and movement with anxiety and worry. You find your words and gestures are more steady, calm and fluid as you leave the environment of rejection for one of acceptance. Your focus is only on whatever issue or desire is present in the moment.

And finally, when all the parts of you that have forever been denied and buried are allowed into the light of acceptance, you can begin to heal the wounds and pain of your childhood. It is only within this space of mutual acceptance that your love, growth and true humanity can flourish.

PART III

JOINING

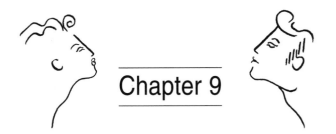

Chapter 9

FROM DENIAL TO ACCEPTANCE
The Mutuality Continuum

Dear Diary:

It's finally happened! I can't believe I'm saying this, but at last I've found Mr. Right! He's perfect! Okay, I know he's not perfect, but you know what I mean. He's everything I've ever wanted. He's cute, he's polite, he's straight. He isn't fixated on his mother, or his ex, or himself. It's as if I'm the only thing he cares about.

We love the same things, he makes me laugh, he's great in bed, he listens to me and he has this adorable way of putting his arm around me when we're walking. It makes me feel like he's really with me. We spent the whole weekend together, and it was heaven. It seemed like it was over in a moment. We couldn't be more alike. I just know he's the one. . . .

A couple's ability to embrace their unacceptable desires and feelings will largely determine the prognosis for their relationship. And their ability to accept those unacceptable experiences will depend a great deal on where the couple stands on the relationship continuum.

Stage I	Stage II	Stage III
Pseudo-sameness	Reject sameness	Recognition of sameness

New Relationship -X- - - - - - - - - - - - Intimacy

Accept the superficial/ deny differences	No acceptance/ focus on differences		Accept the unacceptable/ move beneath differences

The Couple's Dilemma

STAGE I: PSEUDO-SAMENESS

This is your honeymoon period (although, unless you elope quickly, it's likely to come and go long before your wedding). This is that magic time when every glance, every whisper, every touch is electric. As illustrated by the diary entry at the beginning of this chapter, during this blissful "falling in love" stage, the two of you are one, and it seems as if there are no differences between you whatsoever.

I label this stage *pseudo*-sameness because the equality you feel is largely illusory. You're so caught up in being in love that you deny all difference, and are blinded to any separation at all. You want what he wants; you are what he is. You exhibit nothing but sameness. Acceptance isn't even a question because there's no feeling or behavior that seems remotely unacceptable.

You usually experience this stage at the beginning of your relationship. You're in love with love, and illusions run rampant. You have found your dream person, and you certainly don't want any differences, no matter how obvious, to disturb that wishful picture.

Some couples maintain this stage forever. They are determined not to let the honeymoon end because they can't tolerate anything *but* sameness. They fuse together like two peas in a pod. No dissonance is allowed, and they are rarely apart or in disagreement. They just sort of blend together for as long as they can.

These fused couples exhibit a lot less drama, conflict and emotionality than most marriages. Their relationships lack any dynamic passion or growth, but they sustain a level of familiarity, contentment and safety.

You may wonder why I place these pseudo-same couples at such an early stage of the continuum. They apparently aren't playing the difference game, and their equality seems obvious.

But, even though they choose not to focus on their differences, these "honeymoon" relationships lack real mutuality. By denying their differences in the same way that others deny their equality, these couples are using their sameness as a shield to protect themselves from real emotional risk. Their connection lies on the surface level of actions and appearances, not within the unexplored depths of their love, pain and vulnerability.

Just as with all couples, these pseudo-same partners truly are the same at some deep level because both partners struggle to hide their mutual fear of exposure and conflict. But like difference game players, they go to great lengths to avoid recognizing or acknowledging that level of sameness. Instead, they create a surface illusion of shared acceptance.

So what's wrong with that? So what if they are just living out a surface level of sameness, as long as they get along, love each other and don't hurt each other?

Nothing's wrong with that. In fact, there's nothing "wrong" with any of the ways couples adapt and interact. But if the goal of their relationship is to experience the passion and deeper connection that comes from real intimacy, a relationship committed to maintaining a cozy façade just won't cut it.

And if either partner in such a relationship ever confronts the feelings of stagnation or loss that lurk under the surface of such pseudo-sameness, the couple's whole illusion will crumble, and they will move on to Stage II.

STAGE II: REJECTION

The primary objective at this stage of the continuum is to magnify all your differences and use them to validate your favorite position, either up or down. Above all else, you will reject all sameness. Acceptance and equality don't even merit a passing thought. You are consumed with judging, maneuvering and hiding.

Let's return to the person whose diary opened this chapter, and look at the way the rejection stage is described. The following entry could have been made only days later, or it could have taken years for her to move on to this stage.

Dear Diary:

I can't believe this guy! How did I ever get involved with this jerk? This past weekend seemed like an eternity. He doesn't listen, he's boring, he never gives me any space. He has this awful way of clutching me whenever we walk along. And our lovemaking—it's all I can do to get through it.

If he'd only back off. Doesn't he have anyone else in his life? It's as if he can't stand to let me be on my own. I give him plenty of space. Why can't he do the same? We're like night and day. . . .

This is the stage where many couples live, especially those in troubled relationships. The difference game is played full tilt, drama is high and distance is maintained.

When you're in Stage II, so much energy and skill is devoted to protecting your egos by maintaining your differences that others are usually convinced of them as well. It's as difficult to find any sameness at this level as it was to find any difference in Stage I. The end result is the same, but the form of camouflage has changed.

Of course, with so much defensiveness and name calling, a lot of pain will ensue. And pretty soon you have to ask the question that your friends and relatives are already wondering: "If we're this different, and we're this unhappy, why are we even together?"

The Couple's Dilemma

Here's where you come to the fork in the road on your journey because before you can ever reach real acceptance and intimacy in your relationship, you will have to make a commitment to a particular path.

Dear Diary:

I don't know what to do anymore. We keep going through the same routine of fighting, then ignoring each other, then making up, then fighting again. It's hopeless. He keeps saying he'll change, but he doesn't.

Maybe it's me, but I've tried being closer, I've tried being more independent, and I've tried talking about it. Nothing works. I hate to say it because deep down I really do love him, but I think it may be time to end this relationship. . . .

When you face the couple's dilemma, you have three choices:

1. *Split up* because the tension and pain are too much to endure.
2. *Continue the way you have been* because no matter how bad your relationship is, the risk of either complete separation or greater exposure is too great.
3. *Risk experiencing the unacceptable* because however frightening the exposure and vulnerability of the unknown, it's preferable to both the pain you're in now and the pain of divorce.

Choice 1 is a commitment to separation. You will leave the continuum, but will probably go back to the beginning of the journey sooner or later with a new partner.

Choice 2 is a commitment to the difference game. You will stay where you are and continue your conflict.

Choice 3 is a commitment to mutuality. This is the only way you will move forward toward greater intimacy and joining.

In case you think you can avoid any commitment at all, and somehow "slip into" intimacy, I'm afraid that's impossible. Refusing to make a choice is identical to Choice 2.

STAGE III: ACCEPTANCE

When you shift your perception out of the difference game, sameness again appears. But unlike Stage I, where sameness is sometimes used as protection, here the sameness speaks to the inner truth of who you are as individuals and as a couple. Your equality grows out of the humble recognition that the differences you share with your partner need to be to accepted, expressed and integrated into your relationship.

Every part of you is valued and invited to participate because in Stage III you recognize your sameness and are ready to accept the unacceptable. You no longer need to worry about being rejected or fitting into a box that can't possibly hold all that you are and all that you offer.

Dear Diary:

For the first time in a long time, I think there's hope for us. When I told him I was thinking of leaving, he didn't get defensive or react in his usual way. He just started crying. He said that he knows he crowds me, but he's so afraid of being alone that he needs to feel I'm there. I'm the only one he has.

When I saw how frightened he was, I realized that what really bothered me was being needed so much. When I finally admitted this, it was the first time in ages that we really connected. He didn't say anything more, he just held me. Only this time it wasn't in a clutchy way, it was just tender. I know now that I'm just as scared of his needing me as he is. I guess we're not so different after all. . . .

The core sameness that you now see runs deeper than appearances and habits. It's within the wounds you carry, the fear you feel and the capacity you share for risking increasingly higher levels of intimacy, love and connection. In this stage, you are finally able to recognize the humble truth of the equality that forms the heart and soul of your relationship.

Wherever you are on the continuum, opening this book probably indicates that at least a part of you is facing or anticipating the couple's dilemma, and you're struggling to decide whether your relationship is worth continuing. Or perhaps when you bought the book you were certain that intimacy was your primary goal, but you were hoping it didn't take quite so much work and exposure to get there. Now I've presented you with a dilemma you didn't know you had. Sorry.

In either case, you now know your options:

If you select Choice 1, simply skip the next three chapters and go directly to Chapter 13.

If Choice 2 is for you, return to Chapter 1 and fire away.

And, if you truly want to continue the journey toward greater intimacy, acceptance and equality, Choice 3 is your only option, so continue reading.

In making a commitment to mutuality, you are acknowledging the fact that healing the wounds of a lifetime will require truly accepting the unacceptable. You realize that starting over with a new lover won't help you accomplish real growth and change at such a core level. You recognize that this can only be done by facing your fear of the unknown with the partner you now have.

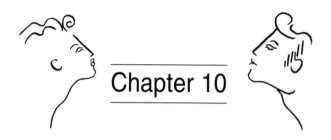

Chapter 10

MOVING INTO SAMENESS
The Steps to Intimacy

I didn't realize how hard this would be. I want to be closer; I want to see us as the same. And I certainly want to end all this pain and fighting. But whenever I begin to feel how close or loving he is, this voice in my head starts warning me, "Watch out! You're just going to be hurt again." And pretty soon we're back where we were. It's as if I'm being pulled in two directions at once. . . .

To help you on your journey to greater intimacy and mutuality, I first must introduce you to another entity who resides in your psychological community.

You already know your *protector*, whose sole objective is to maintain the status quo and guard against the unknown, and your *connector*, whose only goal is to help you join with an intimate partner. But if these two seem always to be pulling you in opposite directions, wouldn't it be wise to ask if there's anyone running the show? Do your protector and connector just battle it out in some kind of territorial dance to see who gets primary control, or is someone in charge here?

While it may often seem that your psychological community is without a leader, and you simply follow the most persuasive voice, your behavior is in fact under the watchful eye of your *director*.

This may seem a bizarre notion to many of you because most of us don't even acknowledge the presence of this part of ourselves. When I suggested this idea to one of my clients recently, he didn't like the concept at all. "I hate being a boss in real life," he said, "because then I have to be in charge of people, and I don't want to be responsible for others. So why would I want a boss inside of me?" His reaction made it clear he was rejecting this part of himself out of his fear of responsibility.

Another client actually was a boss: a corporate director who supervised a very large staff. But she denied this part of herself in relationships because she saw it as intimidating to men. She thought, "If I don't show my director, men will see me as more approachable."

Your director's job has two major functions: observing and managing. It notices everything that goes on within you—your needs, fears, movements, expressions and desires—making no judgments about anything, but using all this information to then select some action for you to take.

When your director is fully present, it will call on your protector, your connector, or whatever other part of you that needs attention, listen to what is needed, and suggest to you what is best for your entire community. When engaged in this way, your director will ask for evidence to support the positions held by your protector or connector, so that actions are not based on empty warnings of danger or abandonment. The more concrete the substantiation for any stated situation or need, the more your director will allow that evidence to influence your behavior.

Your director oversees everything from a place of unconditional acceptance. It does not impose idealized images of safety or joining, but instead develops actions and solutions based on who you really are and what you're ready for. So if your protector reveals a fear of exposing sexual desires and your connector expresses a longing for physical intimacy, your director is the part of you that will search for some way to take care of the fearful part, while pursuing a partner to satisfy your sexual needs.

In previous chapters I have shared with you that when your protector is absent you risk being exposed to the unfamiliar, and when your connector is gone you risk emptiness and deep longing. But when your director is ignored, neglected or absent, you risk paralysis or chaos in your entire psychological organization.

When you fail to call on your director to listen to all your fears and desires, you bounce back and forth between involvement and separation, or you deaden all your emotions and retreat completely. With no one managing your various needs, you'll follow the path of least resistance and go in whatever direction you're pulled hardest. And because your protector has the loudest voice, you'll likely spend most of your time in the difference game.

If your desire is for a deeper level of acceptance and intimacy, you can no longer turn a deaf ear to your director. It's time to trust this key member of your organization.

THE MUTUAL ENVIRONMENT

If your commitment to move out of the difference game and into Stage III of the sameness/acceptance continuum is to mean anything, you must create a space for joining to occur. Intimacy can't be caught on the fly, or attempted on some hit-or-miss basis when the spirit moves you. It requires an emotional environment worthy of your relationship.

Your goal is to change perceptions and attitudes that have gone unchallenged for years. To unlearn a lifetime of thoughts, feelings and behaviors requires real energy and commitment, and half-hearted attempts at closeness that suit the whims of mood and convenience will merely indicate your overall disregard for your relationship.

Before initiating any change, sit down with each other and openly share your commitment to reducing your destructive conflicts and to becoming more intimate. Discuss your feelings of hope or fear, and your trepidation at trying these new ways of approaching and interacting with each other. Openly express your desire for real change in your relationship and your willingness to risk some tension and discomfort in order to recapture what you once felt for each other.

Even if you are involved with someone who is unwilling to participate in any of the exercises or methods of interaction that follow, it's important for you to read this chapter anyway. There are a number of activities you can initiate on your own that will have a striking effect on your relationship even without your partner's cooperation.

You should anticipate some repetition and overlap in several of these exercises and experiences. You are challenging beliefs and attitudes that have been deeply ingrained in your psyche, so confronting them in as many ways as possible is a necessity. There is no magic to these steps. Their effectiveness will depend mostly on your level of commitment to the process and your willingness to risk.

Begin in a loving, open atmosphere consistent with the relationship you both desire, and reconfirm that you share the same goal of greater intimacy and fulfillment. The actions and experiences outlined in this chapter ask for increasing exposure and vulnerability, so half-hearted agreements and guarded commitments will never sustain the new level of tension that you will encounter.

HONORING YOUR RESISTANCE

Whatever reluctance you feel in completing each step of this process will become evident quite quickly, as feelings that have always been unacceptable are brought into the open. I especially want you to be conscious of the negative, protective attitudes that control many of your movements and decisions.

As you move through the mutuality process, pay particular attention to any of these signs of your protector in action:

• Your voice becomes impatient.

- After completing a step you immediately make comments such as, "Okay, we've done that. What's next?"
- You skip steps in the process or try to push through experiences quickly.
- Emotional drama begins to emerge.
- You begin to "fog over" or feel overwhelmed.
- Your body becomes restless or you want to turn away from your partner.
- You approach the process with resignation rather than commitment: "Okay, I'll do this stuff, but it won't make any difference anyway. Sooner or later you-know-who will screw it up."
- Your thoughts are bombarded with a barrage of discouraging comments such as:

   "Don't let anyone tell you what to do."
   "Don't depend on anyone else."
   "This is just psychobabble."
   "This couldn't work for you."
   "This will make you look ridiculous."
   "He won't stand for this."
   "This is really going to hurt her."
   "This isn't who you are."
   "This is hopeless."
   "Doesn't he have anything better than that?"
   "I've never been good at this psychological stuff."
   "I already know this."

I want to once again make absolutely clear that I know how scary and strange moving out of your familiar feelings and reactions can be. And I want you to know that I am constantly holding a space of honor and acceptance for your fear, and for the courage you show in even contemplating these new ways of revealing yourselves to each other. So don't give up or put yourselves down if you're exhibiting any of these normal defensive or protective reactions.

Remember, your protector doesn't believe you can emotionally survive anything beyond what you're already doing, so he'll make up any statement he can to keep you from taking a risk. If you don't call on your director to challenge your protector, your ability to even complete an experience, let alone give it your full passion, will be greatly diminished.

This is why so many people buy books such as this one and enjoy reading the theories, but never put them into practice or achieve real change. I want our relationship to be more than a one night stand. I'm going to do my best not to become another buy it/read it/put it on the shelf experience for you.

Within that spirit, I want you to create a personal, passionate and responsive relationship with your protector. He expects your blind obedience because most of the time you don't even respond to what he says. If he tells you the unknown is dangerous, you silently shrug "Okay" and slink back to your comfort zone. How can you possibly bring passion into your relationships from such a passive stance?

Throughout this process, I want your director to fire all kinds of questions at your protector. When any internal warning is raised, tell your director to ask your protector precisely what and where the danger is, how he knows it will be dangerous, and what the specific consequences will be.

It's a waste of time to polarize with the protective part of yourself by ignoring, debating or criticizing his warnings. Any combative response to your fear and reluctance will just create a standoff, and your protector loves clouding your commitment with a good debate or an angry encounter.

Instead, address this entity clearly and firmly, with an attitude of invitation and respect at all times:

> "Protector, I appreciate your protection, but I want to do this, and I need you to provide me with the space to do it."
> "I know you feel differently about this, but I'd like to learn about it for myself."
> "I hear your statement that none of this is any good, and I'd like to know what your specific objections are."
> "I hear your warnings, but I want to know exactly what the

negative consequences will be if I do this, and precisely how they will hurt me."

"I understand doing this will expose me. Do you have an alternative way to help me accomplish my goal?"

When you address the protective part of yourself so firmly and openly, you are more likely to hear all the noise subside, and you can choose your behavior from a space of clarity rather than confusion

There are only two basic attitudes that will silence your protector:

"I don't need your protection right now."
"I am willing to be afraid."

Anything less direct than these two stances is an indication that you're not really serious and you still want his protection.

Stay alert and prepared for the clever things your protector will try to do. You need to be aware of the difficulties you face, but not dwell on them. Your protector will latch onto any obsessive attitude in an instant, and he loves having you absorbed in anything negative. Your clear perception will be your best ally against slipping back into the unconscious difference game.

Sometimes couples I work with are mentally ready to move ahead, but emotionally they aren't so sure. In these instances, I suggest that they give themselves temporary permission to act as if they are ready and see what happens.

SETTING THE PACE

Most of us have a love affair with speed. This is frequently true with couples who come to me for help. Round after round of the difference game has left them miserable and frustrated, and they're desperate for change. But, they want that change to come quickly and easily.

It is vital for you to understand two things about the speed of the journey toward intimacy. The first is that *none of the steps can be skipped*. Each one takes time and needs to be experienced fully. The amount of time required depends entirely on your own commitment, vulnerability and capacity for acceptance. Trying to jump directly into integrating mutuality will only put you back where you started.

The second principle of pacing grows out of the first: *the voice of impatience lies to you.* When your protector speaks with this voice, he wants you to believe that he is so interested in change that he insists on achieving it instantly.

Your protector is only interested in maintaining the same old merry-go-round. He knows that you won't be as devoted a listener if he tells you the truth that if you try to zip through the process of mutuality, you'll miss the entire journey.

Instead of being honest, your protector maintains the façade of wanting change and tells you what you want to hear: *"I really want things to change, too. In fact, let's change everything immediately! Let's not waste any time. We should be there already!"*

Such impatience will earn you no change, no loving relationship, nothing except your protector's deep appreciation.

RECOGNITION AND EXPRESSION

The movement out of the protective circle of your comfort zone and into an attitude of acceptance will require two recurring behaviors: *recognition* and *expression.* As you leave your comfort zone and gradually integrate mutuality into your lives, you will repeatedly be asked to recognize and express whatever you are experiencing.

Mutuality is built on perception and acceptance. The steps and exercises that follow are designed to help you perceive both your protective behaviors and your underlying sameness, and to accept all of your thoughts, feelings and desires in the presence of your partner.

If you don't acknowledge your hierarchical nature, you'll never be able to let go of it. Only by recognizing your judgmental style, the fears you are protecting and the vulnerability and sameness the two of you share can you leave the drama of the difference game. And only by expressing your judgments, fears, perceptions, beliefs and equality can you experience the intimacy and connection you desire.

I want to connect with you where you live. If you're someone who's become very attached to your difference game stance and are locked into that attitude, the only way any real movement will occur is if we can bring your game playing into the light. At the very least this will make the difference game a lot more fun for you. Once you have permission to fully express your superiority or inferiority, you won't have to waste so much time and energy disguising what you're doing.

If you want to go forward, all the parts of yourself must move with you. You can't leave some behind and expect to make much progress. I want to help your director bring your hidden parts out into the open, where you can acknowledge them, embrace them and give them a proper place within your psychological community.

Instead of "getting out of" whatever you're struggling with, your director must get you more *into* the hidden parts you want to deny. This means standing up and showing up in your relationship with all the parts of yourself, especially those you regard as unacceptable.

In addition to our desire to evict our unacceptable parts from our community, we are also prevented from exposing these parts by our inability to fully express anything. We have been conditioned to dilute our passion and modulate whatever feelings or desires we want to express. It's simply not proper to cut loose and let fly with whatever we're experiencing. Such a thing would be childish, improper and an affront to proper behavior. We wouldn't fit in.

As a result, few of us really know what it's like to express something 100%, even if it's an "acceptable" feeling such as love, joy or happiness. Can you imagine how diluted our expression becomes when we try to expose one of our unacceptable parts?

The key to truly expressing ourselves is congruence. The word congruent means harmonious or compatible. When you move into complete harmony with an experience, when you and the experience coincide, you will then be able to express it 100%. When you're congruent with your feelings, you put your entire being into them. Your thoughts, emotions, body and spirit are all present.

We often feel mediocre, numb or dead in our lives because we only allow ourselves to put a toe in the water, rather than plunge in with everything we've got. It's not that we're not passionate; we all have the potential for great passion. It's just that we can't reach our passion because it's either beyond our acceptable boundary altogether, or we don't give ourselves permission to experience parts of ourselves fully.

For the remainder of this chapter, I will offer structured exercises and guidelines for interaction that will lead you through the steps of mutuality from protection to connection. To whatever degree you are able to use these experiences to increase your level of awareness and the expression of your behavior, your consciousness will be correspondingly impacted. As you become more awake you will expand your ability to make active, rather than reactive, choices, and to experience real intimacy with your partner.

Spend as much time with each experience as seems appropriate for your relationship. Ten to fifteen minutes will usually be sufficient, although you may need longer periods for some of the exercises. Often you will need to repeat certain experiences, or return to them when new issues and feelings arise in your relationship. An effective indication that you're ready to move on to another exercise is when you are comfortable enough with a task that you no longer need to disguise or avoid the feelings it brings up. But don't get too caught up in worrying about your speed or your overall progress; each encounter will bring some new part of yourself into the light, and will draw you closer to each other.

Leaving Your Comfort Zone

Until you know exactly where you are, you won't be able to move on to other spaces. Recognizing and expressing how and why you have kept yourself protected is vital to beginning the journey outside your comfort zone.

STEP 1: VIEWING YOUR PROTECTIVE WALL

How have you been protecting yourself in your relationship? What particular façades and maneuvers of the difference game do you employ to remain in your comfort zone?

I sometimes refer to this step as "seeing your hand on the knife."

I can be sitting with a couple who are quite bloody after stabbing each other with accusations and put-downs, but they'll each swear to me, "I never touched the knife." They'll even question that there is a knife. And if there is one, they never saw it.

"Well I did say that, but that was only because. . ."
"Well I was only pointing out the facts."
"I was just sharing my feelings."
"Well sure, but I never intended to put him down."

There is no way you can stop playing the difference game if you can't even see that your primary goal is to appear better or less than your partner. You can't let go of a knife when you don't even realize it's in your hand.

In your own relationship, if you're not willing to admit that you're an active difference game player, then at least ask yourself, "What façade would I prefer if I *did* have something I didn't want to expose? What approach would I find most comfortable if I wanted to appear either superior or inferior to my partner?" After you've come up with this imaginary action or attitude, ask your partner if you ever do that.

A wide range of possibilities present themselves. Do you like to attack? Criticize? Coach? Or do you prefer the down position: turning helpless, being "the problem" or getting depressed, confused, sleepy or overwhelmed? Do you usually use the knife on your partner by putting her down and blaming? Or do you favor stabbing yourself by minimizing your strengths, demeaning yourself or seeing yourself as undeserving?

At different times, you and your partner will take turns displaying both your superior and inferior stances. But each of you has one that you're more comfortable exposing. If you're usually the overtly superior member of your relationship, you probably prefer to take the role of the "intelligent one," the "faithful one" or the "emotionally mature one."

But recognizing your covert attitudes and styles is equally important. If you secretly get depressed about how impossible it is to change your partner, that's your covert style.

When you put out to the world that you're the victim in the relationship, then overtly you prefer the down position. Your covert style emerges whenever you privately seethe about how much more righteous, worthy or normal you are than your husband. Whether you're a covert superior or a covert inferior, I want all your difference game façades to come out of the closet.

The anchoring experience that follows will make it much easier to recognize and express your difference game modes and disguises. When your interaction is repeatedly grounded in the two back-to-back chairs, your favorite methods of overt and covert protection will become increasingly apparent.

Exercise #1: The Anchoring Experience

Many of the exercises in this chapter involve arranging chairs to represent different attitudes, stances or parts of yourself. The most important of these is the anchoring experience. This technique allows you to anchor certain attitudes and behaviors to a particular place and time. This enables you to recognize exactly what you're doing by isolating it from all the drama and confusion of your many difference game encounters.

For the basic anchoring experience, set up two chairs back-to-back in some out-of-the-way place. Every time either of you senses any reactivity beginning to occur, announce that you want to "move to the chairs," or "anchor this," or whatever prearranged signal you've agreed to use. Do not continue your interaction until you are sitting back-to-back in the chairs.

By reactivity I mean any interaction where one or both of you are in a difference game stance, and you're reacting to your partner rather than simply taking care of your own needs. Whenever one of you is speaking with a raised voice, talking in paragraphs, using "you" statements, defending or making any one-up or one-down comments, you are in a reactive state.

Resume your interaction in the anchoring chairs, and remain there until you recognize that you're playing the difference game, or until you have nothing more to say from this position, and the reactivity has abated.

If either of you isn't willing to acknowledge that you are playing the game, you can still leave the chairs, but you have to agree to stop interacting. *Don't leave the chairs and continue talking.* Simply move apart for awhile and focus on other things. Don't return to whatever issue was the focus of your difference game behavior until you can bring it up without your protectors. If it again leads to reactive behavior, return to the chairs and resume the anchoring process.

If your partner is caught up in the drama and refuses to go to the chairs, you should move there alone because sooner or later you'd be hooked into the game anyway. This of course should be done without any attitude of blame or superiority ("See? *I'm* willing to anchor and you're not!"). You are simply demonstrating your unwillingness to participate in this kind of exchange unless you're in the appropriate place. Your partner can then continue the drama alone and unacknowledged.

If nothing else, this approach will greatly shorten the time you spend in endless arguments and debates. It's amazing how deflating it can be to difference game players when, instead of confrontation, they're given permission to do their thing.

The anchoring experience has several other benefits: it will help you become more conscious of your particular protecting style; it will contain your reactivity by confining it to one particular spot; and because the chairs are back-to-back, it will diminish your erroneous belief that this is a real dialogue where you're truly trying to solve something.

It's possible you're already thinking that this experience is too silly for you to do. *"Talking back-to-back? Are you kidding? It would be too awkward. We'd look ridiculous! And my partner would never go along."*

I find it fascinating that most of us don't hesitate for a moment to react to, comment on and judge precisely the way our partners eat, dress, crack their knuckles and go to the toilet. We're willing to create entire soap operas out of the way our spouses talk on the phone or refuse to pick up their socks. Yet, we're still worried about being silly.

I'm afraid I have some bad news. If you're playing the difference game, you've already exhibited a willingness to be ridiculous. It's built into the game. Your only real choice is to continue spreading your silliness all over the house, or to confine it to one spot and become more conscious.

Exercise #2: Expressing Your Comfortable Role

Whatever difference game behavior you exhibited in Exercise #1, it was designed to validate some comfortable image of yourself. In this exercise, you openly express that favored role or quality in a pure and unadulterated way, rather than hiding behind camouflage.

"When I criticize you it makes me feel superior."
"It's a lot easier for me just to feel helpless."
"I'm into pleasing you to show you what a wonderful person I am."

If expressing one of your preferred images in this way feels too blatant and uncomfortable, it means you're doing the exercise correctly. We don't like to own our desire for superiority or inferiority, so we never proclaim our comfortable roles so honestly. Doing so, however, is much easier on your relationship than all your usual put-downs or underdog routines.

Exercise #3: Owning Your Stance

After moving your difference game encounter to the anchoring chairs and blatantly expressing your comfortable role, it's time for you to take full responsibility for your stance. One of you can suggest that it's time for both of you to own your positions. Turn your anchoring chairs so that your facing each other because you want to take in the passion of whatever you offer each other.

Express your position for five minutes with as much passion as you can. Let go of whatever you consider "presentable" and allow yourself to enjoy your attitude totally. Get out of your chair. Wave your arms if you want. Yell, scream, cry or overact in whatever way you can. Just be there with your entire mind, body and spirit.

Openly declare, "I want to be better than you are," "I choose to be less than you," "I enjoy being superior to you," or any other passionate expression of your desire to be up or down towards your partner.

It is vital that you express your stance without hesitation or justification, regardless of whatever you think is going on with your partner. If your selected position is that of the "responsible" partner, express that position with all the enthusiasm you can muster. Say anything that emphasizes just how responsible you are, how much your partner lets you down, how good you are at taking care of everything. Don't let any thoughts of appearance or presentability get in the way; I want your "responsible superiority" to fill the room.

Don't assume these exercises only fit the up position. If your favorite stance is victim, I want you to express *that* stance fully. No more hiding your inferiority in the corner; bring it out into the open. Crawl up in a ball if you have to. Make your voice as mouse-like as you can. Let your partner see a 100% victim.

When your time is up, or when you've exhausted your passion, sit quietly for a moment and then let your partner do the same exercise.

Don't worry about the content of what you're saying or hearing. And don't respond or react to your partner in any way other than to take in what's happening. I want you both to focus on the energy that comes out of your passion, not the verbiage or internal judgments.

You will soon begin to enjoy letting out what you've always had to disguise or justify. You may even find yourselves laughing at how attached you are to your favorite positions. If the exercise isn't fun, you're probably still trying to look and sound presentable.

When you express your difference game stance with no hedging, you will hear and see for the first time exactly what you've been doing. Then your director can help you decide whether you want to continue playing in this way or move on to another stage of the process.

One of the advantages of finally expressing your difference game positions so openly is that you begin to realize that all those horrible things your protector said would happen don't necessarily occur. For the first time in your life, you've let loose with how superior you really are. You didn't hold back or dress it up to look more proper and acceptable. Yet you haven't been assaulted, arrested or abandoned. Your partner is still breathing, still conscious, still willing to stay in your presence.

Exercise #4: The Accountability Experience

The primary objective of the first three exercises is to expose the enormous amount of reactivity you usually exhibit, and to create a safe environment for fully and openly expressing your difference game stances. In this exercise, you increase your level of recognition by becoming truly accountable for your protective behavior.

With your anchoring chairs facing each other, each of you is to take 15 minutes a day to share how your protectors have persuaded you to maintain the status quo. Whatever thoughts, behaviors or feelings you experienced, whether overt or covert that supported your up or down position are to be expressed.

"I admit that I was under the influence of my protector when I accused you of exaggerating situations."
"My protector convinced me that you're not dependable."
"I agreed with my protector today that you haven't been fair with me."
"I let my protector persuade me that you don't really care about me."

These are all pieces of evidence that you were under the influence of your protectors.

The focus of these first four exercises is the wall you've built between the two of you, and the specific roles and disguises you use to stay within your comfort zone and maintain a safe distance. Now it's time to go behind the wall and find out what exactly you're hiding.

STEP 2: LOOKING BEHIND THE WALL

After acknowledging, expressing and taking responsibility for when and how you play the difference game, the next step is to determine the source of all this intensity. What is the deeper fear or pain you're avoiding, opposing or rejecting? What unacceptable experience makes all this camouflage necessary?

When either the drama or the deadness of your relationship increases, you can assume that you've touched some thought, desire or feeling that you consider unacceptable. You are now doing whatever is necessary to avoid that unacceptable experience.

The list of possible sources for your behavior is endless, but it usually arises out of some form of powerlessness: helplessness (having no control over a situation), disappointment (having no control over the outcome of a desire or interaction), sameness (losing the uniqueness that gives you some feeling of control over your world) and impasse (feeling deadlocked in solving a problem between you and your partner in a way that will satisfy both your needs). These experiences can lead to a frightening sense of vulnerability that we all tend to reject and avoid.

Any time an encounter is moving into either drama or deadness, you can use your interaction to reveal what is hidden by your wall if you simply stop and say, "Wait. What are we really protecting here?"

Remember, it's "we," not "you." Both you *and* your partner are doing the protecting. One of you may have the more overt role, but it's a shared, unconscious decision. Asking your partner, "What are you protecting?" will accomplish little other than moving you into the up position and shifting your focus to a new issue for the difference game: *we'd have a great relationship if you'd stop protecting.*

At first these exercises may seem scary for both of you. You're breaking your unwritten agreement to avoid unacceptable feelings of independence or insecurity.

But think about it. Are you really safe and secure when your partner is keeping his feelings from you? Will either of you benefit when he feels both his freedom and his passion are encumbered? Won't you both encounter these conflicts eventually, only in disguised forms? At the very least, these exercises will allow you to hear things that are already coming between you, and that are probably leaking all over your relationship in different ways.

We all temper or hide our needs and desires out of fear of our partners' responses. We have logbooks full of evidence supporting their anticipated pain or anger, and we use those examples to justify not expressing ourselves. These exercises remove those excuses.

Exercise #5: Honoring Your Mutual Impasse

As you saw in Step 1, there are times when you both become extremely attached to your perceptions of both yourselves and your relationship. Despite your good intentions, these occasions will result in the two of you reaching an impasse where each of you will be equally absorbed in protecting your positions. The temptation to take a difference game stance will be very strong since neither of you are getting your needs met and at that moment you both feel hurt or helpless. Such an impasse will test your ability to see the sameness that lies beneath your pain and frustration.

My friend and colleague Robert Strock offers two steps to using any such impasse as a path to mutuality. The first involves recognizing and expressing your impasse in order to avoid any escalation of the conflict and drama. Instead of putting each other in a win-lose position (*"I'm right, you're wrong."*), you need to place your emphasis on the ways you are locked into your mutual opposition.

Perhaps your partner sees you as insensitive and unavailable, while you perceive her as frequently demanding things in an angry and aggressive way. While you may each be willing to give lip service to your partner's perceptions, neither of you is willing to acknowledge the real validity of the other's views or feelings. This is leading you into confrontation and conflict.

When either of you recognizes such a mutual impasse, you need to say any one or more of the following to your partner:

"It seems like we are not able to meet each other's needs at this time."

"Our suspiciousness and guardedness won't allow us to hear what each other has to say or be together right now."

"We seem to have reached an impasse because we both feel so strongly about our individual views."

Whatever the statement, it must honor the realization that neither partner can make room for the other and that the best solution is to move apart temporarily and take a break. Such a movement neither denies the validity of your feelings and perceptions nor forces some solution from a stance of conflict and judgment.

The second step suggested by Robert Strock is to come back together at a later time when the negativity has subsided, and when you are now available for a deeper intimate connection. In order for this to occur both of you need to see and feel the needs and views of both your partner and yourself. If you are not yet ready to do so, your temporary separation should continue.

The goal of this step is to express your individual feelings in an inclusive, connecting way. You want to recognize and accept the validity of both your views and the effect they have on your relationship. In the example above, your statements would sound something like these:

"I can see that my insensitivity and your anger can equally cause hurt in each of us, and my heart is open to being touched by your pain, as well as my own."

"Your need for sensitivity and caring is as deep and important as mine, and I can feel your disappointment as much as my own."

When you realize that your equal wounds and your equal ability to wound are the same for both of you, your impasse will have become a source of intimate bonding rather than another justification for conflict and distance.

Exercise #6: Exploring the Past

Often the specific feelings we struggle to avoid grow out of painful or frightening experiences from our past. If you were held down against your will as a young child, for example, you might feel tremendous anxiety in any encounter that provoked images of help-lessness. If you were a child who always had to live up to others' expectations in order to be loved, then any experience of another's disappointment will probably trigger some intense reaction inside you. And if you've idealized yourself from birth as the one others can count on, then seeing yourself as undependable will be highly unacceptable.

Take turns with your partner sharing three childhood memories. With each recollection that you offer, add the phrase, ". . . and that left me believing that _____ was unacceptable." Fill in the blank with any behavior, desire or image of yourself that frightens you or takes you out of your comfort zone.

"I remember my father ordering me around and yelling at me if I ever talked back to him. Being raised by a tyrannical, dominating father left me believing that expressing my own thoughts and feelings was unacceptable."

"Whenever I wanted to play instead of doing chores, my mother called me selfish and gave me the silent treatment. That left me believing that putting my own desires first was unacceptable."

Continue in this way until you've revealed the source for several of your beliefs about what is unacceptable for you. Then write these beliefs down so you can refer to them in later exercises as you explore the ways these beliefs are affecting your relationship. Exploring childhood memories in this way and sharing them with your partner is an opportunity both for recognizing what you regard as unacceptable and for experiencing greater closeness as you expose some of your hidden pain.

Exercise #7: The Invitation Exchange

In the invitation exchange, you invite each other to bring up any thoughts, feelings or desires you regard as unacceptable, and give them full expression within a context of love and safety. As you will see, this activity carries a wider range of possible responses and results than the previous exercises, depending on your mutual capacity. The way you and your partner complete this exercise will vary with the level of commitment you each feel ready to express.

Your willingness to change your level of commitment regarding some frightening part of yourself will vary each time you participate in this experience. As this activity moves you deeper into your unacceptable parts, you will need to remain open to whatever degree of expression, and ultimately acceptance, you are capable of experiencing at that moment.

Sit opposite your partner in a space of love and trust. (Unlike Exercises 1 through 4, this should not grow out of any conflict or negative exchange.) Ask your partner, "What unacceptable feeling, thought or image did you struggle with today that kept you from connecting with me?"

Listen to whatever he offers. You can even take notes if it helps to have a visual reminder of what was said. If your partner describes a thought or behavior that doesn't reveal an unacceptable feeling, ask, "What was that protecting you from?" Help your partner with gentle probing questions to recognize the unacceptable feeling he wants to avoid.

Perhaps he replies, "I found myself wanting to find things wrong with you." When you probe for the source of this protection, he answers, "I'm afraid of really letting myself love you." So for him, the unacceptable feeling is allowing himself to love.

It's possible your partner will respond directly to your first question with some unacceptable feeling, such as, "I didn't want to let you see my desire in bed" or "I didn't want to disappoint you."

Whenever your partner opens up about an unacceptable feeling, concentrate on taking in all his energy. Try to hear with your whole body, not just your ears. The content of what he says is always secondary to his passionate expression.

However and whenever the unacceptable part is revealed, express your own appreciation for the risk he is taking, then respond by asking him, "What makes that so frightening?"

He might then respond, "If I love you, I won't have any justification for leaving you. So if I keep loving you without keeping the door open to leave, I'll lose my freedom. I'll be trapped."

If your partner is willing to continue, invite him to express the unacceptable thought or feeling he revealed as completely as possible, bringing his entire mind, body and spirit into the experience. This is where his capacity for sustaining his vulnerability will determine the level of commitment he is willing to make toward exposing his fear and sustaining the tension. A commitment at:

Level 1 means simply *expressing his fear* and the part of himself he's protecting as clearly as possible.

Level 2 means *imagining doing the unacceptable*. Ask your partner if he could imagine sustaining his love for you without having to find anything negative. Or ask him, "Could you simply imagine letting your 'back door' close?"

Level 3 means *saying the unacceptable as if it's true:* "I don't need to find something wrong because I don't need a way to leave. I will just love and enjoy you."

Level 4 means *committing to the unacceptable feeling for a longer period of time* than has been sustained before: "I will allow myself to love you with no escape clause for two weeks."

Level 5 means *fully committing to experiencing the unacceptable:* "I have closed the back door. I no longer need to keep myself from sustaining my love for you. I simply love you."

Each of these levels of expression and commitment involves greater exposure and vulnerability. The attained level is to be honored and appreciated by both of you as you move gradually closer to each other.

And I hope it goes without saying that these levels should never be used as a basis for judgment or defensiveness ("How come you can only express and you can't commit?"). By now you're skilled enough at both the difference game and the game of mutuality to recognize that attitude for exactly what it is.

When your partner has finished exposing some unacceptable part of himself, and has expressed whatever level of commitment is appropriate, thank him for having the love and courage to share it with you.

After you have quietly held this connection for several minutes, reverse the roles and offer your own unacceptable feeling to him.

Schedule 15 minutes on a regular basis for this exercise. One of the primary benefits of this experience is that you're inviting your unacceptable parts to enter the relationship directly, rather than sneaking through some back door. As they are brought lovingly into the light, they lose their power to terrify you. When revealed openly in this safe, loving attitude, your unacceptable feelings won't disrupt your entire relationship, as usually happens when they are allowed to sneak up and surprise you.

Exercise #8: The Purpose Question

At times your partner will be so caught up in her own anger, right-eousness or helplessness that she won't consider breaking her momentum with any structured encounter. So, if she keeps coming toward you with a lot of intensity and no awareness but won't partic-ipate in any of these exercises, simply ask the question, "What is the purpose behind what you're doing or saying?"

You are not to engage in any dialogue or debate. And don't accept any answer that doesn't reveal your partner's underlying intent. Just keep asking, "What is the purpose of you yelling at me?" "What is the purpose of you criticizing me?" or, "What is the purpose of your accusations?" until the feelings behind the aggressive behavior are revealed.

Any justification by your partner based on your behavior is insuf-ficient. When her response is, "I'm yelling because you drive me nuts" or "I have to do this just to get you to pay attention," simply repeat your purpose question until she understands that you're not intimidated by her outbursts and you won't participate in any other exchange.

Exercise #9: Your Protective Beliefs List

Any protective attitude is being fed by a set of underlying beliefs about what is unacceptable. To expend so much energy and endure so much conflict just to avoid certain thoughts and feelings, you must truly believe that these unacceptable experiences will have horrible consequences. Now that you recognize precisely *what* you're disguising or avoiding, your next goal is to understand the underlying beliefs that make you so afraid.

Powerlessness would not be so unacceptable if we didn't link it to weakness, or if we didn't believe that losing control of our world meant we would be hurt or destroyed. Believing that commitment takes away our freedom, or that sameness destroys our autonomy and unique identity, will certainly reinforce our fear and fuel whatever behaviors enable us to avoid those experiences.

Which of these other familiar beliefs are reinforcing your protective behavior?

- If I let go of my caution, I'll be destroyed.
- Disappointment means I'm not enough.
- If we're at an impasse, things will always be miserable.
- If I don't do what he wants, I'll be alone forever.
- If I show my fear, I'll fall apart.
- I have to take care of things because that's who I am. If I stop I will lose my identity and disappear.

The more terrifying the result you believe will occur, the more you will attempt to avoid the unacceptable behavior.

This next exercise helps you recognize the beliefs that drive your distancing behavior. Only when you can state a belief clearly can your director question its validity and observe how it is affecting your relationship.

Begin by separating from one another and asking yourselves, "What behaviors or feelings do I experience on a repeated basis?" Make a list of all the actions and attitudes you exhibit with any degree of frequency. Your list can include just about anything: organizing your tasks, being late, rushing through an experience, blaming or criticizing, complimenting or praising, manipulating, submitting or controlling. This isn't a judgment list; put down everything, whether you regard it as "good" or "bad."

When you've found at least half a dozen recurring behaviors, ask yourself these questions about each one:

- "What belief of mine would create or result in that kind of behavior?"
- "What would happen if I stopped that behavior?"
- "What consequence would I have to experience that I don't want to face?"

You might find that your constant praise arises out of a belief that you must make everyone else feel good about themselves, and if you don't, they won't want to be with you and you'll be alone. Or part of your personal belief system might be that if you slow down, things won't get taken care of and you'll be a failure.

If you want to expand your list, ask yourself what behaviors are most often the source of reactions or complaints from your partner. If you're stuck, you can even enlist your partner's help by asking what you do on a repeated basis. But do this within a real space of acceptance; if the answer is offered with an attitude of judgment, or if you defend or react at all to what is said, you'll move away from recognition and into the difference game.

Another way to discover the beliefs that drive you to avoid the unacceptable is to look back again at your childhood:

- "What was absolutely forbidden in our home?"
- "What experiences would most likely result in discomfort, pain or punishment?"
- "What issues weren't even spoken about?"
- "What would have happened if I (or anyone in my family) had done that?"

When you know the taboos from your childhood, you will have a good indication of many of your own negative beliefs which now play a vital role in everything you do. As you examine each of your responses to the questions above, ask yourself, *"What core beliefs protect me from the consequences of my taboo behaviors and perceptions?"*

By core belief I am referring to those internal dogmas which dictate the choices you make and the paths you pursue. If you confine yourself to being withdrawn, passive, and verbally contained, a possible core belief would be, "If I really express myself, I'll be destroyed." If you are very inhibited sexually, a core belief might be, "If I'm open sexually, I'll be thought of as a whore."

Exercise #10: Sharing Your Beliefs

When you've each discovered two or three core beliefs that seem to carry a lot of power for you, share them with one another. With no guilt or blame, discuss how these beliefs have affected your attitudes, the ways you interact and the ways you feel with each other. When you recognize how your feelings and behaviors have grown out of what you each believe, you will be much closer to seeing the sameness in the fears that you share, and your equal need to protect against them.

STEP 3: BRIDGING THE WALL

Thus far, this process has helped you recognize and express both your difference game stances and the parts of yourself that these attitudes keep safely hidden. Step 3 begins the transition away from what you pretend and into what is real for you. These next two exercises provide a physical experience of this movement from a level of intensity that you can't support to one that you can, as well as the movement from the difference game to mutuality.

As I discussed in Chapter 6, couples whose fighting and drama make them appear too distant are usually, in fact, too close to one another. The conflict is a result of their deep involvement and dependency on one another which causes each to be hurt by every movement and expression of the other. The following experience is especially designed to replace this intensity with a level of involvement that honors each partner's individual capacity for emotional intimacy.

Exercise #11: The Chairs of Integrity

In their efforts to speed up their relationship and reach some desired image, couples often "get ahead of themselves." This in turn exposes them to a greater level of emotional intensity than they are capable of sustaining.

By intensity I mean the magnitude and power of any emotional experience. If a feeling or experience touches you too deeply, it has become too intense for you. Regardless of the limitless number of qualities which can become too intense—anger, closeness, sexuality, sadness or tension—if the intensity of any situation is beyond your capacity for acceptance, you will need to respond in a way that honors your limits. Otherwise you will be led into recurring patterns of "flight or fight."

Unlike the previous exercises in this chapter, here the two chairs you use need to be moveable. This will enable you to place yourself at different distances from each other. The distance is to symbolically reflect how far apart you need to be in order to support the intensity at a particular moment. Support is defined as your ability to take care of yourself in relation to those feelings. When the intensity is too much for you, you will move your chair back; when you can absorb a greater amount of intensity, you can move it closer.

To begin this exercise, sit opposite your partner and select a topic that has been a source of emotion or conflict for you in your relationship. Then move your chair in relation to your partner until you reach a distance that reflects the level of intensity which you can support. As you modify your distance, ask yourself, "Can I experience this level of intensity without running away, creating emotional drama or denying my feelings?"

Now share with your partner whatever you are feeling or thinking about this area of discussion. As you do, ask yourself if you can support or comfort yourself in relation to what you are experiencing. If you can, then you are at a distance that is appropriate for you. If you need your partner to take care of you or if you find the experience intolerable, then you need to move your chair back far enough so you can feel comfortable.

Perhaps your husband has been bringing home lots of anger and frustration about his job, and the situation has created a great deal of intensity for you. Or perhaps you choose to discuss your desire for more affection, and this brings up a lot of fear. Such situations might require you to move your chair to the far side of the room in order to reduce the intensity to an acceptable level. If you begin to feel more comfortable and can absorb a greater degree of intensity, then move your chair closer to your partner.

As both of you share your feelings about the issue in question and move your chairs to the appropriate distance, neither of you is to comment or give advice about the other's position. There are no weak or wrong positions, only ones that you can or cannot support.

Each time you do this exercise, you will discover a different distance which is mutually comfortable because the feelings you are sharing and the intensity those feelings possess will constantly change. Your only concern is that you allow yourself to be touched by the experience in a way that honors the integrity of your capacity without drama, denial or judgment.

Exercise #12: The Four Chairs

It would be nice if we could just demolish our walls and be done with them. But in reality we will constantly move from protection to connection and back again. This exercise reflects this dynamic process, and illustrates how much of your time you spend exchanging difference game rhetoric in order to stay superior or inferior. It will also reveal just how hard it is to sustain an attitude of loving equality.

Place one pair of chairs facing each other and another pair beside them back-to-back. The facing chairs represent loving mutuality; the other pair are the judgmental/difference game chairs.

Sit face to face in the vulnerable mutuality chairs and begin discussing anything. The topic doesn't matter, I'm only interested in whatever attitude you're maintaining at any given moment.

As long as you're truly holding an attitude of loving vulnerability and sameness, with no desire to judge, move up or down or reject any thought or feeling, you may remain in the mutuality chair. But, as soon as you experience any defending, hiding or movement toward superiority or inferiority, move to your difference game chair.

Each of you can be in either of the chairs. It doesn't matter which one you're in, as long as you can support that chair 100%. No thought, word or gesture of vulnerability or sameness may occur in your negative/judgmental chair; no internal or external expression of up or down can be experienced from the mutuality chair.

Let's say one of you brings up the subject of money (although it could just as well be a discussion of sex, in-laws or doing the dishes). If you say, "I'm frightened about money," from a position of real exposure and vulnerability, you belong in your mutuality chair. If you think to yourself, "I'll never get her to balance a checkbook" or "If I start talking about our finances, she'll get all emotional," then you should immediately move to your protective chair.

Be especially alert throughout these exercises for statements that sound like offers of connection but are really disguised judgments. If you're in your mutuality chair, there can be no if/then comments: "If you'll agree to keep to a budget, then I'll stop criticizing you" or "If you were more responsible, then I could relax a little."

Similarly, don't try to make your attitude acceptable by justifying your behavior. "Somebody has to take responsibility for our finances." These are just ways of focusing on your partner. In this exercise, the focus is on you.

And, if you feel or utter any self-deprecating put-downs, jump over to your judgmental chair. "I'm afraid of going broke," is an honest statement of vulnerability. But when it's followed by, "I'm worthless when it comes to money," you're simply protecting yourself within the down position.

When you're in the matching back-to-back chairs, you both can talk or shout at once. What you're saying is irrelevant, and you aren't really going to listen to your partner from that position anyway. So, go ahead and drown out her babbling with your own. You'll still know the basis of your stances, which is the real benefit of the exchange.

When the two of you are not in matching chairs, you need to stop talking to each other. There is to be no diagonal conversation because there can be no real communication between opposing attitudes. You can remain in your chair and fully experience either your own vulnerability or your own inferior/superior position. And it's okay to talk to the empty chair in front of you, as long as you're congruent with the chair you're in.

Continue moving back and forth from one chair to the other until two things occur:

1. You are both able to express and be aware of your superiority or inferiority positions without justifications.
2. You both sustain your feelings of connection, vulnerability and sameness 100% from the mutuality chairs for some definite period, however brief.

The primary purpose of this exercise is to help you recognize how hard it is to sustain a loving position when you've become so accustomed to your hierarchy. Whenever the tension of the unfamiliar becomes too great, you'll get blown out of your mutual chair and back to the difference game.

Repeating this exercise gives you a clear sense of the flow between connection and protection that we experience every day, but which is normally obscured by the noise and smoke of all our drama.

The beauty of this experience is that it allows you to honor both parts of yourselves, the loving and the protective, without getting into the usual polarizations when you try to avoid something. In this exercise, when your negative protector wants the floor, you can openly give it to him with no guilt or resistance. And when your connector wants to be heard, she can be supported in a safe, loving environment. You simply have to switch chairs.

STEP 4: DISMANTLING THE WALL

Acceptance occurs on two levels: within yourself and between you and your partner. They are mutually dependent; you will only accept your partner to the extent you have accepted yourself, and an attitude of acceptance between you and your partner will have an impact on your openness to experiencing your own unacceptable parts.

With each unacceptable part of yourself and your partner that you can accept, another brick is removed from your protective wall. As the wall lowers and your acceptance increases, the sameness between you and your partner becomes clearer.

Because experiencing your sameness usually means leaving the familiar, accepting these deeper levels of awareness into your behavior and consciousness is a gradual process. You will pass through several levels of acceptance as you embrace your fear and move from distance to connection:

Level 1. Allowing your sameness intellectually. At this tier, you are strong enough to give verbal recognition to the sameness between you, at least when you're not in heated conflict. But, despite this new awareness of your equality, you won't yet be willing to take full responsibility for this realization, especially with each other.

You might say, "Of course we're similar in the way we're wounded." But you still won't experience this together, or be able to say, "I see how our mutual wounds created that fight last night."

Level 2. Allowing and experiencing the sameness momentarily. At this level, you will mutually own and feel your sameness, but you won't sustain it. You've become more courageous and are not as dependent on your ego images, so you're willing to humbly accept your equality. But, you will lose this ability whenever your fear of exposure and vulnerability becomes too great. You'll then revert to focusing on your differences in order to elevate or lower yourself in your own ego mirror.

Level 3. Allowing and sustaining the sameness. Here you will be able to hold the tension of your equal pain, equal fear and equal responsibility for whatever protective behaviors you've exhibited. You will allow the discomfort and helplessness of leaving your comfort zone for increasing periods of time.

I want you to be aware of the particular level of sameness you are supporting as you go through the following exercise.

Exercise #13: Same-Level Intercourse

Pick some issue about which you and your partner are very sensitive. Choose something that frequently results in one of you feeling less or more.

A common situation might involve a husband coming to bed and asking for sex after a gap of a week or more. His wife responds that she is feeling too pressured and would rather just cuddle. The man feels undesired, whereas she believes she is being used. His underlying belief is that by not being desired, he is less of a man. She believes that being used means she is not really cared for as a woman.

Whatever the loaded issue is for you, limit your dialogue solely to statements that express a need, and avoid those that imply that one of you is less or more than the other. Comments such as, "I feel pressured," or, "You're not there for me," are out of bounds because they either inflate you or imply some shortcoming in you or your partner.

You may only offer statements such as, "I understand," "I share that feeling," "I can appreciate that," or any direct statement of desire or of a real feeling, such as, "I want to make love," or "I'm afraid."

Whatever you say must allow you to stay on the same level as your partner. If you can't think of statements that meet this criterion, simply tell your partner, "I have nothing to say."

The purpose of this exercise is not that it result in any particular action or outcome, but that you experience the challenge of remaining equal to your partner and realize how much of your usual interaction is dominated by up or down comments.

Our lives are filled with expressions of difference. It will take time to see and hold the sameness that lies underneath all that fog. The more often you are willing to face each other in a space of quiet acceptance for the mutual feelings you share, the more you will be able to sustain your equality.

Exercise #14: The Unacceptable Qualities List

There are two keys to accepting the thoughts, feelings and desires you both consider unacceptable: seeing the positive aspects of whatever you are struggling with and embracing and appreciating the hidden parts of yourselves. The more you welcome experiences that you regard as negative, dangerous, embarrassing or unworthy into your psychological family, the greater will be your ability to connect with each other.

On your own, list five qualities in your partner that you don't accept and that serve to interfere with your ability to join. One by one, allow yourself to be touched by these qualities. Really let them in without any judgment or critical comment.

When you have fully experienced a quality without letting your defensiveness or judgment shade any part of it, ask your director to look for where that quality exists inside yourself, even if it is in some other form.

Let's say you're focusing on your partner's hostility. Ask yourself where hostility fits into your own community. Perhaps it has taken the form of quiet resentment rather than bursts of anger. Find the place where your own experience of hostility can connect with that of your mate. Keep letting this experience in without any judgment or resistance.

Deal with one quality at a time. Continue the process until you can begin to see each one reflected inside yourself, and can recognize something positive in all the particular qualities you're focusing on. How have they added positively to your relationship? Can you appreciate the way your partner has taken responsibility for outwardly displaying the qualities you both possess so that you won't have to?

You'll go through several starts and stops with this exercise, as your protector keeps muscling in. That's fine, just stay with it. When you have explored all five qualities in this way, rank them in order of increasing unacceptability. If you are not sure of the order, ask yourself, "Which one of these creates the most resistance and tension for me? Which would I like to avoid more than any other?" That one goes last.

Now share with your partner the first, least difficult quality on the list. Share your awareness of how this part of her manifests inside of you. Tell her how much you appreciate that aspect of the two of you.

This needs to be a genuine appreciation; if you're giving lip service or are unable to do it, return to the first part of the exercise and go back through the list alone. Continue in this way for as many sessions as are necessary until all five qualities have been shared.

Exercise #15: The Second Invitation Exchange

It is now time to further help each other accept the parts of *yourselves* you are hiding, and invite them into their rightful place within your relationship. For this exercise, you will begin by sitting in two chairs side by side with two empty chairs facing them.

The empty chairs represent your attitude of mutual acceptance. From these chairs nothing is judged and no one is seen as above or below you. The chairs you sit in at the beginning of the exercise represent your judgmental/protective style.

Whoever feels ready moves first to one of the mutuality chairs. From here, invite your partner to join with you and be your equal as you reach out your hand to him. Regardless of what your partner says or does, you are to hold this position of mutuality and connection. Give no energy to any negative comment or gesture on his part. Simply stay with your invitation.

If your partner accepts your invitation, he is to move to the other accepting chair, take your hand and respond in his own words or the ones I have provided below:

"I fully acknowledge that. . .
   we are the same;
   we are equally wounded;
   we are equally frightened;
   we are equally unavailable . . .
   and I share this relationship with you from a mutual
place of love and responsibility."

His responses can vary, as long as they are offered from a place of complete equality. As soon as any element of resistance or any unacceptable feeling arises for him, he must move to his protective chair and express his unacceptable part as in the earlier invitation exchange.

In response to any feeling or expression of inequality, you simply repeat your invitation, while acknowledging the other's feelings: "I hear that you feel unworthy (or superior to me), and I invite you to bring that part with you into our family. You are joining me on equal ground, where all the parts of ourselves are acceptable."

When the invitation is accepted and your partner can sustain it, or when it is declined and he openly states that he isn't ready to take that risk, the exercise is over and it's time to switch roles.

These invitation exercises will be an ongoing process as you face your fears together and gradually welcome more of your unacceptable parts into the relationship. The more comfortable you become with risking this level of vulnerability and exposure, the closer you will be to integrating acceptance into your entire relationship.

Exercise #16: Balancing the Imbalance

You are familiar by now with the idea that any time you reject a part of yourself, you create an imbalance. You are then tilted in favor of the more esteemed members of your psychological family. This exercise is designed to correct this polarized situation.

In this exercise, one of you is the "giver" and the other is the "receiver." Begin by having the receiver select an unacceptable part of herself that she wants to focus on, such as selfishness, loveability, innocence or gentleness—whatever quality the receiver regards as too unknown or frightening to expose.

You both agree to focus on that one quality for a period of a week. The giver is to sincerely look for every opportunity to recognize and express that quality in the receiver. So if the unacceptable quality is selfishness, and the receiver always tries to appear unselfish, the giver might say, "I appreciate how selfish you were in taking care of everyone so you could feel comfortable."

Or, if the selected quality is being powerful, and the receiver usually hides behind a mask of helplessness, the loving statement might be, "I see you as very powerful," or, "I admire how powerful you're being right now." The key is to frame the statement in a way that is exactly the opposite of what the receiver is used to hearing or believing. If the receiver reacts that she still feels helpless, you are to respond by saying, "I know you feel that way, and I see you as powerful." Continue in this way for the entire week, then switch roles and focus on some new quality.

This experience can be one of the most cherished gifts you'll ever give your mate because you are sustaining your recognition and acceptance of your partner's unacceptable part without any conditions or reservations. It will also bring up your own fear as you look at your partner in this new way and honestly express your appreciation for an unacceptable quality you have both conspired to keep hidden.

The more you can assist your partner in healing her imbalance, the more you will increase your own acceptance. And when you are the receiver, you will finally understand that those inner voices that try to create separation, both within you and between you, are simply aspects of your mutual fear. With each new element of acceptance that you can integrate in this way, the support for your sameness becomes stronger.

Exercise #17: Sustaining Mutuality

This final exercise brings you back to your invitation chairs one more time. You're alert and perceptive enough now to recognize the ways you shift from connection to protection without needing extra chairs. So simply face your partner and say, *"I truly see and feel that our capacity for intimacy is the same."*

Hold this attitude until thoughts or emotions come into your awareness that discount or dilute that statement. The moment that happens, tell your partner what has occurred, close your eyes until you are ready to open them and return to the original statement 100%.

Continue this experience until you are able to sustain the statement with your entire consciousness, or until you have expanded your original capacity for an intimate connection.

STEP 5: KEEPING THE WALL DISMANTLED

In this final step toward greater equality and acceptance, you incorporate an attitude of mutuality into all your interactions with each other. You replace your desire to protect with a desire to live. Here there is much greater support for experiencing the underlying equality that you share, and your list of unacceptable feelings is greatly diminished. You move more easily between closeness and separation, and sustain the tension of exposing and sharing the integrity of all the parts of yourselves.

A wonderful measure of the extent to which you have integrated acceptance into your lives is in the way you now handle the everyday problems and challenges that confront every relationship. When you find yourself working through tasks fairly quickly and smoothly, without either of you trying to score ego points or prove anything, then you know you've come a long way. If issues that once consumed or crippled your relationship now can be dealt with simply as tasks, with no underlying drama or posturing, then your capacity for acceptance has clearly expanded.

You are now ready to move into the ongoing process of experiencing more intimacy and accepting even deeper parts of yourselves.

I hope it is obvious that the steps toward mutuality are not separate and exclusive. We flow in and out of all of them, sometimes stuck in one, then occasionally drawing closer to our partners and moving on to deeper levels of connection and intimacy. Because this is a dynamic process, as soon as new situations and difficulties arise that tap into our fears, or as soon as we become complacent and less alert, we will again slide back into the difference game. So always take note of the issues and tasks that throw you back into judgment and protection. These point to feelings that you still find unacceptable, which you still need to welcome into your relationship.

Although living fully in the last stage of mutuality is humanly impossible, we can steadily increase our ability to sustain our acceptance and equality as long as we can find the courage to let go of our protective identities.

PART IV

OBSTACLES

Chapter 11

THE JOY OF UNSATISFACTORY SEX
Mutuality in the Bedroom

"Do you want to have sex tonight?"

"Didn't we have it last night?"

"Yea, but that was the only time this week."

"Well if you want to."

"What about you?"

"I'm fine if you initiate."

"I started it the last three times."

"Are you sure you want to do this?"

"I thought I was."

"Why don't we wait until the morning?"

"I've got to get up early."

"Why don't we just cuddle?"

"Frankly I'm about cuddled out."

"Then let's do it now."
"Do what?"
"I don't know."
"Well good-night, dear."
"Good-night."

Of all the settings where we strive for mutuality in our relationships, the one that's most threatening is the bedroom. Who among us comes to bed truly naked? The clothes slip off, the coverlet is thrown back and our insecurities and attachments are suddenly very present and extremely obvious to us. It is harder to hide from ourselves here than in any other area of our lives. It is little wonder that ego trips, guilt and the difference game permeate our sexual encounters.

As if our own fears and expectations weren't enough, culture comes to bed with us, too. We absorb its images, messages and illusions. Advertisements, books, magazines and movies exert a not-so-subtle pressure: *be potent . . . be orgasmic . . . be sensual . . . be gentle . . . be open . . . be turned on . . . be natural . . . be . . . be . . . be . . .*

Figuring out who we're supposed to be becomes even more bewildering when these cultural ideals transform into their opposites. In one decade open, free, experimental sex is in; in the next decade it's love, commitment and caution. Ideas about male and female roles change even faster than society's morals and taboos. This ever-shifting subtext adds to our confusion and makes sexual satisfaction and fulfillment seem impossible.

But ultimately all of these pressures, attitudes and fears, whether they originate from within or without, are just other versions of the difference game in action. The bedroom is simply our grandest arena for playing out the judgments and disguises of up and down. With all the exposure and vulnerability that sexual intimacy requires, is it any wonder that our protectors will snuggle up right next to us every time we come to bed?

THE JUDGMENTAL BED

All of the pressure to be something other than what comes naturally results in a continual desire to rank everything we bring to bed. *"That's good. That's bad. Long and sensual is okay. Quick and dirty isn't. Orgasm is king. Impotence shouldn't even be mentioned."*

This sexual ranking system is the essence of what I call the *judgmental bed*. This is a bed where certain thoughts, desires and experiences are selected as acceptable, while others are rejected and kept out of sight. In the judgmental bed, perfectly normal human feelings such as awkwardness, anger, insecurity or boredom, are labeled unacceptable and shoved under the bed. The only qualities allowed into the bed are the ones that both partners agree are acceptable that night.

As you can imagine, this bed is pretty empty because only the most highly favored experiences are allowed in. But it's very crowded underneath the judgmental bed, where you and your partner have been stuffing all the parts of yourselves that don't meet your high sexual standards.

The judgmental bed is one where:

- Parts of you are good and parts are bad.
- Parts of you are at war with other parts of yourself.
- Parts of you are never openly expressed.

It isn't hard to see how such attitudes thrill your protector. As with any version of the difference game, all this judging and rejecting not only robs your sexual relationship of your full vitality and passion, it creates a climate ripe for conflict.

Consider a couple locked in the classic sexual conflict: He wants sex more often than she does. Even when they compromise by agreeing to have sex a certain number of times a week, they're not able to carry through on their agreements. Why?

Because all their negotiation doesn't address the real issue: that underneath their outward "desire" differences, they are each hiding some very real fears that are too uncomfortable for either of them to expose.

Perhaps the husband equates sex with his power and manhood. In his own mind, if he doesn't score on a regular basis, he sees himself as weak and less of a man.

The wife may see sex as an opportunity to feel that someone cares for her. So, any thought of being used as a sex object by her husband would be unacceptable for her. If she believes she is just fulfilling his needs without receiving love, affection and attention in return, her own worth is diminished and she feels she is less of a woman.

As with many couples, the bedroom becomes a stage where they act out their need to protect themselves from their deeper fears. When bedtime rolls around each night, the pressure for both of them becomes enormous. He worries that once again he won't get to display his power, and she sees withdrawal or submission as her only two alternatives.

Whether or not they have sex, the result is often disappointment and resentment. The only real winners are their protectors, who have kept their unacceptable fears safely hidden under the judgmental bed.

Such distance is inevitable whenever you favor some desires and behaviors over others. Intimacy in the judgmental bed is always of secondary importance. Your primary objective is to find ways of building yourself up or putting your partner down, in order to gain control of the bed and protect your image. So, in the midst of what is purported to be a place for passion and intimacy, you'll think or hear such expressions as, "I'd be more sexual if you were a more sensitive man," or, "I've been amazingly tolerant putting up with someone like you." In other words, *"We'd have great sex if it weren't for you."*

Many popular sex therapy treatments unknowingly collude with this ranking system. This will occur any time certain behaviors are labeled as dysfunctions or are given a lesser value. Frank Hajcak and Patricia Garwood, authors of *Hidden Bedroom Partners*, distinguish between truly sexual behavior and behavior that uses sex for various underlying agendas, such as validation, dominance, control, social pressure or as a buffer for depression. These "hidden agenda" behaviors are considered destroyers of sexual pleasure because they divert energy from the pure intimate experience of sex.

These authors offer various ways to stop the "deleterious effects" of using sex for hidden emotional needs. Their approach is in sharp contrast to what I am proposing here. I maintain that *the only interference to our sexual pleasure is refusing to accept whoever shows up in our bed.*

When even the experts regard certain experiences as "problems" and label them dysfunctional, inappropriate, dispassionate, unromantic or inconsiderate, what choice do you have but to stamp them *unacceptable* and shove them out of sight? And with so many parts of yourselves squeezed into that little space under your judgmental bed, you're bound to feel tremendous pressure, anxiety, guilt and fear of exposure.

Of course, it is possible that some sexual issues have a physiological basis. When I work with such clients, I refer them to people with expertise in that area because such conditions are beyond the scope of my practice or of this book. My only concern is that no sexual situation, emotional *or* physiological, be used as a basis for judgment and distance.

When so much of your energy is channeled toward hiding your unacceptable parts, or criticizing those of your partner, there's almost nothing left to give to your sexuality. Your passion is neutralized, and it's only a matter of time before you feel empty, mediocre and numb.

This deadening of your sexuality will usually result in three common issues I encounter repeatedly with the couples I see: *unsatisfactory sex, lack of interest in sex* and *infrequent sex.* In almost all such situations, one partner takes the role of wanting more or better sex. This partner feels increasing frustration and hidden resentment. The other partner, who resists sexual encounters or is seen as "the problem," shoulders the guilt or blame for not being more sexual.

These judgmental bed roles are neither exclusive nor gender defined; in my practice I see men and women on both ends of the continuum. But whatever form these outward differences take, focusing on them eventually results in tremendous anxiety or no sex at all. Sex becomes a mountain the couple must futilely climb, knowing they will never reach the top.

I find it very interesting to see how each of these issues has been more prominent in our culture at different times. In the 1970s, the emphasis was on enhancing sexual performance and finding the precise G-spot for bigger and better orgasms. In the 1980s, with the growing prominence of dual-career couples, many partners despaired over their vanishing sexual interest and desire. Now, it's quite common to hear couples going several months or more without any sex at all.

Infrequency, pressure, conflict and dissatisfaction are all symptomatic of couples who have denied or ignored their various sexual personalities. When my female clients fail to support their personalities which need emotional foreplay, these women can easily lose their sexual desire. When my male clients fail to support their insecure personalities in bed, these men can turn into erectile robots, always having to keep it up. And when a couple's constant concern is scoring a 9.9 in the Sexual Olympics, the bedroom becomes an arena only for winning and losing, rarely for joining and loving.

Each of these issues offers fertile ground for declaring one partner "the problem": "We'd have a great relationship if you were a better lover." "The only way we have sex is the missionary position." "I'd like to have sex more often, but she isn't interested." "We're lucky if we do it on national holidays."

The other partner can now regard herself as better or less: "He just doesn't know how to be tender in bed." "I guess I'm just not desirable anymore." The resulting conflict can go on endlessly, with one partner taking one end of the quality/interest/frequency spectrum, and the other arguing for the other end: "I'm a better lover." "No, I'm better." "You're oversexed." "You're frigid." "You expect sex too often." "We don't do it enough."

As each partner's position is judged good or bad, right or wrong, better or worse, the intensity of the game escalates until they're both fighting for their ego lives. Meanwhile, their passion and sexual intimacy has been buried in the rubble of the battle.

Making Our Selections

Within your judgmental bed, your protector will insist that you deny, disguise or reject any thought, desire or experience that will cast you in an unflattering light. So it's good-bye to fear, sadness, insecurity, impotence, frustration, inadequacy, awkwardness, powerlessness, anger and fragility. And at all costs, you must never be caught committing one of the Big Three sexual felonies: manipulation, obligation and faking it.

The sexual experiences we deem unacceptable greatly outnumber the ones we celebrate. The sad part of all this selectivity is that many of the richest parts of yourself remain off limits and unused. In *Constructing the Sexual Crucible*, David Schnarch describes the way couples eventually come to a consensus about what is mutually tolerable in bed, while all the rest of their feelings are discarded in one way or another. Anything that creates discomfort for the partners is gradually pushed away.

It is usually acceptable, for example, to be orgasmic and potent, sensitive and loving, passionate and desiring, confident and secure, and to have great endurance and lasting power. As long as you can perform within these parameters, you're happy to slide between the sheets. But can anyone truly manifest these qualities night after night? And what do you do when you can't?

What happens when you're making love and the part of you that doesn't feel turned on starts to whisper, *"I'm not feeling anything. I want to get out of here,"* or, *"I'm bored. Hurry up and get this over with."* Or what if that voice starts saying, *"I'm losing my erection! Quick, get it up! Push harder! Thrust faster!"* You try to ignore these voices, but they only get louder and the feelings get stronger.

Or maybe your partner starts to make sexual overtures, and you feel frightened and awkward. You hope the feeling will go away, but it doesn't. The thoughts flash through you: *"If I tell him how I feel, he'll think I'm crazy or frigid and he'll turn away or make fun of me. I'll feel foolish. It'll be better if I don't say anything. I'll just fake it and hope he doesn't notice."*

Will you share any of these thoughts with your partner? Don't be ridiculous! You have to shove them under the bed where they belong!

So, you ignore your feelings and grind away until you somehow make it to the finish feeling drained and dissatisfied. And with each episode, the unexpressed feelings and thoughts accumulate. After awhile there's a lot more energy and intensity below your bed than there is in it.

Your primary motivation in the judgmental bed is to preserve your false self. Whatever sexual image you've created to protect you from the unacceptable, you will preserve that image at all costs. So, if your personal façade is to be strong, any sexual weakness will be ostracized to the underworld. If your persona is that of the pleaser, then any selfish need is hidden.

As in all aspects of your relationship, your capacity for intimacy is the same as your partner's. The specific *list* of what is sexually unacceptable for each of you may vary, but there are sexual rejects under both sides of the bed. Even though one of you may seem confident in bed while the other is insecure, those are just your agreed upon roles.

If you want to bring some tension into your judgmental bed, just watch what happens if the insecure partner displays some aggressiveness, or if the confident partner expresses insecurity. As soon as you switch roles and move outside your familiar comfort zone, your equality will quickly become apparent.

Support for the Judgmental Bed

The legs of the judgmental bed consist of four attitudes that reinforce our need to rank and hide many of our sexual parts. These attitudes overlap a great deal, but it is their cumulative effect that forms the foundation of our protection from real sexual intimacy.

The first of these attitudes is *lack of acceptance* for whatever thoughts, feelings and behaviors we regard as unworthy, inappropriate or downright shameful in bed. Years of conditioning make it all too easy to play favorites with the aspects of ourselves we choose to express when we're in a sexual relationship. As long as we can't accept all the parts of our sexual selves, we'll continue putting down at least half of who we really are.

Just consider the following list of feelings and attitudes:

Awkward
Frightened
Inadequate
Impotent
Uninterested
Needy
Boastful
Selfish
Guilty
Pressured
Dishonest
Joyful
Using
Manipulative
Powerful

All of these are normal, natural qualities that most of us have experienced repeatedly. Yet how many of them do you accept in yourself? Which ones would you feel truly comfortable bringing to bed and sharing openly with your partner?

The second leg of the judgmental bed is the tendency to *favor some parts of ourselves* over their opposites. With every pair of opposing qualities, we regard one as more valuable than the other. Our shyness doesn't equal our openness, our passivity doesn't equal our aggression, our weakness isn't as good as our strength.

For any pair you can conceive, the "valuable" end of the spectrum will be one you'll bring to your judgmental bed; the opposite will be disguised or denied.

The third leg holding up the judgmental bed is *lack of respect* for the unacceptable parts of ourselves. When we treat our fears, desires and weaknesses like strangers who aren't deserving of our attention, we alienate a part of ourselves. Our fear of losing control of the bedroom, exposing too much of our true selves and seeming inferior makes us turn our backs on half of what we are.

Instead of providing a space for these feelings, we deny them expression, and we miss useful messages that could add enormous depth to our lives.

The following two stories illustrate this point:

When Alan came to see me, he was so ashamed of his premature ejaculation problem, he could barely discuss it. He considered it responsible for the breakup of his marriage, and he wanted more than anything to get rid of it.

But instead of moving away from his "problem," I asked him to communicate with that part of himself, and listen to what it might have to tell him. When he entered into a dialogue with the premature part of himself, he discovered that he repeatedly moved too fast in relationships, and had never paid sufficient attention to his fears or to the level of involvement he was ready to experience.

So, the literal act of ejaculating too quickly was actually a metaphor for Alan's impulsive actions. This unacceptable sexual behavior was really his body's way of asking him to slow down and get in touch with who he really was: a vulnerable, shy, sensitive man. Realizing this enabled him to stop calling that part of himself a problem, and motivated him to pay much closer attention to his own needs in his next relationship.

Steve was distraught over becoming impotent with his new lover. As we explored the nature of their relationship, he revealed that her lack of commitment caused him great pain. When I heard this, I said it sounded like the same position his penis was taking: "I will not be firm in this relationship."

Although the statement startled him at first, he began to recognize the message his body was sending. This new respect for his impotency meant it no longer needed to reside under the bed, and could instead be accepted and appreciated.

The very next time I saw Steve, he reported that he was again able to have intercourse, but that he planned to terminate the relationship anyway because it wasn't the level of commitment he wanted.

In *The Hazards of Being Male*, Herb Goldberg discusses the wisdom of the penis, and talks about all the different messages men can learn if they pay attention to their sexual organ instead of judging it. I would like to go even further and invite you to appreciate the wisdom of the vagina as well, and to listen to *all* the attitudes and feelings you encounter in the bedroom, not just those emanating from your genitalia.

The final corner of the judgmental bed is held up by the *heaviness* we bring to the bedroom. When it comes to sex, we take ourselves so seriously that it's surprising we ever have any fun in bed at all. If we could laugh a little at all the physical and emotional gyrations we go through to become sexually intimate, we'd find a lot more basis for joining. As long as seriousness is the order of the day, any failure to perform up to standard will be another basis for rejection.

The Consequences of the Judgmental Bed

As with any other version of the difference game, the judgmental bed offers safety and protection instead of risk and exposure. And even in the judgmental bed, you sometimes get to bump and grind just like they do on the Playboy Channel.

But the price for these rewards is high, and only you can decide if it's worth all these other consequences.

Loss of sexual energy—Restricting at least 50% of who you really are siphons off a lot of your energy and passion. Every part of you has energy to contribute to your sexual relationship. When most of those parts are kept under the bed, much of what you have to offer is missing. And a good portion of what's left will be directed toward hiding and suppressing those unacceptable feelings.

An information gap—Since every part of you has something to tell you about your true needs and desires, pushing parts of yourself away will deprive you of important information. This will lead you into actions that are futile, destructive or simply outside your capacity. Sooner or later you'll look around and say, *"How'd I get into this mess?"* You got into it because you were cut off from voices that would have guided you elsewhere.

Pretense—If you're studying to be an actor, you couldn't ask for a better drama school than your judgmental bed. If not, you may get weary of the continual need for imposture and disguise. Constantly displaying what you consider acceptable, rather than what you really want and feel, is a lot of work.

Distrust—An added result of your Emmy-winning performances is the growing suspicion that maybe your partner is also faking it—not just with her 8.5-on-the-Richter-scale-orgasms, but with whatever feeling or thought she exhibits. How can you trust your partner if you can't trust yourself?

Boredom—When only the same, acceptable feelings and behaviors are paraded out every night, pretty soon things can get routine and predictable. Spontaneity, variety and excitement become increasingly difficult when every new thought, action or emotion must be screened for acceptability before it's brought into bed.

Pressure—As you're probably starting to realize, the judgmental bed isn't just a place for lovemaking—it's a job. You've got a lot of work to do here: evaluating and ranking all your thoughts and feelings; selecting only those that are acceptable; hiding the other parts of yourself under the bed; guarding against exposure; staying turned on (or else denying any sexual desire so you can roll over and go to sleep); performing up to expectations; reacting properly to all your partner's movements; and keeping all this up for just the right amount of time. What a lot of responsibility! No wonder you're under so much stress. Air traffic controllers aren't subjected to this much organization, selection and pressure.

Distance—In the judgmental bed, you get to be buck naked and still avoid real risk, exposure and vulnerability. You can tie your two bodies in a knot and still not be connected on a deep level. And this is probably the reward most of you are interested in: the safety of intimacy without exposure.

Or perhaps not. If these prizes are no longer to your liking, maybe you're ready for the alternative. . . .

THE ACCEPTING BED

The internal and external conditioning that supports a sexual status system is extremely powerful. To reverse these deeply ingrained attitudes and behaviors, a new kind of bed is needed—one that offers you many more options and has room for the numerous unique human qualities that emerge in your sexual relationships.

This new *accepting bed* supports your mutuality. Here you're allowed to feel and express all the unacceptable parts of yourself that you've been hiding from your partner. And here your energy and passion are channeled entirely toward your partner in an attitude of loving connection. Sexual pleasure and satisfaction come not from matching some image of what you should be, but from exposing and sharing everything that you are.

> *Like many women, Terry was struggling with thoughts and feelings that seemed highly unacceptable. After 15 years of marriage, she was turned off sexually. She kept hoping for a certain responsiveness from Ed, and when it wasn't there, she felt frustrated and disappointed.*
>
> *Her frustration was now turning to resentment, and she was becoming sexually numb. She began dreading his sexual approaches, and was constantly searching for ways to avoid sex altogether. Her excuses ran the gamut of fatigue, work, headache and "Just not tonight." If she kept this up for too long a time, her frustration and resistance would turn to guilt, and she'd finally submit to passionless, dutiful sex. But all the while she was "servicing" Ed, she would tell herself, "Just get through this, and the pressure will be off for awhile."*

Terry began hating the parts of herself that created this cha-rade, even though she saw this solution as the only way to keep things comfortable and normal.

When I heard Terry's story, I said, "Don't you think it's time to bring your obligatory self out of the closet? Why not just be straight about it with Ted and tell him you're having sex because you feel obligated?"

She looked at me like I'd ask her to wear a fish on her head, but by now I'm used to that expression on my clients' faces. She start-ed getting nervous and retorted that she couldn't possibly do that. "Ed would get angry."

I knew Ed was a very reticent and passive guy, who Terry was always wishing would be more passionate. So I responded, "What's so bad about that?" She smiled as she realized that such a concern was nonsense.

Then she tried to escalate her resistance. "Well, what if he leaves me?"

Even she had to laugh at that one.

"But it will hurt his feelings," she then added.

"Maybe," I said. "But how happy do you think he is now, with you faking it most of the time? Do you really think he isn't already aware that you're not happy or satisfied? And if you do this out of love, how do you know he won't like it? Do you really have that much to lose?"

She thought about it a minute, then finally blurted out, "Well, what exactly are you asking me do?"

"I want you to go home tonight and say to Ed, 'I want to have obligatory sex with you.' No matter what his objections are, I want you to passionately declare, 'I'm getting behind in my obligation. I owe you sex, and I don't want to get any deeper in debt.' Whatever he responds, I want you to start taking off his clothes, insist on sex, and in an excited, pleading voice say how important it is that you repay him. And while you're doing this, I want you to thoroughly enjoy your obligatory self."

At first she responded, "You've got to be kidding. Who says those kind of things?" I answered that the only choices I could see were either this or sexual deadness. Then she replied, "Even if I was willing, I'm not sure I even know how."

So I said, "All you need to do is allow yourself to be your obligatory self, and trust that you intuitively know what to say and how to do it. You're already giving him obligatory sex, so I'm only asking you to be yourself. Only this time I want you to do it openly, with no defensiveness."

Finally, she agreed to give it a try.

At bedtime that night, Terry did what we had discussed. At first Ed was surprised and a bit reluctant. But because she played it straight and was passionate about her obligation, he got turned on fairly quickly. They ended up having obligatory sex twice that night, and she felt much greater freedom and excitement at no longer having to hide what she dreaded. The next night Ed said, "Can we have obligatory sex again? That was the best sex we've had in a long time."

I wonder how many of you could even imagine that open, obligatory sex like this had any place in your intimate sexual relationships. In the beginning, Terry had the same struggle. She expressed all kinds of doubts and concerns that this approach could accomplish anything, or that it might even make things worse. But, it was only natural for her to feel frightened about this unfamiliar behavior that violated a lifetime of conditioning.

So, if the approach I describe here sounds outrageous, unacceptable or impossible, I certainly appreciate your feelings, and I don't really expect you to think otherwise at this point. I only ask that before you reject the qualities of the accepting bed, you ask yourself:

Is our present bed big enough for all the needs and desires I would like to express and fulfill?

Is our present bed an honest reflection of who the two of us really are?

Is our present bed a place where my partner and I come together on all levels to experience real intimacy and acceptance?

If your answer to these questions is no, and you're tired of a bed filled with grades, restrictions and all kinds of judgments, then I'd like to invite you into the accepting bed, where everyone is welcome.

To further help you choose the bed that's best for you, here are their basic differences:

Judgmental Bed	Accepting Bed
Protected	Vulnerable
Safe	Scary
Familiar	Unknown
Routine	Varied
Judgmental	Welcoming
Partial expression	Total expression
Divided energy	Full energy
Restrictive	Free
Honors prescribed images	Honors all parts of you
Separation	Connection

If you're still uncertain, either because you question the validity of this new approach to sex, or because it simply sounds too risky and frightening, let me make one more suggestion: pick one night a week to try the accepting bed, just to see what happens. The rest of the time you can continue with whatever your usual routine is. But one out of every seven times you go to bed, give this alternative a shot. Who knows what might happen?

MOVING INTO THE ACCEPTING BED

Once you've decided to experience a sexual encounter where every part of you is welcome, and your passion grows out of whatever you're feeling at any moment, what exactly do you do? How do you overcome the rules and attitudes that have been drummed into you since puberty, and learn to connect with each other in this new way?

The Principles of Sexual Mutuality

Your first step is to consider a new set of rules and parameters, not only for your sexual relationship, but for defining exactly what sex is. I know many of these may sound odd or frightening, so have your director tell your protector that you appreciate his diligence in guarding you from risk, but you want to explore something new. Unless your protector has specific objections or concrete evidence that these principles won't work, ask him to be silent.

Sex is whatever you bring to bed

In the accepting bed, sex is no longer limited to the hot parts of R-rated movies, or to the encounters you heard about in the locker room. It's not what your parents warned you about, and it's not just what you read in the letters to *Penthouse*. In other words, sex is no longer the narrow group of images you have been carrying in your head for most of your life.

Sex is any exchange of energy between two lovers. It is any expression, internal or external, that emerges when you interact with your partner. Sex becomes a *total* connection whenever you allow the intercourse of all of your parts.

There are no exceptions to this all-encompassing definition. Any restrictions reduce the total capacity of your sexual energy. Under this new definition, sexual expression can take a multitude of forms. When sex is perceived in this expanded way, rather than merely as two bodies rubbing together, then any exchange of energy with your lover is recognized as a sexual experience.

With this expanded view, all sexual expression is elevated to the same level. Any form your energy takes, any particular way you feel and behave, is as welcome and respected as any other. In the accepting bed, you'll never think or hear, "This is sex but that's not." Here it's all sex, and it's all equal.

Roger had resigned himself to having sex only once a month.
He saw himself as someone who had never had a very big sex

drive. As a result, he felt both guilty and unsatisfied in his rela-
tionship with Helen.

I asked Roger to try expanding his concept of sex. "Instead of
waiting until you feel turned on in a certain way," I said, "find
some way to engage your wife every night. It doesn't have to be
anything you regard as sensual or sexy. Just start with whatever
feelings emerge for you."

Roger came back to me the next session and confessed that he
hadn't done what I suggested. "I just felt too uncomfortable and too
pressured. It was easier just to forget about sex like I always do."

It was important to honor that what I had suggested was
beyond Roger's capacity at that time, so I asked what he would be
willing to try, other than simply tuning Helen out and avoiding
interaction entirely. After some exploration, Roger said he would
be able to fantasize to himself for ten minutes in bed each night
about what he had to offer her. This exercise felt much safer to him
after so long a period of denial.

At our next session Roger revealed he had been able to carry
through this time. Even though the sex was only on the fantasy
level, it had stimulated more desire than he anticipated.

The door to his sexuality was now open, and Roger became
much more conscious of all that he was capable of bringing to bed.
He felt much more open and excited about being with Helen, and
the old feelings of fear and intimidation began to subside.

Once Roger was no longer hooked into a limited definition of sex,
he was able to see beyond his previous perception of himself. Instead
of believing that nothing was going on, he began to recognize the
level of desire that was true for him and appreciate his own sexual
nature.

Everything is an opportunity for intimacy

At the very heart of the accepting bed is a loving space where
every part of you is present. Removing all imposed values and

judgments from your sexual encounters expands your perception to one of equality and celebrates all that you are.

Think of Terry, the client I described earlier, who was struggling with her feelings of obligation. Or Roger, who regarded himself as lacking in desire or sexuality. Such feelings would usually be considered deficiencies in the bedroom, which Terry and Roger should do their best to eliminate.

However, I consider obligation and lack of desire to have as much value in the bedroom as any other experience, so long as they are used as a basis for acceptance and joining. That is why I counseled both of them to bring these feelings to bed, to express them, value them and appreciate their own vulnerability. I wanted them to experience the powerful intimacy that comes from being multidimensional.

Relationships that have lost their passion, energy and satisfaction need to begin the journey toward change with this new attitude. Unfortunately, most of our rejected sexual experiences are labeled "problems" and regarded as obstacles to intimacy rather than avenues to it.

Orgasm is 100% of anything

In opening up your sexual relationship, it's important to regard every part of you that emerges as capable of providing an orgasm. I know such a concept is difficult to embrace because we have formed such conditioned images to the word *orgasm*. But to me, orgasm is more than just breathing heavy, curling your toes and achieving a *grand mal* seizure with your lover.

Orgasm is the all-consuming rush of energy that comes from surrendering and giving yourself fully to any action or feeling. You will have an orgasmic response whenever you lose yourself completely in *any* emotion or experience. So, two people allowing themselves to experience 100% of their awkwardness together from head to toe will experience an orgasm just as powerful, and just as valuable, as the one that comes from total surrender to sexual intercourse.

The "awkwardness" orgasm won't set off the same kind of whis-
tles and fireworks as the copulation one does, so if that's all you're
looking for you might miss it. You have to be open to something
more subtle and fragile in nature. But I promise that if you allow
yourself to bring every ounce of your mind, body and spirit to your
awkwardness, your fear, your lack of interest or any other experience,
the result will be a powerful and delightful release.

This new orgasm will provide a real sense of substance and
depth. The more fully you allow yourself to experience some unacceptable feeling, without any desire to run from it, the more peace
and serenity you'll feel. Just stop to consider: how often do you let
yourself experience what you're feeling for even 60 seconds without diluting, resisting or avoiding it? What might happen if you
did? All it takes is conscious awareness and giving yourself
permission.

Laughing at ourselves is loving ourselves

In the accepting bed there is an appreciation for the absurd. Taking
ourselves very seriously becomes suffocating, and the bedroom is
especially vulnerable to such heaviness. By the time we've made certain we're physically, emotionally, sexually and politically correct,
we may as well phone in what's left of our passion.

Bringing the unacceptable to bed becomes much easier when an
air of lightness and fun surrounds you. And appreciating the humor
of our sexual tango is the most direct route I know to closeness and
connection.

*Doug and Lisa came to me with their chins on the floor
because of their troubled marriage. Doug was very frustrated
and unsatisfied over the frequency of their lovemaking, and they
both agreed that Lisa's sexual desire was next to nil. She
expressed some resentment at the pressure Doug was putting on
her, but she felt too guilty about her "problem" to express any
anger.*

I asked them if they were willing to try something a bit lighter and take a break from the heavy, oppressive routine of him being up and her being down. With some uneasiness they agreed.

I suggested that they go to bed that evening and express their positions more openly and directly, with no hedging. Doug was to become blatantly demanding about the amount of sex he required. He was to insist that Lisa satisfy his needs. I told him to drop any pretense of accommodation, propriety or respectability, and just live his desire fully.

Lisa was to stop defending and feeling guilty, and instead was to fully live her role as "the problem." I wanted Doug to hear her say, "It's a shame you didn't get the throbbing, gotta-have-it woman you need. Instead you got me, the problem."

Even as I was sharing the instructions, the room came alive and they both started laughing. The excitement and lightness continued as they did this at home, and the door was now open to approach their relationship from a very different place. The heaviness of judgment and selection had been replaced with the lightness of the accepting bed.

A person who can laugh at herself in the presence of another has no need to defend or prove anything. She recognizes that whatever her disguised behavior is protecting, the disguise isn't who she really is. When you appreciate the absurd, you can look at yourself without judgment, and there is no alternative but to love yourself.

When the four principles described above are brought into your consciousness, your sexuality can grow and blossom in the light of acceptance. Then you'll be ready to face the biggest sexual taboo of all. . . .

Unsatisfactory Sex

What do you think is the sexual experience we absolutely must avoid at all cost? What behavior in bed makes men tremble with fear, makes women turn their eyes away and is considered forbidden in every corner of our society? What single act is so loathsome that we'll do anything to avoid even the hint that we might be guilty of it?

That's right. Some of you may be ashamed to even say the words, but the biggest sexual taboo we will ever encounter is *unsatisfactory sex*. Can you imagine anyone standing up and proudly declaring, "I'm lousy in bed!"

This is our most dreaded enemy in the bedroom, the experience we'll do anything to avoid. Read, study, practice or hide. Do whatever it takes to make sure we can never be accused of performing unsatisfactory sex.

Keeping this monster at bay isn't easy, no matter how hard you try. For one thing, there are so many things that can make sex unsatisfactory. Is your partner in the right mood? Is your approach too bold? Too meek? How's your speed? Your thrust? Your volume? Your tenderness? Your endurance? Did you come too soon? Did you come at all? Did your partner?

And you'd better be up to par on whatever it takes to satisfy your partner. Of course, I'm not just talking about what satisfies your partner tonight. What about tomorrow night? Or what about a different partner? Satisfaction could require something different every time. You'd better study some more.

In the accepting bed, *unsatisfactory sex is no longer taboo*. In fact, it can be one of the most uninhibited, liberating experiences you have ever known.

Let's say you get into bed feeling uneasy and uptight, not really in the mood or worried that your lovemaking won't be that enjoyable. You try to hide these feelings, but then your partner asks what's going on. What do you say? Struggling to cover up your feelings makes you even more awkward and insecure and you figure you're really in trouble and . . .

Stop!

This is the old scenario, in which there are good guys and bad guys. Tonight you're going to experience something different. I want you to drop that internal monologue and decide to simply enjoy all these thoughts and feelings, and declare this to be "unsatisfactory sex night."

Since the whole notion of celebrating unsatisfactory sex is no doubt foreign to the two of you, begin by simply letting yourself pretend that what I'm about to describe is perfectly normal. Tell each other that tonight you want to make unsatisfactory love. For the first time in your sexual lives there will be no turn-offs; absolutely nothing you feel or say will be wrong, incorrect or unacceptable.

Tonight you're going to take a night off from your usual quest for great sex. Instead, you're to applaud anything that will make you're lovemaking unsatisfactory. So, if his initial approach is a bit too fast or abrupt, that's good. If you're taking too long to get into it, that's good, too.

Perhaps this new approach is making you uncomfortable. Terrific! Tell your partner that following these guidelines is distracting you, so you can both share your success at making things even more unsatisfactory by doing so much thinking. You both welcome any action that can create a feeling of dissatisfaction.

As your unsatisfactory lovemaking continues, you celebrate every word and movement that reduces your satisfaction. So now you cheer your partner's limp penis, and you love his insecurity and its many nuances. If you're unable to get wet, you both applaud your ability to stay dry. If he touches you too firmly, too lightly or not at all, you respond, "Thanks, that was really awful."

The two of you probably can't believe that everything is okay. You even *try* to make a mistake that is unacceptable. But that only adds to the pleasure of performing unsatisfactory sex. So you simply continue your lovemaking however you wish, sharing and enjoying each and every moment that keeps you unsatisfied. And you finish whenever you please because your dissatisfaction will be even greater if one of you comes too early, one of you comes too late, or best of all, if you don't come at all. Just be sure to thank each other for some of the most unsatisfactory sex you've ever had.

Does all of this sound silly? Of course it does. It violates every rule of sexuality you've ever heard. The fact is, having unsatisfactory sex *is* silly. That's the point! Silly is good! So do it anyway. A session of unsatisfactory sex that ends in laughter or giggles isn't unusual.

Remember, you want to bring lightness, fun and humor into your bed to replace all that pressure and judgment you've had to endure.

The question to ask about this experience is not whether it was weird, awkward or silly. Instead, ask yourselves, "Were we freer and lighter?" How did it feel to climb into bed when for once there was nothing you couldn't feel and nothing you were supposed to do?

Now that you've openly experienced unsatisfactory sex, think of the effect on your future lovemaking. There isn't nearly as much to worry about in bed because you've already been through your biggest nightmare. You have experimented with the most shameful parts of your sexuality, and you've survived letting go of your own particular sexual image. There is really nothing more for you to fear. After all, your partner has witnessed the worst you have to offer.

THE NINE STEPS TO SEXUAL FREEDOM

As you shift your perceptions and beliefs from those of the judgmental bed to those of the accepting bed, you will begin to see a transformation in your sexual relationship. Like all movement from protection to mutuality, there are specific steps and stages to making this powerful shift in your attitudes.

The guidelines that follow will help you develop the new consciousness necessary to change your sexual relationship to one of equality, satisfaction and real intimacy. The more these new attitudes become an integrated part of you, the less power your protector will have to challenge your openness and vulnerability. A mutual attitude in the bedroom will free the sexual energy you've kept smothered under your bed.

As with any movement toward mutuality and the unknown, these steps should be taken slowly, one at a time. You can't push or rush yourself into the accepting bed any more than you can sprint into any other form of exposure and surrender. As the two of you move closer, you will gradually begin to express the parts of your sexuality that once caused you shame or fear. Simply hold a space of humble acceptance as you allow your many selves to emerge.

While it is certainly preferable to have both of you committed to an accepting bed, it is not mandatory. The foundation of this approach is to expose and accept all your feelings and behaviors in bed, *regardless* of any real or anticipated reaction from your partner.

So you don't have to hear your partner say that he'll cooperate; if you're showing up passionately with whatever feeling or desire is true for you, he'll have no choice but to participate in some manner. As long as you can maintain your own attitude of acceptance, some shift toward intimacy will occur. This was illustrated earlier in the case of Terry, whose passionate desire for obligatory sex brought an immediate change in Ed's initial reluctance to participate in the exercise.

STEP 1: RECOGNIZE YOUR DOMINANT IMAGES AND STYLES.

The first step toward an accepting bed is to become fully aware of whatever image or style you're bringing to bed. What feelings and movements dominate your lovemaking? What role, personality or pattern of behavior is already comfortable or familiar to you?

Any time you crawl into bed there will be one part of you that will be dominant at that moment. It could be rough or tender, flirtatious or demanding, seductive or resistant, wild, scared or sad. It really doesn't matter what image or style you're displaying, as long as you're fully aware of it. It's critical that you remain tuned in to whatever part of yourself most needs to be expressed at any given time.

Sometimes recognizing your sexual persona isn't too difficult, if it's an image you maintain repeatedly, and if it's one that the two of you find easy to accept. Let's say tonight's dominant need is tenderness. If this is a style that you and your partner already deem a "good" one, as society currently seems to, recognizing it in yourself probably won't be that tough.

But what if your dominant desire is to be selfish and demanding? We don't see too many articles these days discussing how great it is to ignore your partner's needs in bed. If you and your partner regard such behavior as unacceptable, you may not want to consider that it's a part of you, and you'll push it under the bed before you're even fully conscious of it. If you hide it in this way, you've already slipped out of the accepting bed.

If you ignore or deny your strongest desires or feelings, you'll create resentment and alienation in bed, and you'll be unable to experience your full passion. Before you can begin to intertwine sexually with each other, you each have to ask, "What do I want, need or feel right now?" and then honor and support that part of yourself.

STEP 2: BRING YOUR DOMINANT STYLE TO BED.

When you know which thoughts and feelings hold the greatest energy for you, stand up 100% for those parts of yourself. Whatever your sexual style, live it fully in bed with your partner. If tonight your hesitant and uncertain part is dominant, I want you to fully experience those two qualities.

I've already discussed the difficulty of fully experiencing anything with our entire being, and how we all tend to temper and dilute our feelings and desires in any situation. Now I want to prepare you for two added obstacles to taking this step: *opposing styles* and *unacceptable styles.*

Opposing Styles

While I am very supportive of each partner's unique sexual needs and expression, your different desires, habits and movements will always affect each other. If you're unaware or unaccepting of these differences in your individual styles, you can easily be hurled back into the judgmental bed.

Let's say "slow and romantic" comes to bed with "Wham-Bam-Thank-You, Ma'am." If the difference between these two styles takes you by surprise, you can expect a tricky matchup. You'd better acknowledge that your images or needs are different. Otherwise, frustration, disappointment and resentment are bound to result. If a boxer is about to climb into the ring with a 210-pounder, he'd better know who his opponent is before the match begins. The same holds true if you're meek and mild, and you slide between the sheets with a sexual heavyweight.

Often I talk to clients who recognize that their partner has a different style, but they continue acting as if they could simply wish it away. "He never wants to just cuddle," or, "She's so inhibited in bed" are regarded as problems that, given enough time or complaining, will somehow miraculously disappear.

When your partner's sexual image clashes with your own needs, you must accept that, like it or not, that's his style. Most of us will verbalize our sexual differences, but we're unwilling to fully acknowledge who we're really in bed with.

If you're squeezing any kind of emotional drama out of your different sexual styles by complaining, hiding or rejecting, you're not allowing your differences to coexist. Instead of denying them, you need to find some way to relate to them. Only then can you move closer and hold a space of intimacy and acceptance.

Perhaps you can negotiate a space for both styles: "I'll do 'get-it-over-quick' with you now, but later (or next time) I'd like you to do 'slow and romantic' with me." Or, maybe the two of you can bring your passion into the differences themselves, so that all the while he's saying, "Let's just do it," you're whispering sweet nothings and doing your slowest sexual movements.

Or perhaps you just say no to each other's desires, and then you come together in your shared disappointment about the impasse. Remember, if your goal is greater passion and intimacy, a 100% "disappointment orgasm" is just as good as a 100% "intercourse orgasm."

Unacceptable Styles

The second obstacle to bringing your personal images and styles to bed occurs when the behavior itself is unacceptable. What if the dominant part of yourself is anger, impotence, obligation, fatigue or some other feeling or style that you'd rather deny and shove under the bed?

When this occurs, your goal will be the same: to invite this part of yourself into bed, where it can be passionately experienced, accepted and embraced. The goal simply becomes more frightening as we encounter the images of ourselves we find most unacceptable. And this experience leads us directly into Step 3.

STEP 3: RECOGNIZE AN UNACCEPTABLE PART OF YOURSELF THAT YOU'RE HIDING.

To recognize some part of your sexual identity you are excluding, you need to take your eyes off what your partner is doing and give up any efforts to change him. Discovering what is under your own judgmental bed is a full-time job.

Often, Step 2 alone will be all it takes to reveal what's under your bed. If you find it frightening simply to stand up for your style, then it's pretty obvious what you're hiding. Any dominant desire you feel but resist exposing to your partner is in some way unacceptable.

It may be that you're each comfortable with your own individual images, but the fact that your images differ from one another is causing lots of drama or tension. This probably means that you regard feelings such as disappointment, resentment, anger and sadness as unacceptable, or that you're avoiding seeing yourself or your partner as submissive, domineering or selfish.

Another way your sexual personalities can point toward what's under your bed is when these images and behaviors become unvarying. Then, you must ask yourself what would happen if the opposite styles slipped into bed with you. For example, if the only roles the two of you ever assume are gentle and considerate, is it because selfishness or wild abandon would be too terrifying? Or if every night in bed you become Mr. and Mrs. Sex Machine, where have you both hidden your vulnerability and insecurity?

I often have clients who give endless accounts of how worried they are about revealing some behavior or feeling in bed, when in fact it's a role they assume most of the time. "I'm afraid of being manipulative," they might say, even though every one of their sexual encounters is a carefully orchestrated attempt to control their partners.

"I don't think you're scared of that at all," I'll reply. "You've been manipulating your husband for years. You just don't want to be up front about it. I think what really scares you is losing control. What would happen if you allowed yourself to surrender fully, and let him do whatever he wants?"

This is a tricky situation, because it's certainly unacceptable to such a person to openly experience her manipulation. But it's the vulnerability of exposing it that would be frightening, not the manipulation itself. And an even more unacceptable experience would be to bring out whatever it is that the manipulation is hiding.

As with any area of our lives, the feelings and desires we find unacceptable are those that frighten us by moving us into the unknown. Look for the experiences in bed that seem unthinkable, that would leave you exposed, helpless and vulnerable. Those are the parts of you waiting under your bed.

STEP 4: RECOGNIZE THE CONSEQUENCES OF HIDING THAT PART OF YOU.

Once you discover a part of yourself that is unacceptable, ask yourself what price you're willing to pay for hiding it. What effect is it having on your sexuality, and on your relationship, to maintain your disguise?

I know all the pretense makes your bedroom feel safe and familiar. But is it allowing you to get closer to your partner? Are the two of you feeling alienated or distant? Is your lovemaking truly fun and passionate? Or has guilt, hostility, resentment or anger begun showing up in bed? Is coming to bed still new and exciting? Or is it possible that one of you is looking to some other partner for adventure and variety?

And what about *within* you? What has been the cost of shutting down a part of yourself? Is your desire as strong as ever, or are you losing interest in sex altogether? Has the stifling of your energy and passion spread beyond the bedroom and taken the form of physical problems, emotional tension and just a general dullness to everything you do?

Keeping your bed entirely within the routine familiarity and judgment of your comfort zone is bound to affect your entire relationship. So, every time you recognize another part of you under the bed, keep asking yourself the cost of keeping it there.

STEP 5: INVITE THAT PART OF YOURSELF INTO BED.

Once you've recognized whatever experience you've kept hidden under your judgmental bed, it's time to risk exposing that part of yourself to your sexual partner.

> *Julia was a client of mine who became aware of how covert and manipulative she was with her passive-aggressive behavior toward Hal. "Do we have to?" she would whine. "Tonight? I have a lot of work."*
>
> *By listening to her own wimpy excuses, she began recognizing the strain of acting out all these little oppositional numbers in response to sex. "It's even making me nauseous," she told me. "It's no wonder Hal's getting turned off."*
>
> *It seemed to me that she was ready to move on to Step 5 by welcoming the resistive part of herself into bed. So I said, "Why don't you get on with it? You don't want to let Hal in sexually, and that's all there is to it. So be openly rebellious. Stop tiptoeing around and tell him, 'No way! You can pout, complain or lay on a guilt trip, I'm still not letting you in.'"*
>
> *That night she tried to do as I said, but I'm sorry to report that she failed. Because of her openness and passion, Hal got excited, and she was feeling her newly channeled energy so much she chose to make love with him after all and really enjoyed it.*
>
> *Some clients are hopeless.*

What occurred with Julia is a beautiful example of the power of acceptance, and how it creates movement. Because she was willing to openly accept her rebellious and resistive part that aspect of her no longer needed to fight for space or prove anything. She felt much more free to willingly surrender to Hal.

None of us is able to recognize and accept all the aspects of our sexuality that we've spent so many years rejecting. But if your *intention* is to accept these unacceptable parts of yourself, at least you won't be jumping out of bed and running down the street every time they show up. And, if acceptance of any particular feeling is beyond your capacity at that moment, simply acknowledge to yourself, "I'm feeling scared right now, and I'm not ready to expose that part of myself yet."

Step 5 works best if it carries a commitment for acceptance from both you and your partner. It is usually unrealistic to expect that one of you is capable of exposing all that is beneath your bed, while your partner does nothing. That would entail a lot more courage and self-esteem than most of us have.

But even with an uncooperative partner, you will be able to shift to an attitude of acceptance as long as you honor and respect who you are. Begin with the hidden parts of yourself that are within your capacity, and changes will occur regardless of your partner's reactions.

Show your partner that you are serious and that you are going to support with full passion whatever experiences are true for you. Remember, your partner is only used to seeing your acceptable feelings and reactions. At first he may be startled or put off by your sexual independence. But, he will almost always respond to your honesty and passion.

STEP 6: SUPPORT THE TOTAL EXPRESSION OF THAT PART OF YOURSELF.

Until you experience a feeling or desire with your entire being, you're hedging your passion. One foot in and one foot out just won't cut it in the accepting bed.

Anger is an excellent example. Many of us say we're expressing anger, when instead we're merely displaying some substitute emotion like resentment, hostility or disgust. We rarely offer our partners our pure anger.

A truly passionate expression of anger would usually last five minutes at most. Content would be irrelevant, and the heat of our passion would burn out quickly. But the behavior we pass off as anger goes on forever, diluted down to an endless series of snipes, jabs and hostile glances.

The bedroom is especially vulnerable to partners hedging their passion by waiting for just the right set of circumstances for it to occur. We firmly believe that until our partners look, sound and feel exactly like some prescribed image we hold, we can't possibly be passionate. It's as if we had to work ourselves up to a state of passion, with no chance of liftoff until all systems are go. Otherwise, we continue feeling turned off, uninterested, numb or dead, waiting longingly for our opportunity.

In the accepting bedroom there is no need to wait because passion is not limited to certain qualities or situations. In my practice, I can find passion in any relationship, because I am not looking for it in selected places. I don't even have to search for it. I simply invite couples to bring their passion to whatever is already there, rather than waiting for the "right" experience to show up.

I am only interested in the energy shared by the two of you, not in whether it looks or feels a certain way. To me, passionate resistance is as exciting as passionate lust. The only question I ask is whether you want to give your passion to your partner.

Passion must be conscious and purposeful. If tonight you're feeling "turned off," you can't just slip passively into being turned off and call that passion. In the accepting bed, you must actively choose to put your full energy into this feeling.

So, with all your conscious energy behind the experience, you tell your partner, "I'm turned off to you, and I'm going to look for anything I can find in your lovemaking to keep me turned off. And it probably doesn't matter what you do anyway, I'll still be turned off."

The essential component of this experience is participating 100%. Change will occur only when you surrender totally to whoever you are in that moment and offer it fully to your partner. If you fight or dilute your own experience, you'll stay stuck.

STEP 7: EMBRACE THIS UNACCEPTABLE PART OF YOURSELF.

Most of my clients are amazed that anyone could truly embrace something they have always considered impossible to even acknowledge. "In the past, I never even wanted to admit that these parts existed. Now you want me to celebrate them?!"

Embracing the unacceptable means looking for what is actually there, rather than what is missing. There is always something to embrace. We just have to focus on it, rather than on some idealized quality or experience that isn't a part of us right now.

Joanne had been self-conscious and uncomfortable for years because she couldn't have an orgasm, and would frequently put herself down and express embarrassment over her problem. All her energy was directed toward the "acceptable" orgasm that she thought she was supposed to be having. She was ignoring or denying what her body was really feeling and needing in bed.

What surprised me about Joanne was her obvious sensuality and sensitivity. Her descriptions of her sexual relationship made it clear that she was quite responsive in bed. I realized that if I went along with her negativity about not having orgasms, I'd be colluding in rejecting this part of her.

Instead I coined a new sexual term: mini-orgasms. I told Joanne that anytime she felt any vibrational moment in bed on any level—physical, mental or emotional—we would regard that as a mini-orgasm. "Let go of worrying about textbook orgasms for awhile," I suggested. "Right now I want you to notice any rush you feel at all. Even the least surge of energy, sensation or pleasure qualifies."

I believed focusing on mini-orgasms would allow Joanne to find real value in what was actually occurring, and not be bound to some narrow image of "The Orgasm." This way she could begin to embrace many of her sexual experiences without so much judgment and frustration.

However, the next time she came to see me, she reported that when she made love this time, nothing new had happened. It was only after we explored her experience in more detail that she revealed that there were indeed several vibrational moments of pleasure for her. "Those were mini-orgasms," I declared. When she could no longer maintain her usual negative perception, she smiled and displayed a loving appreciation of the part of herself that was able to experience this amount of pleasure.

As her acceptance continued and she stopped judging it against some external image, her sexuality emerged even more, until her lovemaking became much more pleasurable and free. Eventually she stopped worrying about whether her orgasms were "mini" or "maxi," because she had embraced the part of herself she once regarded as limited and unacceptable.

Embracing means putting your arms around every part of you that has something to express in your sexual relationship. To experience your awkward little boy or your timid little girl, you need to allow yourself to welcome whatever elements of these characters are present in a given moment. You can only do that if you allow yourself to be impacted by whoever shows up in your bed.

I will often hear someone say, "Okay, I'll try it. But I still don't really like that side of myself."

"Then you're not ready to accept," I'll reply. "Until you can truly embrace the feeling or desire you're keeping buried, you'll remain separate and removed from whatever experience you're having."

Impotency is a good example. I've counseled men who have been impotent for many years, who throughout those years have continually hated their impotency, felt ashamed about it, and endlessly hassled themselves over it. But despite their enormous struggle, they haven't really experienced impotency for a single moment. They have never allowed themselves to truly see, hear and feel themselves as impotent without any judgment or rejection. All that they have experienced is unending *opposition* to their impotency.

Step 7 doesn't mean forcing yourself to accept every hidden part of who you are. If there is a part of your sexual personality that you can't yet embrace, you need to honor that limit to your capacity and look for some other need or feeling that would be easier to accept. Your acceptance is what matters, not the particular part of yourself on which you focus.

George was feeling guilty about his decreasing interest in making love to his wife Elaine. As the frequency of their lovemaking decreased, the awkwardness and pressure he felt in bed were becoming unbearable.

As we explored his feelings, I asked him, "Which hidden part of you would most likely show up in bed with Elaine?"

"I'd be frightened," he answered. So, I asked if he could bring his fear into bed openly, and stand up for it 100%. "I don't think so," he replied uncomfortably. "I'd be afraid I'd just slip away."

It was obvious that embracing his fear was currently beyond George's capacity. So we had to discover what part of him was more present at this moment. I suggested that avoidance seemed to be where most of his energy was. This time his response was different. Some of the tension left his body, and it seemed clear that this would be an easier feeling for him to support. "I avoid sex all the time anyway," he said with a relieved sigh.

George and Elaine then began their shift to an accepting bed as he started expressing his avoidance openly, no longer trying to reject or disguise it. As he embraced that part of himself and saw that Elaine neither jumped out of bed nor screamed in terror, his willingness to share his vulnerability expanded. Eventually he was able to risk bringing out the fearful part of himself that had once been beyond his capacity.

All I did with George was keep tracking back until I found the quality that he was capable of supporting. You can do the same thing for yourself. Just remember that you're not focused on any particular outcome, and you are to honor whatever limits you have right now. Embracing a part of yourself is all that matters.

When both of you are able to embrace your unacceptable parts, the change in your sexual relationship can sometimes be astounding. Just imagine this scenario:

> *Your husband comes to bed tonight wanting sex, but you're not really interested. So you ignore his advances, or make up some reason why tonight isn't good for you. He then turns over in frustration, or perhaps gets angry about not having his needs met.*
>
> *Or perhaps you want to avoid such a scene, so you halfheartedly lay there and service him, giving little energy to the experience other than wanting it to be over. He may consciously or subconsciously detect this, but he goes along, figuring a crumb is better than nothing.*

I would guess this scene plays out in a thousand bedrooms every night. But the script becomes vastly different within an accepting bed, where all feelings and experiences are given equal status. In seeing each other through the eyes of mutuality, lack of interest carries no lesser sexual status than being turned on or wanting sex. It's just another behavior, no better or worse:

> *Your husband comes to bed tonight wanting sex, but you're not really interested. So you reveal your lack of interest as something you have to offer, not as a problem, a weakness or something you have to hide.*
>
> *Now there's just one question: are "interested" and "uninterested" willing to go to bed together? This is where you let go of all your conditioning, which tells you to view sex from a very narrow perspective. As you recognize that sex is any exchange of energy between lovers, many possibilities present themselves. Interest and lack of interest can share the bed openly after years of competing and sneaking around.*

Within this new attitude of acceptance, every action of his is a passionate statement of his desire. He wants sex with all his mind and body. He caresses, he fondles, he whispers to you of his longing.

And every thought and action you experience is a passionate statement of your lack of interest. As he kisses your neck, you look at your watch. As he begins to penetrate, you ask him, "Please hurry, I've got a meeting in the morning." All the while he's expressing his interest, you continue a running monologue of whatever is occupying your thoughts and keeping you from being interested. In response to each thrusting movement, you ask, "Are you done yet?"

As your conflicting passions try to drown each other out, you're finally reduced to mutual laughter. Whether your pleasure stems from orgasms of desire or orgasms of disinterest, the two of you come together.

The freedom to express thoughts such as these is tremendously exhilarating. By accepting and embracing whoever comes into bed, you achieve greater closeness, passion and real intimacy.

STEP 8: APPRECIATE WHAT THIS NEWLY EXPOSED PART HAS GIVEN YOU.

I know that what I've been describing may sound so foreign or frightening that it's hard to imagine you'd look on such an experience as a gift. But just imagine for a moment what it would be like to regard every thought, feeling or desire, even those you've kept hidden since adolescence, as a positive contribution to your sexual relationship. Think what it would mean if all your sexual expressions had equal status and were welcomed into your bed.

This attitude brings tremendous freedom to the bedroom, a place where freedom is often discussed but seldom truly experienced. Everything you and your partner have to offer is now cherished and enjoyed, and nothing remains hidden in the closet. Would such a place not be a gift?

Let's say you feel inadequate one evening. In the old judgmental bed you did whatever you could to hide this from your partner, hoping with all your might that it wouldn't be detected. But, pretending that all this camouflage would improve your sex life was one of the biggest jokes your protector ever played on you.

I'd be willing to bet that you or your partner feel inadequate at least ten times a year. Attempting to hide, disguise or ignore all of these instances can only leave you frustrated, angry, unhappy or numb. And this in turn pushes you further from each other and makes you even less "adequate" than you are to begin with.

But in an accepting bed, your inadequacy is seen as making a truly positive contribution to your relationship. Think of the benefits of allowing your partner to see and feel who you really are on so many occasions. . . .

- You begin to feel less alone, and you experience the intimacy of sharing a mutual experience.
- With each new exposure, the trust between you builds, giving you the courage and strength to share more of yourselves.
- Variety and adventure come back into your lovemaking, as so many more facets of who you are move into the light.
- With so much less energy used to maintain your sexual façades, you have a lot more to direct toward your passion for each other.
- Coming together without your false selves gives you an opportunity to feel loved just for who you are, and not for some familiar routine.

All this occurs because you openly share your inadequacy without making it a problem.

STEP 9: INTEGRATE THIS PART OF YOURSELF AS A POSITIVE CHOICE.

Every feeling and behavior that you can recognize, accept, express and embrace becomes a new member of your sexual family that can now be welcomed into your bedroom. The more choices you allow yourself, the more opportunities you have to connect with your mate. As each newly accepted quality is brought into the light, your capacity for acceptance expands, and your bedroom becomes a loving and passionate home for real intimacy and connection.

THE CONSEQUENCES OF THE ACCEPTING BED

You may find it hard to believe, but underneath all the rewards of the accepting bed, there are two core consequences: *no conflict* and *no dysfunctions*.

Ending Conflict

While they take a variety of specific forms, most sexual conflicts boil down to three basic issues: the quality of lovemaking, sexual interest and sexual frequency. As I described in detail at the beginning of the chapter, these concerns form the basis of an endless cycle of difference game arguments, accusations, silences and conflicts.

But quality, interest and frequency become irrelevant in a mutual bedroom because whatever desires, feelings or movements you bring to bed are accepted in their own right. It doesn't matter if you measure your sexual encounters on your watch or on a calendar, and it doesn't matter if you like the missionary position or could provide the illustrations for a sex manual. Whoever you are is welcome in this bed.

So what is left to fight about? As long as you can sustain the tension that comes from accepting all the parts of yourselves, you'll be giving great sex all the time.

Dispelling Dysfunctions

Because there is no judgment or hierarchy in the accepting bed, no part of yourself needs to be ostracized. Inhibitions, premature ejaculation, frigidity and impotency are no longer seen as dysfunctions. As Kenneth Wapnick says in *The End Of Injustice*, "The power of a problem is that we believe it is a problem and we then have to defend against it."

In the mutual bed, all behaviors are considered expressions of your sexuality, so *there is nothing you have to hide or defend.*

After nine years of struggling with his shame and embarrassment about being a "premature ejaculator," Kevin came to see me. This shy, innocent-looking man confessed, "This is so uncomfortable for me that after coming too quickly the first time, I have to wait five minutes before I can get another erection."

I jokingly replied, "You're a better man than I am. I'd be happy to get a rise out of mine after only five minutes." I supported his courage in sharing his pain with me, and told him I'd like him to try something new, even though it might seem a bit odd. He said he was willing.

"Tonight I want you to have sex a little differently," I said. "I want you to come as quickly as you can. If you really put your mind to it, you should be able to ejaculate even quicker than usual.

"I also want you to ask your wife to cheer you on toward this goal. As you keep shouting, 'Ready or not, here I come!' I want her to keep yelling out for you to hurry up.

"Then in your next sexual encounter, I want you to share with her whatever your body and penis are feeling in the moment. I want her to hear things like, 'I'm not able to contain my excitement at being with you. It's too much, and I'm really worried about penetrating you. I'm afraid I'll come before I even enter you.'"

In performing these exercises, Kevin's "problem" became a positive goal, welcomed into the bedroom for the first time. And the lightness and fun that had been introduced around an issue that had always been heavy and intolerable alleviated the pressure and guilt that had permeated his lovemaking.

Soon he was able to extend the time he took to reach orgasm. And more important, time was no longer a problem because he had achieved greater intimacy and satisfaction in bed.

In my final session with Kevin, I had an image, which I shared with him, of a man attempting to balance all his weight on his penis. This relatively small part of himself was expected to hold up the enormous burden of his need for power, validation, security and adequacy. Only when people with Kevin's courage allow their total beings to come to bed are their sexual organs relieved of all this pressure.

It is very often the "problems" you embrace and bring into bed that will bring the greatest closeness and trust to your lovemaking, adding enormous depth and richness to your entire sexual nature.

THE LAST EMBRACE

All of the experiences I have been describing in this chapter involve your conscious participation. There is no sneaking around, nothing is covert, and both partners are free to think, feel and do whatever is true for them, as long as neither violates the other physically.

You may be concerned that such actions will be perceived as inconsiderate or demeaning, and that someone will get hurt. But in my experience, pain is rarely the result of honestly expressing who you are. It is more often covert manipulation that will truly wound your partner. When you hide your feelings and desires, you send an unconscious message to your partner that he or she is too weak or too inadequate to be in bed with the real you. And what could be more demeaning than being regarded as an emotional or sexual cripple?

You may wonder about some of the examples I used to illustrate this new approach, and whether the couples eventually had intercourse. They may or may not have. All that really matters is that they supported who they were in bed and made an intimate connection based on whatever they had to offer each other at that moment.

Many of the anecdotes throughout this chapter involve a good deal of humor. This is often the result of bringing the manipulations of our inflated egos out into the open. But humor isn't always the form your closeness takes. In the mutual bedroom, nothing is good or bad, right or wrong, or better or worse than anything else.

You may feel frightened and extremely vulnerable about having sex with each other. Perhaps each of you has been hurt by something the other did, or you may be exposing past wounds and scars to each other for the first time. One of you may have been a victim of childhood sexual abuse, or maybe one of you sees yourself as inexperienced in bed. In these instances, you may come to bed with great delicateness and deep respect for your pain and fear. Each of you may simply want to share the ways you are fearful, the negative fantasies in your head and the helplessness you feel.

You will then want to move toward one another very slowly and tenderly. There could be many instances when you'll stop, say nothing at all and gently hold each other or lie side by side while you feel what is occurring. This is the nature of fearful and vulnerable sex. But out of your compassion and joining can come a sexual encounter as passionate and fulfilling as any other.

There will also be many instances when neither of you wants any sexual contact, no matter how freeing it might be. This desire is also embraced and regarded as another form of loving expression, no better or worse than any other. You honor and appreciate this movement away from each other with the same acceptance that defines all your lovemaking.

In the mutual bedroom, the question of having or not having sex becomes irrelevant because everything is regarded as sex, and everything can be felt and done with passion. Problems, dysfunctions and conflicts are replaced by loving expressions of who you are.

As a therapist, it is my function to help each couple shine a light under their bed so that all of their unacceptable parts can be recognized. It is also my task to help each couple recognize when the light is too bright and must be turned off.

I am sometimes asked, "If there are no problems, how do you know when you have completed the process of accepting whatever unacceptable feeling you were focusing on?" Your answer is revealed by your responses to these three questions:

"Do I no longer want to place this unacceptable thought, feeling, desire or behavior under the bed in order to hide it from myself or my partner?"

"Do I fully accept the positive contribution of this particular part of myself?"

"Do I now embrace this part of myself as one of my friends in bed, and see it as a choice I may freely express?"

If you can't answer yes to all three questions, then you're still hedging. Better look under your bed. A part of you is there waiting.

Chapter 12

OTHER
TOUGH ISSUES
Threats to Mutuality

Sure, it's fine to talk about equality and loving.
But I'm a compulsive eater who's 50 pounds overweight, I'm married to an alcoholic, I'm co-dependent with my mother, and I think my spouse is still having an affair. If we went to therapy, which we can't afford, the shrink would take one look at us and wonder where to begin.

Moving from protection to an attitude of sameness and vulnerability is a delicate, frightening process that requires consciousness and commitment in even the best of times. So, what happens when we're confronted with life's major hurdles, and we have to deal with the controlling, judgmental behavior of friends and relatives, or the pain and despair of issues such as money, infidelity, addictions, substance abuse, physical or sexual abuse and depression? Is it possible to find a basis for acceptance and equality in the face of such overwhelming threats to our mutuality?

One of the biggest problems with most of the difficulties we encounter, even the heavyweights listed above, comes not from the challenges themselves, but the ways we try to deny, disguise or compensate for our fear and pain. As complex, dramatic and truly painful as these experiences can be, they are primarily alternatives to exposing our hidden selves.

Every one of the problems I discuss in this chapter is symptomatic of some hierarchical perception. All are the result of rejecting some part of ourselves and then hiding under the cover of our addiction, hostility, depression, or the judgments and behaviors of outsiders. Any such behavior is a sign that we have gone beyond the limits of what we consider acceptable, and now those unacceptable parts of ourselves are dictating the direction of our lives.

OBSTACLES FROM THE OUTSIDE

Your relationship doesn't exist in a vacuum. It must endure the challenges that enter from the outside world and expose your fears and vulnerability. As you turn to each other for protection from these new forms of the unknown, this added exposure can thrust the two of you back into the difference game as easily as if the conflicts had originated between you.

I want to offer a few ways of dealing with two of the most challenging issues that seem to originate outside your relationship: financial pressure and the negative influence of friends and relatives.

Financial Pressure

One of the reasons money can easily sabotage greater closeness and intimacy is that it is often regarded as something separate from your relationship. It's as if money were a fence that had to be climbed over or knocked down before any other issues could be dealt with:

"We're facing bankruptcy—I can't worry about our sex life now!"

"If I don't work all the time we'll go broke."

"We can't afford to go to therapy."

As long as money is awarded this singular status, controlling all attempts to face other issues and join with each other, then it will lock you into the status quo.

This is not to say that financial problems cannot be serious, painful and truly threatening. But, the only way they can ever be addressed effectively is when they are approached like any other difficulty within your relationship: by recognizing and accepting the unacceptable feelings that the issue of money is hiding.

Whenever money is a source of conflict between you and your partner, and not simply a shared problem to be faced together, it's because you're focusing on your outer differences. For example, one of you might be seen as the "spendthrift" and one as the "tightwad." Maintaining these roles is a joy to your protectors—even an amateur difference game player can come up with a dozen or more judgments, put-downs, dramas and helpless victim attitudes in response to these two images.

Your only way out of this conflict is to recognize the mutual fear that lies underneath the differences. A husband who wants to save and protect his money might feel insecure and frightened about going broke, and will feel extremely inadequate. His preoccupation with earning money and holding on to his security protects him from these unacceptable feelings of inadequacy. He sees his wife's spending as an abandonment of his need for security.

A wife who wants to spend money may hope her purchases will protect her from feeling lonely, emotionally deprived and unloved. She feels very insecure about her own worth beyond the value of the things she can buy. She sees her husband's preoccupation with frugality as an abandonment of her need to be valued.

The "hoarding" husband feels responsible for taking care of their future financial needs. The "extravagant" wife feels responsible for taking care of their present emotional needs. These mutual fears may take different forms, but they are identical in their intensity, in the vulnerability they create and in the ways they control both partners.

So, if you and your partner experience repeated conflicts over finances, you can initiate the most precise budget you can think of and clip all the coupons you can find, but until you recognize your underlying sameness about money, your drama will continue. No financial plan or discussion will ever get anywhere unless you both feel your fears have been honored. Until then, you'll just keep banging into each other with every new bank statement and credit card bill.

Judgmental Friends and Relatives

For every couple, the support of those around them can make an immense difference to the closeness and intimacy they achieve. Unfortunately, the opposite is also true: the judgments and attitudes of parents, children, stepchildren, in-laws, friends and associates often seem to conspire to extinguish the slightest glimmer of mutuality. In most relationships, it's all the couple can do to hang on to whatever closeness they have when faced with the judgmental chorus of those surrounding them.

When you allow yourself to be drawn into positions of superiority or inferiority, you send a message to everyone outside your relationship that you have never completely left home, and you're both still dependent on others' advice and approval. But, when you maintain an attitude of joining with your partner, their comments will have little effect.

Whenever an outsider exposes some problem that you and your partner struggle with, you need to listen to your own response. Does your reaction reveal an attitude of connection or protection within your relationship? Any drama, judgment or reactivity on your part means you've joined them in the difference game. But when you hear yourself answer, "Yes, we have a problem with that," or, "We're working on that situation," your attitude of mutuality has sustained. As you learn to perceive outsiders as opportunities for recognizing your own unacceptable feelings, these friends and family members become less negative or frightening for you both.

Another way to diffuse outside threats to your equality and acceptance is to use divisive friends and relatives as a basis for moving closer to each other, rather than as an excuse to initiate your own judgment and distance. Whenever either of you anticipates any kind of attack or exposure from an outsider, share your fears with your partner. Then, mutually agree that whenever such an instance occurs, you'll hug each other, hold each other's hands or make some other gesture of joining. This will literally bring you closer, and it will symbolize your commitment to connect around any potential threat.

Let's say one of you is upset about your mother-in-law's repeated snipes at your parenting. Share with your partner that these comments hook into your unacceptable fears of inadequacy, and pull you toward your protective position. By moving through the process outlined in Chapter 10, the two of you can use this as a basis for increasing your recognition and acceptance.

Then, when your partner's mother hits you with one of her not-so-subtle put-downs, you have no need to get defensive or depressed, or argue or react in any way because whatever inadequacy you feel is acceptable, a valued part of yourself and your relationship. Choosing to hug each other in response to the attack will change the whole dynamic of this interaction. You'll be amazed at how deflating it is for an outsider when behavior designed to keep you distant only brings you closer together.

Try this approach with anyone outside your relationship who threatens your attitude of acceptance. The next time your children hook into your fears of impotency or inadequacy by behaving in an out-of-control manner and provoking a situation that can easily lead to tension, conflict and distance, remember your pact and move into a hug with your partner. Do the same when friends start comparing their child-rearing methods to yours.

Another way of neutralizing the power of outsiders is to recognize that their focus on your relationship is often a difference game tactic of their own. Remember, they also possess unacceptable feelings and fears of exposure that are as great as yours. If they can unconsciously move up by affirming their superiority to you or your mate, their own protectors are thrilled. Just don't let your protector suck you into their judgments.

Most friends and relatives offer their advice and opinions out of love; their judgments are rarely conscious attempts to hurt or divide you. So, your own mutual attitude can transform those close to you into a valuable support system, as long as you keep their focus on both you *and* your partner, rather than one or the other. Outsiders can often be helpful in seeing what really scares you, or in recognizing how the two of you match. And there are many unacceptable feelings that are easier to first expose to your best friends before you offer them to each other.

DESTRUCTIVE BEHAVIORS

This chapter is not about treating or curing powerful and deep-seated addictions. Such complex issues as alcoholism, substance abuse, compulsive behavior and physical abuse require a level of examination and understanding that goes beyond the scope or objectives of this book. But I do want to provide an approach that will help you come to terms with these destructive behaviors within your own relationship. I want to assist you in exposing the unacceptable feelings that lie beneath the surface behavior. With an attitude of mutuality, it is possible to move through the myriad of drama and disguises to deal with these challenges directly.

Recognizing the connection between your addictive behavior and the unacceptable feelings that are being buried is the first step toward coming to terms with the behavior itself. Once you strip away the camouflage and drama from any behavior, and are no longer consumed by judgment, guilt, victimization or helplessness, you are better able to choose the response that is most appropriate: continuing to accommodate the behavior, treating it or moving on from the relationship.

If you're getting stoned or drunk six times a week but you don't see it as having an impact on your relationship, then we probably can't get very far. Any such denial means you have chosen to substitute numbness for pain. You don't feel any hurt because you don't feel much of anything.

If this denial is bringing you satisfaction, joy and everything you want in life, terrific. But if it's not, perhaps you're ready to consider an alternative. You won't be willing to risk real change until you recognize that the numbness you're committed to will end up killing all of your passion, and all hope of real connection. If you're in doubt about that, glance over at your partner. Are the two of you really alive together? Or can you look deep enough into her eyes to see the pain that you've been covering up?

Once you admit that there is a problem affecting your relationship, you are ready to ask yourself the primary question about your behavior: "What is so frightening that I would rather continue my destructive behavior than experience that pain?"

What is so unacceptable that you'd rather eat than face it? What experience is so terrifying that you prefer to allow outsiders to control your life? What part of yourself is so unworthy that you are willing to abuse someone you love in order to keep it hidden? When you find the answer, you'll know what the real issue is for you.

Barbara's chain-smoking was creating increasing stress in her marriage. She repeatedly complained about the effect on her health and her husband's attempts to control her by nagging, telling her to go outside and making sarcastic comments in front of others.

When I asked her what would be so bad about quitting, she kept insisting, "Nothing. If I could only stop, things would be perfect."

I told her I found that pretty hard to believe. "You want me to accept that this ongoing pattern of behavior is motivated by nothing and has no purpose. That even though you feel the pain it's causing you and your relationship, you continue smoking for no reason at all. I just don't buy it."

As I repeatedly challenged Barbara in this way, she finally admitted that if she stopped smoking, her husband would come toward her more often, and probably want more sex. This would leave her no easy way out, and she'd feel exposed and naked. Cigarettes were a way of clouding her unacceptable fear of being sexually desired. Only after we uncovered her fear of intimacy in this way could we begin dealing with the addiction that was protecting her.

You must confront the illusion that your own destructive behavior comes from nowhere. You wouldn't have dedicated your life to this recurring pattern unless you believed something really awful would happen if you quit. Whether your fear is based on reality doesn't matter. Your imagined pain may only apply to the person you were at age three. But as long as you still carry that belief, it will control your life.

The list of specific problems that can overwhelm a relationship is endless; anything can be a basis for judgment and separation. But there are a few issues that are given so much weight by society, and can be the source of so much pain, that I would like to offer some specific suggestions for looking at them from an attitude of mutuality.

Addictive Behavior

All addictive behavior grows out of a desire to numb some form of pain. By drowning our feelings with drink, suffocating them with smoke, stuffing them down with food or deadening them with drugs, we stay safely away from the unacceptable.

The nature of alcohol is to dilute experiences that are uncomfortable. The alcoholic acts under the illusion that he can drown out whatever he doesn't like in his life. Unfortunately, these unacceptable feelings float back to the surface, where they get bigger and bigger, and must then be flooded with more drink.

To confront this behavior directly, you must ask, "What is so painful that I'd rather dilute it with alcohol than experience it?" You must passionately demand an answer to this question until you get one. At least once an hour, ask your director to insist on learning what is being protected.

At first you might not get a response. Keep at it. Your protector hasn't taken you seriously for a long time and doesn't believe you really want the answer. He'll even toss you false answers: "I wouldn't rather drink. I'd love to not have that in my life." But allowing yourself to believe such a lie will only keep you in numbed denial, and prevent you from confronting your behavior directly.

The same process holds true for any addictive behavior. When you recognize there is a problem, ask yourself, "What is so painful that I'd rather fog it over with cigarette smoke, dilute it with alcohol, numb it with drugs, force it down with food, hide it under layers of fat or purge it out of my system?" Until you are willing to accept the tension of bringing your answer into the open, you're unlikely to give more than token responses to the behavior itself.

I work extensively with clients who expend enormous energy struggling with food. Eating disorders are a primary interest of mine, both because of my own struggles (I'm a diabetic with a smorgasbord consciousness) and because food has the unique quality of being the one addiction we can't live without.

One of the first steps I take with any of these clients is to create a map of her eating and weight. This diagram consists of several concentric circles, each one representing a level of weight loss or gain. At each circle a person addicted to eating confronts some unacceptable experience. If he is not willing to experience what lies within that circle, then it will be a stopping point for her.

Let's say that 150 pounds is a weight that fits a person's comfortable image of herself. So, anything moving her into a smaller circle would be unknown and unacceptable. She might will herself down to 145 pounds, but until the experience of being there is accepted, sooner or later the old weight will return.

With the majority of my female clients who have weight issues, the most unacceptable feeling that they place within their smallest circle is experiencing their own sexuality. It is frightening to them to see themselves as sexual, and to face all the ramifications of being sexual. "If I'm sexual, he'll want to have sex with me even more," or, "What would I do if other men besides my husband were attracted to me?"

Dealing with too much or too little weight becomes familiar and manageable, whereas living one's full sexuality is unknown and terrifying. So, the food addiction or eating disorder serves to weigh down the unacceptable experience.

Half of you reading this book are probably breathing a sigh of relief right now because you're not the ones who are addictive, co-dependent or abusive. Clearly it's your partners who display the destructive behavior, and you'd have great relationships if it weren't for them.

This fantasy is one of the insidious aspects of these dramatic issues: they make it so easy to adopt the difference game attitude that one of you is "the problem." The other can then easily assume the position of superior righteousness or hopeless victim.

But remember, your partner is a mirror, not an object. No matter what his outward behavior, you have exactly the same capacity for acceptance. He's simply taken most of the responsibility for hiding whatever frightens you both.

It certainly appears that the sober partner is different than the alco-holic, or that the "stable" spouse is superior to the "depressive" one. But, those surface differences are illusions. They simply mean that one partner has a more presentable cover than the other.

If you're complaining about what your partner does, there's a place where the two of you connect. There's something you both find unacceptable, and the complaint covers it up. I want to awaken you to this connection so you can make a real decision about your rela-tionship. I want you to be able to respond to your partner's addictive behavior directly because your conscious desire is to accept it, to facilitate treatment of it, or to move away from it. I want your own behavior to grow out of an honest choice and not out of your wish to avoid something unacceptable.

When you're involved with a partner who exhibits addictive behavior, your best hope for real movement and change is to find the unacceptable feelings you've both unconsciously agreed to disguise. As long as you see your partner and his addiction as the only prob-lem, you'll remain in the unending drama and conflict of the differ-ence game.

If you're with a smoker, ask yourself, "What am I doing to fog over my own feelings?" If your partner is an alcoholic, ask yourself, "What am I doing to dilute myself?" If you're with an overeater,

"What am I indulging in or weighing down?" For spouses of workaholics, "What am I busying myself with?" and substance abusers,
"What am I avoiding or numbing?" As with any other attempt to
move out of the difference game toward real change and fulfillment,
a movement inward is the first step.

For any form of addiction your partner exhibits, ask yourself:
"What am I doing that matches my partner's behavior on a deeper
level? What unacceptable part of myself is so painful that I'd rather
collude in my partner's addiction than face it?"

When you answer these questions honestly, you will recognize the
method you have chosen to deaden, abuse or run away from your
relationship, or from yourself. Your method of rejection and disguise
will always parallel your spouse's more obvious addiction. If you're
addicted to television rather than drugs, you may not get arrested, but
you're numbing some pain nonetheless.

If your husband is co-dependent toward his mother, where is *your*
dependency? Are your icy silences and isolation any different in their
ability to keep you from connecting with him?

If your wife is depressed, what do you do to depress your feelings
and desires in more subtle ways?

In other words, how do you collude in your partner's attempts to
avoid pain or exposure at all costs? Once you have accepted your
own unacceptable feeling, you'll no longer need to put your partner
down or play the role of victim.

If you're married to an alcoholic, for example, once you are no
longer diluting yourself, you can face your partner directly and
regard his addiction as a problem to be dealt with, not as a basis for
judgment or drama. Only when you move out of your own protective
behavior can you then make a real choice about whether you want to
remain with this alcoholic. If his capacity for acceptance has
increased along with yours, your mutual ability to deal with the alcoholism will probably have strengthened. If he chooses to return to his
own comfort zone, then your capacity may now be greater than his,
and you may choose to move out of the relationship.

Depression

Much of the power of depression comes from regarding it as an entity rather than an action. The logical response to "I am depressed," or, "I'm in a deep depression," is "What are you depressed about?" Then the focus is shifted to some issue, rather than the unacceptable feeling that is being depressed.

To confront the problem of depression directly, the most effective question to ask is not, "Am I depressed?" but, "What am I depressing?"

What is so painful or frightening that you want to shut down emotionally rather than expose it? From what is this depression protecting you? What part of yourself is so unacceptable that you'd rather be depressed than deal with it?

As with issues of sex and weight, I am only addressing psychological, not physiological, problems. My interest here is your conscious or unconscious choice to depress your disappointment, powerlessness, fear, anger or whatever other feeling or desire you believe necessitates shutting yourself down.

When your partner is consumed with this dark mood, ask yourself, "What unacceptable experience am I depressing instead of allowing it into our relationship?" When you recognize the ways you are also containing, hiding and depressing some feeling, you will have found your underlying sameness.

Infidelity

A major difficulty in dealing with extramarital affairs is that there's such a huge consensus in society that the unfaithful spouse is wrong. This makes it very easy to miss the couple's matching behavior, and once again they are drawn into judgments and dramas that cloud their underlying sameness.

Infidelity possesses a unique complexity that often makes it the biggest challenge to an attitude of mutuality: a third person has now been brought into the picture, bringing his or her own desires, demands and difference game tactics. Dishonesty and denial are usually included in the package and because sex is already a sensitive and vulnerable area for most of us, the wound to the betrayed partner is deeper and more personal than with many other destructive behaviors.

Extramarital affairs can often be a stopping point for couples in therapy. When the faithful partner's sense of betrayal is so deep, the affair must be confronted before dealing with any other issue in the relationship. If the unfaithful partner is directing most of his or her passion toward the affair and wants to continue the outside involvement, there won't be enough energy left to support moving closer within the marriage. At that point, therapy becomes futile.

But no matter how difficult or complex affairs can be, the underlying issues remain the same as with all sources of conflict. If you are sexually involved with someone outside your marriage, the question remains: "What unacceptable experience does this affair allow me to avoid?" What is it that frightens you so much you'll move outside your marriage to prevent it? Feeling undesirable? Inadequate? Impotent? Powerless? Whatever it is, your affair is helping you disguise some unacceptable part of yourself.

And, as with any other outwardly destructive behavior, the "unfaithful" spouse's partner must also ask the equally painful, and perhaps more difficult, question: "How am I being unfaithful to our relationship?" Because for every wife who's having an affair, I'll show you a husband who's having a "presentable" affair with his golf clubs or his car. And for every husband who's sleeping around, there's a wife whose fidelity to their relationship is also less than absolute.

If your husband is having a fling with his secretary, it's pretty obvious who his affair is with. But what if you obsessively devote all your energy toward your children, and place your relationship with them above the one you have with your husband? Society smiles on an affair like yours, but the result is the same: your passion is turned outward from your relationship; you're covering up some unacceptable part of yourself; and your spouse is left with a feeling of betrayal.

This matching behavior is what Carl Whitaker, in his book *The Midnight Musings of a Family Therapist*, refers to as a bilateral affair. Any attached, compulsive relationship with another that takes priority over the one you have with your spouse is an affair. So, when you're as involved and obsessed with your mother as he is with getting laid, or when you're as consumed by your drinking buddies as she is by her romantic lover, you're having a bilateral affair.

I once had a client who berated her husband for sleeping with a co-worker. But further exploration revealed that she was totally involved with her family. Her parents ate almost all their meals with her and her husband, her sister and nephew moved in for awhile, and the whole brood came along on all their vacations. The result was that she and her husband were almost never alone together. The affair she was having wasn't sexual, but in its compulsive attachment, in its unfaithfulness to their relationship and in the spouse's feelings of abandonment, it fully mirrored her husband's infidelity.

It's also possible to be unfaithful by turning inward. When you become consumed by being the dutiful, victimized wife, or the put-upon, cuckolded husband, and all your energy goes into your hopeless depression, are you really bringing any more energy or support to your marriage than your philandering spouse?

Once again you must ask, "What is his unfaithful behavior reflecting? What is so unacceptable that I'm willing to deny or endure his affair rather than face that part of myself?" Once you recognize and resolve that unacceptable feeling, then you can make a clear choice about what you want in your life, and stand up for those limits. When you come to terms with the way you've been unfaithful, you can face your partner without drama or blame and say, "This will never happen again."

Abuse

All the behaviors discussed in this chapter are simply ways that we "act out" in order to avoid, deny or reject the unacceptable. While mutuality accepts any honest expression of your feelings, thoughts and desires, it does not support acting them out in ways that violate yourself or another. Passionately expressing your anger is quite different from hitting your wife.

Using our unacceptable parts to justify addictive or abusive behavior is directly contrary to a core principle of mutuality: owning all the parts of ourselves, and taking full responsibility for all our actions and their consequences. Nowhere in my practice, or in this book, do I make excuses or justifications. And I certainly don't want to do so with behaviors that are destructive. The justifications, "A part of me was out of control," or, "One of my selves did a criminal act," are pure nonsense.

As difficult and painful as issues of physical and sexual abuse might be, their magnitude and consequences should not obscure the fact that their primary purpose is to protect against some unacceptable experience. The question remains, "What feeling could be so terrible that violating another human being is preferred?"

In almost all cases, the answer is powerlessness. A man who abuses would rather risk jail or death than experience powerlessness. Beating someone, or taking advantage of someone smaller and more helpless, provides a brief moment of denying his fear and believing, "I'm no longer vulnerable. I'm in control. I'm powerful." For all of us, powerlessness is a major issue; for the abusive person, it's a form of death.

Recognition and acceptance are especially tricky for these individuals because if they seek help or admit they have a problem, they risk not only judgment and condemnation, but absolutely terrifying feelings of vulnerability and powerlessness. If they don't get help, they have to keep finding more victims.

For those in relationships with abusive partners, the question remains, "What is so unacceptable that I would rather deny or endure this behavior than face it?" As hard as it may be, you must ask yourself how you are abusing your relationship with your spouse or family. Is your willingness to put up with repeated physical attacks, or to deny or ignore the sexual abuse of another family member, really less abusive? Facing the terror that lies beneath your own denial is the most powerful step you can take towards ending the destructive behavior.

With any destructive behavior, it is only when you strip away the roles and façades the two of you maintain can you recognize the unacceptable feelings you are both attempting to hide. And only then can they be brought into the light of exposure and acceptance.

When you finally uncover the unacceptable experience you've been denying, you then face an even bigger decision. Do you want to confront, experience and come to terms with this unknown part of yourself, or do you prefer to keep running and hiding? By confronting your alternatives directly, you can at least stand up for your behavior without the drama and conflict of your up and down stances.

So, if you're an alcoholic, stop hiding behind a down position of guilt and come straight at your partner with, "I'm an alcoholic. That's the way I choose to live."

And if your spouse has the addiction to alcohol, but exposing the unacceptable part of yourself that is being protected is too painful or frightening, at least leave your superior righteousness or your inferior victimization and stand up for the choice you have made: "I choose to be with an alcoholic in order to protect seeing myself."

There are no tricks here and no easy answers. There is just a choice between the familiar pain and safety of your comfort zone and the long, hard road of bringing a rejected part of you home.

PART V

Endings and New Beginnings

Chapter 13

COOPERATIVE
SEPARATION
Mutuality and Divorce

*F*rank and Gladys had been coming to couples therapy for
several months, yet little change had occurred in their cycles of
conflict and silence. Each week I would hear their problems and
pain, and each week I would offer all the counseling and support
I could think of. But, each week they would return to therapy with
the exercises unattempted and their drama unchanged.

*I finally shared my feelings of frustration and curiosity: "I seem
to have more energy for your relationship than the two of you. It's
as if I'm doing all the work here. I don't mind, but it isn't getting
us anywhere. So, perhaps we need to look at whether you really
want to be together."*

*When neither of them challenged my suggestion, I continued.
"Maybe the two of you really are incompatible. Maybe what you*

are trying to tell me—through your refusal to try the exercises I've suggested—is that you think it would be better if you separated."

They both sat in silence for a moment, until finally Gladys replied, "These things you're asking us to do are too hard. There's just too much hurt between us. I don't have it in me to try anymore."

Instead of protesting, Frank continued to sit in silent agreement. And a few months later they were divorced.

It should be clear by now that one of the core principles of my approach to couples, and of my therapeutic practice, is to support the relationship. I begin with the belief that two partners who choose each other, and who sustain their relationship for any significant length of time, want to be together. Until proven otherwise, I will act on the assumption that the couples I see are uncommitted, not incompatible. But, when I discover that the only effort toward preserving and improving the relationship is my own, I start to question my original assumption.

When I suggest the possibility of separation to most couples, no matter how dramatically they have been hurling judgments and accusations at each other, they will immediately back pedal and resist any suggestion of a breakup. But if such a suggestion goes unchallenged, then we have to explore the possibility that they don't want to be together.

If you are involved in this kind of relationship, and breaking up is really the option you wish to pursue, then mutuality can still be a positive alternative to the anger, hostility, depression, defeat, bitterness, superiority and drama that usually accompany divorce.

Divorce reduces most of us to three-year-olds, and probably contains more rage than any other relationship issue. With an attitude of mutuality, it's possible to move apart with feelings of sadness and disappointment, certainly, but with a sense of genuine completion as well.

I know that with all the pain and anger that usually precede divorce, many couples just say, "To hell with it. We don't care about working at anything anymore. Just let the lawyers handle it." Or,

"The last thing I want is to feel loving or equal to that bitch. I never want to speak to her again." Or maybe, "After everything that bastard did to me, all I'm interested in is taking him for everything he's got, and giving him as much grief as he gave me."

When couples I work with maintain these stances, I feel an enormous sadness. When my efforts to help them achieve a more cooperative divorce result only in my own feelings of powerlessness, I need to let go of the couple and accept that I have no control over their decision, or the ways they are hurting themselves and each other.

But for those of you who want a more respectful, fulfilling ending with someone you once loved deeply, and who want to separate without destroying each other, mutuality provides you that alternative.

RECOGNIZING THAT IT'S OVER

Four different situations indicate that a relationship needs to end. All four result in divorce, but each takes a different path to get there.

We have different values. When two partners disagree over a value that is so important that it's nonnegotiable, the relationship can't continue. It's not uncommon for couples to come together, get married, and only then realize that there are crucial values they failed to discuss or come to agreement on. Their relationships crack in the face of this because these issues are inflexible.

A common crucial value difference concerns having children: one of the partners wants a child and the other doesn't. Perhaps one partner knew this was an issue, but had hoped that once they were married, the other would magically change his view. Now they go around and around about the issue to no avail. All they accomplish is enormous pressure, conflict and guilt. Finally they realize that the impasse is immovable, and they call it quits.

Other nonnegotiable values might include marriage, religion, geography and career choice.

One of us changed roles. When two people come together, they draw up an unconscious contract about the role each will play in the relationship in order to fulfill their deepest needs. It makes no difference if the couple is aware of this unwritten agreement. The contract is nearly unbreakable.

I once counseled an alcoholic client who was married to a nurse. They had been together for years, with her maintaining the role of his caretaker.

When my client stopped drinking, became a member of AA and got his life in order, he violated their unwritten contract. Her primary role was gone because he no longer needed to be taken care of. The foundation of their connection had been broken.

Another such contract I frequently encounter is the one between an insecure "little girl," with no awareness or sense of her own individuality, and a man who is attached to providing for and protecting others. She gets the warmth and stability of being cared for, and he gets to feel important and validated. They are a match because they equally need one another, and enjoy the security inherent in such a relationship.

Everything is fine until the little girl decides to become a woman and express her individuality. She wants to replace some of her comfort and security with independence and strength. Soon she starts looking for her natural match, a man who can stand on his own in the face of her newly felt power, and who will respond to the sexual charge that goes with her expanded identity.

Unfortunately, this man is nowhere to be found within her marriage because her husband is still trying to connect with the person she used to be. She blames him for not meeting her needs as a woman, until finally she realizes that the problem is simply that she has changed and he hasn't. He is still following their original contract. He had never agreed to be the man for her woman, only the provider for her little girl. The only way of overcoming this dilemma and remaining together with greater intimacy is for her husband to give up his identification with being a caretaker, and to see if they can find a new basis for connection.

We are unwilling to move forward. If you reach a point in your relationship where the only way to end the conflict, pain or dissatisfaction is to do something you find too difficult or frightening, your best alternative is to move apart. If the energy and vulnerability that mutuality requires are beyond your limit, you will answer no to any real change, and you'll be stuck. This usually occurs in couples who are both so wounded and reactive that there is no adequate foundation to support even the beginning stages of mutuality.

When a couple reaches this point and doesn't split up, the negative energy continues to increase, and the two of them endure terrible fights or an icy coldness. It's conceivable that they can maintain this cycle of pain and distance for years, but their marriage is essentially over. All that is left is for them to realize it, get off the circular ride and move apart.

One of us has developed a greater capacity for acceptance. As I have stated many times throughout the book, the two partners in any committed relationship are exactly the same in their capacity for acceptance, intimacy and exposure. But if one of you chooses to recognize and accept some unacceptable parts of yourself, and the other does not, you will eventually be a mismatch, and you'll need to let go of your relationship.

Again, you are only in this category if your greater capacity for intimacy contains no element of the difference game. As long as you have energy for anger, judgment or conflict with your partner, you're still a match.

Whichever of these four paths leads to your decision to divorce, it's vital to your future that you end this part of your life and separate without beating each other up.

MUTUAL ENDINGS

The process of divorcing from an attitude of equality and respect consists of four basic steps:

STEP 1: RECOGNITION AND RESPONSIBILITY

Your first step toward a mutual separation is to recognize the sameness of your pain, your fear and your mismatch, and accept full responsibility for it. Each of you has a partner whose values are different; each of you has a partner whose role no longer matches your own; and both of you are hurt by the past and afraid of the future.

When you fully accept your equality, there will be no accusers, no winners and losers, and no victims of your divorce. But, if you're not willing to accept your accountability and sameness, there can only be finger pointing, blaming and war. And any divorce you get will be incomplete because you'll still be hanging on to each other emotionally.

STEP 2: EXPRESSION

Once you have accepted your sameness, your next step will depend on the condition that led to the breakup. If you no longer match because one of you has changed roles, or because you differ over some unchangeable value, you need to tell your partner, "I love you and I no longer want to be married to you." Say this in a soft, firm voice, with no drama, hostility or blame. It gives your partner a clean, clear message without also implying that you still have a desire to be involved on some emotional level.

If there is any emotion behind your statement, you are giving your partner two messages: *"I want to leave you,"* and, *"I still have energy for you."* Some people think that hostile energy doesn't count when you're ending a relationship. But it really doesn't matter in what form you give energy to your partner, you're still emotionally involved and your divorce won't be clean. The bottom line is this: if there is any drama in your expressed desire for separation, you're still connected and you're not yet ready for a mutual divorce.

After expressing your feelings and your wish to end the relationship, maintain this attitude for one week. Don't dilute your desire with fighting, blaming, sarcasm or arguing. Any such up or down behavior tells your partner that you weren't serious about your message, and reveals your desire to prove something. If you still have something to prove, you're not yet done with the relationship, and your original statement was nothing more than rhetoric.

Once you have held your desire for a week, undiluted by any difference game maneuvers, you can begin discussing the logistics of divorce. But to do so before you have completed the first two steps of recognition and expression is an exercise in futility. Rushing to this point in the process will merely result in more unresolved drama.

If you are divorcing because you can go no further toward risk and exposure, the process is somewhat different. In this situation, tell your partner, "I am too frightened to go any further with you, and I can no longer accept our impasse."

Again, this statement needs to be sustained mentally, emotionally, physically and spiritually for a week. During that time, both partners accept 100% responsibility for their own limitations, and neither uses the other for justification ("I wouldn't have this limitation if it weren't for you."). If either partner can sustain this attitude for a week, the couple is more than likely ready to move on.

If a week seems awfully short, you're underestimating how difficult it is to sustain a vibration like this in such a congruent manner. The couples I work with who are not ready to divorce are usually fighting again within a day or two. Or else they block out the assignment altogether, and return to therapy claiming they forgot to do it.

If your desire to separate comes from a different capacity for acceptance, you must clearly state and hold that position for a week: "I want to move to a level of intimacy and exposure that doesn't seem compatible with your desires. I love you, but I no longer want to be married to you."

If there is any feeling of superiority or any accusatory tone to this statement, then your "greater capacity" is a fantasy, and your desire to move forward is talk without substance. You will then have to choose between a nonmutual divorce, or returning to Chapter 10 and risking greater acceptance and equality.

STEP 3: HONORING YOUR DIFFERENT PARTS

The next two steps will deepen the process of cooperative separation. After you have sustained your desire to leave the relationship for a week with no drama, it's important to identify exactly *which* part of you wants to leave. Because your entire psychological community probably didn't choose to be with your partner in the first place, it would be unusual if every part of you now wants out.

In one of the previous examples, a woman's insecure "little girl" dominated her choice of a husband. That part of her will always want a daddy to take care of her. But now, the "independent woman" part of her has become stronger and is demanding to be given a higher priority. That's the part that is motivating her decision to leave.

If you fail to enlist your director in discerning and honoring all the different parts of your psychological community, you'll be pulled every which way as each internal need and desire struggles to be heard. You'll face much less internal conflict when, for example, you can tell the insecure little girl part of yourself, *"I know you feel frightened and dependent. But now I'm choosing to support the independent woman part of me who is willing to be afraid. That need is more important to me now."*

STEP 4: THANKS AND GOOD-BYE

In completing your relationship, express your appreciation for what you have shared with the person to whom you're saying good-bye. No relationship is ever without merit, because it brought you further along the path of discovery and growth.

Offering your gratitude for whatever made an impact on you not only honors your partner, it allows you to leave in a responsible, loving way.

THE OBSTACLES TO A MUTUAL DIVORCE

Thus far I have described this journey as a fairly smooth one, in spite of the intensity and disappointments of such a passage. But what happens when you hit one of the many bumps or chuckholes along the road to divorce?

Almost all the obstacles to a mutual divorce grow out of opposition. When two partners remain enmeshed in their accusations, judgments, demands and reactions, movement is nearly impossible. Therefore, the best hope for any real progress comes from removing your combative stance. When you no longer provide each other with walls to bang up against, the drama collapses and the real issues can be dealt with more rationally.

This is tough to do because we usually regard opposition as a way of standing up and taking care of ourselves. But in a divorce, nobody gets taken care of through combat except the lawyers.

This is not to say that the only alternative to big legal fees is to lie down and play dead. I simply mean that especially when you're divorcing a hard-nosed spouse, a continuous pattern of opposition won't work. You need to employ other styles that don't play into your partner's oppositional behaviors.

So, when you're involved in a less-than-amicable divorce, you've got two choices: use an attorney to defend against your spouse, or back up and stop giving your partner a target to fight against.

The suggestions that follow are by no means a cure-all approach. I'm just trying to increase your possibilities. Sometimes these methods enable you to get what you want without it costing a fortune. At the very least you'll experience less turmoil. And if these approaches don't work, and your partner wants to hold on to a hostile or demanding attitude, you can always get your lawyer back on the phone.

The Hostile Partner

When your partner expresses a lot of anger, you can find yourself sucked into battles over the slightest issue. Despite your intention to retain an attitude of sameness and acceptance, each day brings a new encounter about your selfishness, your lawyer's unfair demands or who gets custody of the record albums.

The key strategy for avoiding all this drama and conflict is to refuse to engage your partner over whatever he claims is the issue. Instead, respond to all the blame and accusations by acknowledging your partner's feelings. Instead of arguing over whose fault the breakup is, or what your justifications are, simply say, "I can hear that you really feel hurt by me," or, "I understand that you want me to agree with the way you see things."

Another method of taking the conversation to a different level is to respond, "Let's say I concur with you that the breakup is my fault. What do we do then?" This shifts the focus away from blame and superiority, and channels your partner's energy inward, rather than toward you.

In a mutual approach to divorce, you need to *stop perceiving your partner as the enemy.* If you don't, your only alternative is to defend yourself and launch counterattacks.

To avoid this perception of your spouse, it's important to recognize that:

1. *Your partner is deeply hurt, and is lashing out in order to avoid feeling any more vulnerable.* A divorce is going to propel both of you into the unknown, and your protectors will be grasping at every opportunity to move back to familiar ground.

2. *Your partner still wants contact with you.* If you hook into his polarizing drama, you're giving him the safe contact he wants, but you're violating your own desire to leave and separate. So before joining in, ask yourself, "What is my primary goal here, contact or separation?"

3. *Your partner can no longer fulfill your ego needs.* This points out the most common pitfall divorcing couples face, and the most important one to avoid. You need to stop trying to get your ego needs met by someone you've decided to leave. Maneuvering for approval, reassurance, love, respect and acceptance has no place here. If you want a divorce, it probably means you weren't getting enough of these things before. Why would you assume you could get them now that you're separating?

Recognizing these things about your husband or wife will help you avoid feelings of superiority or guilt. To assume such judgmental attitudes is to reenter the difference game and prevent the separation you desire. You want to perceive your partner objectively because the more you can detach yourself from your partner's emotions (and the more you can remove your partner from your own), the cleaner your separation will be.

The Battle over Assets

Another common entanglement in divorces occurs when your partner uses your joint assets in an attempt to intimidate and control you. Intractable or unfair property demands become the issues that hide the real feelings underneath, and threaten to hook you back into an oppositional stance.

Asset discussions are rarely about assets. In most states the laws are pretty straightforward about who's entitled to what. All the endless arguments about what's fair, and all the expensive, protracted negotiations, are fueled primarily by some underlying negative beliefs.

If your partner believes she was hurt more, gave more, worked harder or was more faithful in your marriage, then the division of assets is going to be her last chance to validate her superior stance. The question you need to ask about all your property arguments is not, "What's fair?" but rather, "What is the negative belief that is keeping the asset discussion from resolving?" If you can shift to a mutual attitude until the negative belief is revealed and addressed, the impasse might break.

Let's say your wife is demanding full title to your house. Instead of standing up for your own demand for half of its value, limit your interactions to those statements or questions that keep you out of the power struggle: "So, it sounds right to you for you to get sole ownership of our house? Tell me how that works for you. How did you arrive at that conclusion? If you get the house, are there other things you'll want as well?"

I hope it's obvious that you need to ask these questions openly, with no flavor of sarcasm, anger or superiority. You're attempting to get the controlling person to engage with herself, while you just observe and avoid any entanglement. When you ask the partner you are divorcing what will satisfy her, she has to question herself, not you. This removes you from the polarization.

Your wife might respond, "Well, you get the boat and the car," or, "You can get by living in an apartment." So you continue probing the basis for her offer: "And do you believe that would be an even split? How do you see that as being equal?"

When the justifications shift from tangible assets to emotions, then you know you have tapped into some underlying belief: "I put all my life into this house, and you were never around. You're the one who left, so why should I give up my home? I'm the one who's been hurt here, not you."

When the discussion reaches this level, you need to focus on these underlying beliefs about who was hurt more, who was more guilty and who deserves more. Respond to them by acknowledging the pain your wife is trying to bury. "I hear that you feel hurt and betrayed by me. I understand that you don't think I have been fair."

Then try to reveal the underlying sameness of your feelings. "Are you under the impression I'm not in pain about this? Would you be willing to let me explain how I feel hurt?" Or, "I know you're in a lot of pain. Is there any way we can take care of how hurt you are?" Or perhaps, "If we accept that you were hurt more, is there any other way we can take care of that besides you getting the whole house?"

Often a spouse is so busy arguing and defying you that he won't ever say exactly what he wants. You're just subjected to an endless series of accusations and demands. In that case, simply ask, "What exactly is it you would like? Tell me exactly how you want to divide this property and what you think would be fair."

If it becomes obvious that, for whatever reason, your spouse has no interest in the concept of fairness, shift the focus by saying, "What unfair divorce agreement would you like in order to justify the unfair way you believe I've treated you?" Encourage him to describe his desired settlement in detail.

The goal here is to dissolve the hierarchy as much as you can so that your partner's energy will be focused more on assets than on proving how much more wronged he is. Then his property demands might not be so unreasonable.

The Unwilling Partner

These same principles apply if your partner won't deal with you about some divorce issue. Let's say that instead of loud diatribes and battles over fault and blame, your spouse just ignores the entire issue, or refuses to take some necessary action to move the process forward. Papers are left unsigned, belongings aren't packed, appointments aren't kept.

Again, leave your own needs out of the discussion. Your angry, soon to be ex-partner isn't really interested in your needs anyway. Instead, make statements that can't be objected to, such as, "I respect your desire to not talk to me about something until you feel ready. Any idea when you will feel ready? If you won't be ready for a long time, what do you suggest we do in the meantime?"

Children

Perhaps the most tragic consequence of divorcing from an attitude of judgment and blame occurs when children become pawns in their parents' power struggle. Ron Supancic, a family law specialist whom I work with on divorce cases, recently told me, "Research has shown that the most important emotional and psychological factor for children in divorce settlements is not who the kids end up living with, but how the parents treat each other."

I've had clients use their kids like ropes in a tug-of-war, and I've heard young children echo the hurtful accusations of their mothers and fathers: "Daddy said you don't really want to be with me," or, "Mommy said you just want to goof around, and that's why you're leaving."

As difficult as it will be to remain nonjudgmental and to retain control of your emotions, the best thing you can do when your partner is pulling your kids into his anger and blame is to remain a nonplayer. As with any other arena, the divorce-and-custody version of the difference game loses most of its charge when there's no opponent.

Again, I'm not saying that you should ignore your partner's actions, or that you should give up on what you want or what is fair. I'm only suggesting that your response will be more effective when it's not reactive and combative. Then you send your mate a clear message that you won't be playing this game anymore, and there's a better chance he'll lose the energy for holding his up position. No one likes to play the difference game alone.

Let's say you're a father who discovers that your daughter has been enlisted in justifying your wife's superiority. Begin by remembering to limit your discussions with your wife to observations and questions about your child:

"Nancy Lynn seems to be very angry lately, and she's been getting into fights at school. Today she said that I'm leaving because I don't love her anymore. Do you have any idea where this is coming from? Do you know where she would get such an idea? How do you think we can convince her she's not to blame for our breakup?"

And what if your wife admits her actions? "Well, it's true. If you really cared about her, you wouldn't be running off. So she might as well know how men really are."

Your best response is again to work through your spouse's underlying beliefs without getting involved: "So you think it's in Nancy Lynn's best interest to tear down her father? How will that help her, exactly? Does she seem to feel happier and safer when you tell her this? How will thinking her father is a bad person affect her in later life? What kind of a husband do you think she'll marry if she grows up believing men are jerks?"

Your attitude here is neither judgmental nor passive. If your spouse remains unchanged, suggest family counseling for your child's sake. And if that suggestion is rejected, you once again will have to draw the line and turn to the court system to help you stand up for your child's needs.

Perhaps more than any other benefit, divorcing from an attitude of mutuality is one of the greatest gifts you can give your children. With most divorces, after the property has been divided, the lawyers have been paid and the smoke has cleared from the battlefield, the kids are the ones who have been hurt the most. The two people who gave them life and who are their primary source of love and protection, have left each other hurt, scarred and abandoned. How else could little ones feel but wounded, frightened and helpless?

Think of the difference when your children can see that even with a painful, frightening experience like the breakup of a marriage, the two of you can see beneath your differences. Imagine how much happier and safer they will feel when you achieve the separation and independence you need without sacrificing your love and respect for each other, or for them.

NEW RELATIONSHIPS
Finding a Mutual
Partner

K̇athy was reeling from the traumatic breakup of her two-year relationship with Bill. She felt anger at him, and anger at herself for getting involved with yet another man who couldn't commit to what she really wanted: marriage, children and til-death-do-you-part.

This was not a new situation for Kathy. For years she had been riding the familiar merry-go-round: alone/available/dating/meeting only jerks/meeting Mr. Right/falling in love/getting closer/asking for commitment/getting dumped/alone again.

She had tried immersing herself in the singles scene, and she had tried backing off and simply waiting for a relationship to present itself. She'd tried the sensitive, evolved type and the old-fashioned macho type. She'd gone for brains and she'd gone for brawn. And at various times she had blamed her looks, her intelligence, her independence, her dependence, her upbringing, her job, Los Angeles, the movies, the women's movement, the men's movement, the Sports Illustrated *Swimsuit Issue and AIDS for her consistent romantic failure.*

With each new failed attempt she felt increasing pressure from her family, her friends, society and her biological clock over her inability to find and keep a loving, committed man.

What was wrong? Kathy, like many singles, was an attractive, intelligent, sincere and fun-loving person. Why couldn't she achieve the relationship she wanted? Why did she always seem to pick the wrong guy? Why was she caught in this vicious circle of involvement and rejection?

When so many people of both sexes profess to wanting close, caring relationships, why is it so hard for potential partners to find each other? What good are all these principles for increasing the love and intimacy in your relationship, when you aren't even in a relationship in the first place?

The single world is full of people who feel like helpless victims. The horror stories surround them: *"Everyone decent is taken." "She's a ball buster." "He just won't commit." "She was picking out our china pattern by our second date." "He's a mama's boy." "She left me a week before the wedding."*

Is it any wonder that the difference game flourishes within this kind of atmosphere? The common refrain I hear from almost all my single clients is, "I dread going into the dating scene again. It's awful." They become consumed with dumping on themselves, other singles, members of the opposite sex or the entire species.

I've heard women talk of parties where all the men were creeps, and men describe dances where all the women were dogs. Pretty soon I'm tempted to ask, "You mean out of dozens of people there, there wasn't anyone who surpassed those low standards?"

As with any other stage of a relationship, finding a partner can be a lot less adversarial, and a lot more fulfilling, when viewed through the eyes of sameness. Mutuality can dissolve the hierarchy of comparisons that seems to consume the dating scene. Perceiving sameness and equality, rather than difference and inferiority, can greatly reduce the chances of becoming hurt and victimized. And an attitude of acceptance can keep you from suffering all the exhaustion, frustration and futility that a judgmental approach to dating will certainly entail.

If you're not in a committed relationship right now, I want you to stop dreading your life as a single. I want you to see your current relationship status as an opportunity for discovery and growth, and another stage in the path to embracing your true self. And I want to help you recognize and achieve all your relationship goals, whatever they may be.

THE PRINCIPLES OF MUTUAL DATING

As in all areas of your life, your protector will do his best to cloud reality and blind you to any truth that might lead to some unknown, unacceptable feeling or experience. He'll feed you any fantasy he can about the singles scene, just so the status quo will be preserved. Until you challenge your protector and recognize the following principles, you shouldn't expect anything other than the same familiar dating patterns you've suffered through a hundred times.

There Are No Surprises

A mutual approach to relationships entails listening to whatever statements and clues are offered by any potential partner. I once had a client who complained that the woman he'd been dating for several months was driving him crazy with her emotional swings. "One minute she seems involved in the relationship. Then the next time I talk to her, it's as if she could care less."

I asked him if she had mentioned anything on their first date that stood out. "Well," he replied, "she did say something about not knowing what she wanted from a relationship. But I figured that once we saw each other for a few months, things would iron out."

Another client expressed her frustration that her relationship never progressed beyond a certain level of involvement. "We see each other a couple times a week and that's it. He seems to like me, but he never has any more time for me."

I asked her the same question about their first date.

"All he said was that his work and his kids were his whole world," she responded. "But I thought that if we hit it off, his attitude would change."

I'm afraid not. What people say on the first date is what you get. So listen for throwaway comments like, "My relationships usually last a couple of months," or, "I don't like to let things get too serious." If you ignore these warnings, you're bound to be surprised.

Of course, your protector *wants* you to deny that you ever heard the other person, so that you can act as if your new partner's behavior came from out of the blue. Because surprise is a lot more presentable a reason for failed relationships than admitting that . . .

You Will Only Get What You Are Ready for in a Relationship

If your capacity for emotional interest and involvement is three months, then any longer a period will take you into the unknown and frighten you. That's why you'll continue attracting three-month daters, and that's why your relationships will begin to deteriorate after about eight weeks.

You can only attract mates who fit your own capacity. As I discussed in Chapter 5, you will only hook up with others who possess your same level of differentiation. Put a single woman in a room with a hundred men she's never met. Ninety-nine are single and one is married. If her capacity is only for safe relationships with very set boundaries and no risk of commitment, then she'll zero in on the married guy every time.

For some of you, your capacity will be defined by the duration of the relationship, and for others by the level of commitment you believe is acceptable. Perhaps getting engaged is within your comfort zone, but you never quite make it to the altar. Or perhaps you only feel comfortable dating married men, unavailable women or alcoholics. Potential partners outside those categories will threaten the safety you feel with what's familiar.

Your limits are often defined by the accessibility of your masculine or feminine parts. If you're a man searching for a more fulfilling relationship, you need the support of the masculine part of your nature—the part of you that "shows your sword" and stands up powerfully for who you really are—without any need to prove or justify anything. If this masculine part of you is absent or disguised by superiority and false bravado, you'll pick mother figures (to please), "little girls" (to care for or be superior to), or victims (to beat up on).

If you're a woman wanting to expand your limits, you need the support of your powerful, receptive feminine nature without the need for approval or outside security. When the feminine part of you is absent, or merely a façade of helplessness, you'll gravitate toward relationships with "little boys" (to take care of), or father figures (to lean on).

I can already hear you lament, *"I want more than I'm getting in my relationships!"* Unfortunately, it makes no difference what you say you want. You will only let into your life what your capacity dictates. But recognizing and accepting your limits, rather than hiding or denying them, is the first step toward expanding your capacity and moving toward more satisfying and fulfilling relationships.

All Relationships Work

Until you integrate this fact into your life, you will continue to feel like a failure each time a relationship ends. But every relationship you've ever had resulted in a period of closeness, intimacy and growth on some level, and was the right relationship for you at that time. It was the one you were ready for, it was within your capacity and it gave you the opportunity to discover and learn about who you are.

A series of three-month relationships does not connote lack of success. If this is your pattern, then you're very successful at creating three-month relationships. You're an expert on who to pick, how to pursue them and how those relationships should develop—one month honeymoon, one month plateau, one month conflict and termination.

Every relationship is successful in its own right. You only think it's unsuccessful because you're comparing your own pattern of dating to the happy-ever-after fantasies that get all the good press. When you can let go of all the judgments, you can see the value in any relationship you've ever had.

I know that a three-monther is not two years. So what? It was never meant to be. If you ask around, you'll find countless people who would secretly love a wonderful, exciting, uncomplicated three-month relationship. When you can maintain this realization, you'll eliminate a lot of pain and surprise from your pursuit of a partner.

You're Afraid of Getting What You Say You Want

Until you can accept that moving into the unknown with some new type of relationship is frightening, you'll remain in a fantasy world where all your past "failed" relationships are due to bad luck or some personality flaw.

Your dating pattern, like every other repeated behavior you exhibit, is a source of protection. You wouldn't violate your stated desires and subject yourself to the pain of unsatisfying relationships if you didn't think changing that pattern would expose you to something even worse.

Your fear is very real. Long-term relationships are unknown if your experience is all with one-night stands. And hooking up with strong, independent partners will be scary if your past is populated with wimps or daddy's girls.

No matter how loudly you proclaim your desire for a fairy tale marriage, if such a relationship has eluded you, it's because this unknown experience is terrifying. If you really want to alter your current relationship capacity, you'll need to begin, as always, by recognizing, accepting and expressing what's true for you right now.

MOVING OUT OF DEFEAT

If you're uninvolved right now, how do you find a fun, loving and satisfying relationship with a partner who's right for you? You dread stepping out into the "singles" scene again, and you definitely don't want another ride on the hopeful/disappointed/defeated merry-go-round. So what do you do?

STEP 1: RECOGNIZE AND EMBRACE YOUR CAPACITY.

To move into an attitude of mutuality, your first step is always the same: to recognize your current behavior and take responsibility for it. There is no way to move out of your familiar patterns if you won't even admit what they are.

Identifying your relationship capacity is easy—just look at your past relationships. What is your dating scenario? How long do your relationships usually last? Months? Years? Hours? What kind of partners are you drawn to? Strong and silent? Weak and submissive? Married? Sexpots? Mama's boys? Individuals who are unable to commit? Once you identify the parameters of your dating comfort zone, then you need to take full responsibility for it and passionately embrace it.

Accepting our limits is just as difficult when we're looking for relationships as it is when we're in them. Our egos aren't that thrilled to hear us announce, *"I'm only interested in short-term relationships,"* or, *"I only get involved with married men."* So we live dual lives, proclaiming a desire for permanence and commitment, then pursuing relationships that will never meet those criteria, but which fall within our capacity.

Denying your capacity in this way leaves you in Never-Never Land, forever landing in relationships without any awareness of how you got there. If you don't accept and own your limits, you remain a sucker for the difference dating game—expending your energy putting down the people you date, or beating yourself up as an emotional or relationship failure.

STEP 2: CELEBRATE YOUR CAPACITY.

I want to support you in whatever relationship feels right for you, regardless of the judgments of others. So, if you want to be involved with married men, celebrate that even if it's just to yourself: *"I like being with married men. It's safer, it has set boundaries, and I don't have to worry about where the relationship is going. I can be romantically and sexually involved with someone and still be single. It's the best of both worlds."*

If your desire and capacity is for brief relationships, then embrace that part of yourself: *"I like short-term relationships. That way, just when things start to get boring, I can move on. I can enjoy the thrill of romantic conquest, but I don't have to go through all the hassles and conflicts of long commitments. I love the variety of being with lots of different people, while married people struggle with the same person year in and year out."*

And, if you like involvements with individuals who have some addiction, such as to alcohol or drugs, I want you to celebrate that desire as fully as any other: *"I love going with addicts because they always need me to take care of them. It allows me to be a savior, and help someone who's pain and need are very deep. And I never have to worry about protecting myself from too much exposure because they can barely see anything through their addictions."*

Let's say your relationships usually burn out after about three months. Up to this point you've been passively slipping into this type of relationship, then acting surprised and defeated when yet another romance failed to lead to marriage and children.

This time, instead of judging your three-month partners as jerks, or yourself as a relationship cretin, I want you to celebrate your skill at finding the right partners: *"I do three-month relationships and I'm good at it!"* I want you to shift your stated goal from what you think it should be to what it is. Enter the dating arena by standing up fully for the three-month relationships that are your strength.

From now on I want you to inform your dates immediately that you're a three-monther. As things progress, keep them posted about the time remaining: "Just two months left to go." "We're down to a month, now."

You may be grumbling to yourself, "I can't do that. I'll look like an idiot, and it will destroy a potential partner." But at worst your proclamation will only hurt your chances for a three-month relationship. Based on what I hear from my clients, there are lots of those available. And you don't want more than a three-month commitment anyway (or did you forget that?).

Since the person hearing this is most likely a three-monther as well, you'll get one of two responses: he'll admit he has the same capacity, and he appreciates your honesty; or he'll deny his own capacity and play wounded. The first response will make you feel good. The second (assuming you know that his track record is similar to yours) will remind you of how you used to play wounded yourself, and can give you a good laugh.

> Arlene was an expert at selecting unavailable men, and getting involved in safe relationships. When I first met her she was seeing Vince, a married man in whom she had little interest beyond friendship, and a guy who couldn't even commit to dating her.
>
> But in spite of the fact that he repeatedly told her he wasn't available for a relationship, the two of them would get into all kinds of intense arguments over their future together. They would yell and scream over Vince's unavailability, Arlene's demands, their hit-or-miss dating pattern and his unwillingness to make any commitment to her.
>
> After hearing about several of these episodes, my instructions to Arlene were to cut out the pretense of these painful interactions and stand up for what the relationship really was: SAFE SEX. I told her to share this with Vince, and to ask him as often as possible, "Do you want to do some safe sex?"
>
> Of course she at first resisted. "Safe sex isn't all I want," she'd proclaim. "I want a commitment just like everybody else."
>
> "Then there's no reason to be with this man," I'd reply. "Because you know he's unavailable for that. So something *must*

*be drawing you to this relationship. I just want you to own it
instead of subjecting yourself to all this fantasy and drama. What
have you got to lose?"*

*Reluctantly, she agreed. And when she began focusing on their
safe sex, Vince responded that he loved her new attitude and did-
n't want her to give it up. Not only did this end her pretense and
hostility, it enabled her to channel her energy toward a more satisfying relationship.*

For Arlene, opening up to the truth and accepting her true capacity was her only chance of increasing her capacity and moving on to
something new.

STEP 3: OWN YOUR FEAR.

In addition to recognizing and celebrating your relationship capacity, you also need to acknowledge the vulnerability you feel at moving outside your familiar comfort zone.

Owning your fear allows you to honor and respect your limits, and
accept your relationships for the ways they serve you, rather than the
ways they let you down. And, if you choose to venture into new territory, you can do so with your eyes wide open. Your willingness to
feel your fear turns your desire for a new type of partner into a real
possibility instead of a disaster.

STEP 4: CHANGE YOUR BELIEFS.

Now you are ready to expand your capacity and risk opening up to
whatever new relationship you want. But, before you head out to the
singles bar or compose a new ad for the personals column, you need
to change your thinking.

A different kind of relationship will require a different belief system in order to be successful and satisfying. So, you've got to recognize whatever old dating myths you've been carrying around, such
as:

"No one I could fall in love with could ever love me also."

This is a great one for sabotaging the relationship you want. How likely will it be that you'll find the partner of your dreams if you don't even think you're worthy of that person?

Millions of people have found relationships with those they truly loved. Are you really so unique that for you alone this would be impossible? Could it be that such a belief was planted in your ear by your protector, who'd really rather you didn't step into the unknown arena of a truly loving relationship?

You need to replace this idea with the belief, *"I can be loved by someone I love."* If your protector raises a fuss, have your director ask for specific evidence that mutual love is impossible for you. The past doesn't count; you're open to a new type of relationship now. So why can't you have it?

"All the good ones are taken."

Right. Of course they are. That's why dating services, personal ads, matchmakers, singles bars, singles clubs, singles support groups and singles bowling leagues have become multi-million dollar enterprises. Because all the people who use them are rejects, and you're the only good one left.

Mutuality is not about judgments. It's about sameness and joining. When you let go of your hierarchical thinking and expand your accessibility, desirable partners appear.

Paul Newman is taken. Meg Ryan is taken. But there are plenty of other attractive people out there offering as much love, fear and longing as you do.

"There's no place to meet new people."

I know you don't like hanging out in bars, and I know you're not thrilled about computer dating and want ads. But what else is there?

The problem with this belief is that it operates on the premise that you have to *find* the new partner you desire, as if he's lost somewhere. But he's not lost, so there's no need to seek him out. He's been here all along, but you haven't seen or heard him knocking because you were unavailable. Since your protector wouldn't allow you to move into this new kind of relationship, how could you have noticed this potential partner? You were too busy with your usual dating routine.

As an experiment, ask ten of your friends who are in committed relationships how they "found" their mates. I'd be willing to bet that only one or two will say they were searching everywhere they could think of for just the right person until finally, *there they were!*

Most romantic relationships of any duration seem to grow out of chance encounters, common environments such as work or school, or existing friendships. That's because, consciously or unconsciously, the lovers in these relationships had allowed themselves to take Step 5.

STEP 5: CREATE THE SPACE FOR A NEW RELATIONSHIP.

As difficult as this might be to accept, the biggest step you can take toward "finding" an appropriate partner is to stop searching and turn inward. You need to create a space for your new relationship to enter your life. Holding this clear image as a real part of your consciousness will do more to bring fulfilling relationships into your life than a month at Club Med.

Begin by making the following statements as you actually visualize your new relationship happening in the present:

"I am ready to receive the partner who's right for me."
"I see the relationship I desire coming toward me."
"I am in the relationship I want."

Repeat these statements every day, and sustain this attitude for a month.

I know this will seem strange to some of you, and you're worried about looking or feeling silly. I'm sure your protector is working overtime to discount the whole process: *"How can what you imagine in your head make any difference to your relationships in real life? You aren't even seeing anyone right now, how could you be in the 'right' relationship? This is ridiculous! You should be out there going to bars and dances and joining the right groups."*

Please thank your protector, but tell him you've tried his way repeatedly, and now you want to trust the power of your internal energy and your receptivity to a new kind of relationship. If your protector is still unconvinced, take him to see *Field of Dreams*.

STEP 6: SUPPORT THE RELATIONSHIP YOU DESIRE.

The visualization described in Step 5 plants the seed for your new relationship. Now you must face the work of creating an open space for this person to enter. As you move through the day, repeatedly ask yourself, *"Does what I'm doing support the relationship I desire?"* Every thought, every action, and every decision you make will either expand the space for your new relationship or violate your commitment.

The opening you provide is very precious, and must be very selective. The door cannot be opened indiscriminately to whoever passes by. Only the one you desire can be allowed in.

As long as you hold the vibration of exactly what fits your desires and needs, anyone else who comes near you will simply move on. Even a date with an impostor will be impossible because she'll be exposed at the door.

As you maintain the image of the lover you're awaiting, monitor your internal progress. In your visualization, does he seem far away or very close? Has he been moving toward you? The more graphic your image, the more real the space you're creating will become.

Don't be surprised by the fears that grow out of these images. You're not used to this kind of relationship, so you're bound to be frightened. *"What if I he doesn't show up?"* *"What if she rejects me?"* *"What if I get hurt?"*

Remind your protector that he's looking at your old lovers, not the new one you are welcoming. Your new partner is someone who truly wants and accepts the person you really are, not the person you were pretending to be.

Everything this book has taught you about the temptations of the difference game will hold true in this new relationship as well. Your protector's only goal is to keep you safe from the unknown. So, of course he'll shout to be heard when you venture toward something you have never experienced before and are afraid of receiving. But so long as you remain alert to this fact and call on your director to challenge these old beliefs, your connector will be able to welcome the love you desire.

Any deep fear you carry is likely to emerge whenever you move into the unknown. I once had a client whose father had died when she was very young. Any serious involvement with a man brought up her fear of loving someone and then having them die. Until she recognized the ways that protecting herself from that buried fear had sabotaged her previous relationships, she was unable to move forward. Only when she accepted her fear and was willing to experience it fully could she open herself to greater closeness with another.

The process of developing a receptive space for receiving what you want is quite challenging. We've spent so many years clogging the space with familiar but unfulfilling relationships that unclogging it will take time and commitment.

STEP 7: HONOR YOUR LIMITS IN ANY NEW RELATIONSHIP.

When a relationship finally manifests itself in the space you've created, it is essential that you move forward only at a pace and level of commitment that are within your capacity. Unless you can support each stage of the relationship mentally, physically, emotionally and spiritually, don't push yourself to some new plateau.

When your physical body can support sex, you need to discover if your emotional body can handle it too. Can you accept the tension of bringing sex into the relationship, regardless of what your new partner says or does?

Are you really ready on all levels to raise the issue of marriage, or are you just coming at your partner so he'll back safely away? Do you really have the support of your entire psychological community to keep sleeping around, or is that a violation of your new commitment to a more fulfilling relationship?

I've seen numerous relationships end in painful disaster when people failed to pay attention to what they could support. Often your protector will push you into sabotaging your relationship by persuading you to move beyond your capacity. Then you're left to stare in amazement as your newfound relationship crashes and burns.

Whatever your fear, and whatever your new partner's imagined reaction, behavior that honors the limits to your capacity for intimacy can only result in greater satisfaction, love and fulfillment in any relationship.

PART VI

INTEGRATION

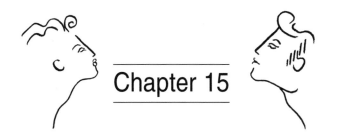

Chapter 15

SEEING THE SAMENESS IN EVERYONE
Universal Mutuality

If any person attempts to elevate your ego by saying:
   "You are not like other men,"
   "You are not like other women," or
   "You are not like other couples,"
tell them to stop. Because sooner or later they will put you down by saying:
   "I made a mistake. You're just like other men,"
   "You're just like other women," or
   "You're just like other couples."

Instead, respond to their praise by saying:
"I'm like all other men,"
"I'm like all other women," or
"We're like all other couples."
Only then will the door be open for all to be
accepted, and no one will be disenfranchised
from the company of men, women and couples.
—Stephen Johnson, Ph.D.

As I was writing this book, a single defining moment united all of Los Angeles. On January 17, 1994, the most destructive earthquake in this nation's history leveled both our physical and psychological homes. No one here escaped its power. In those 40 or so seconds, everyone was hurled into the unknown, and forced to confront feelings of fear, vulnerability and helplessness.

But in response to this indiscriminate threat, there emerged a unifying sense of sameness and joining. With very few exceptions, families were brought together, neighbors helped neighbors and strangers risked their lives for victims they had never met. Crime dropped. Differences of race or class were disregarded. Animosities were forgotten.

Never did one hear, *"I was a better earthquake survivor than you,"* or, *"This was your fault."* No one judged the fear or the love that others shared, no one offered their help and support out of superiority or guilt. There was only a universal feeling of shared pain, acceptance and joining.

This is the essence of mutuality.

Of course, as the aftershocks continued, this experience of sameness passed. Eventually the old judgments and hostilities returned to the freeways, the neighborhoods and the subsistence lines because a lifetime of focusing on differences and protecting ourselves from the unknown couldn't be permanently stopped by ten earthquakes. But that didn't diminish the initial experience of connection that everyone felt.

MUTUALITY IN ALL YOUR RELATIONSHIPS

The same concepts I've shared with you as a couple will hold true for your outside relationships as well. The more willing you are to risk the exposure of your unacceptable feelings, and to recognize the underlying sameness you share with others, the greater the closeness, independence and real power you will experience in all areas of your life.

If you limit the principles of mutuality to your marriage, your movement toward intimacy can be overwhelmed by the powerful influence of our hierarchical culture. Your ability to join with your partner will only increase as you expand your attitude of equality and acceptance in all your relationships.

A narrow view of sameness will make it nearly impossible to overcome a lifetime of conditioning, perceptions and beliefs. Mutuality can't be tried out on Monday, forgotten on Tuesday and then picked up later in the week. Bringing mutuality into your daily consciousness means integrating your expanded capacity for acceptance into relationships with your children, your family, your friends, your co-workers and everyone you encounter.

Achieving real connection requires that you determine your goal in life. Is it to serve your ego, either by expanding it or protecting it? Or is it to feed your relationships and yourself through love, acceptance and a commitment to the truth? If it's the former, the difference game will serve you well. But if your primary desire is for connection, your journey will best be served by seeing all others as a reflection of who you really are, and appreciating the sameness you share.

When we can relate the wounds, fears and desires of others to our own pain and longing, it becomes much harder to stay hostile, righteous, self-indulgent, hopeless or victimized. An attitude of real equality cuts through all the judgments, prejudices, illusions, disguises and nonsense that consume so much of our time and energy. Moving beyond our intimate relationships toward universal mutuality enables us to replace all our drama and protection with real power, passion and joy.

In the coming week, I'd like you to observe all the experiences and interactions you reject and label unacceptable, and to realize that each one was a lost opportunity to learn about yourself and connect with another person. Did you yell at your child when he acted impatient? Then you missed recognizing your own impatience, and you missed hearing the pain that was hidden behind your son's behavior. When your boss made excessive demands on your time, did you passively agree, then ridicule her to co-workers behind her back? If so, you lost an opportunity to bring your own demanding nature into the light, or to experience unacceptable feelings of strength and independence by honoring your own needs. And you passed up the chance to connect with your boss' cry for help about her own vulnerability.

Just as with your lover, when you replace your difference game perceptions with the eyes of sameness, you look for opportunities to join rather than to blame. *"I'd have a great job if it weren't for my boss,"* and *"I'd have a great marriage if it weren't for my in-laws,"* are just two more ways to avoid experiencing the unacceptable parts of yourself.

One of the biggest changes you can make in your outside relationships is to see them all as opportunities for expressing your passion. When you stop waiting for passion to appear and begin discovering it wherever you are, you'll gain control over your life. When your life is defined by actions instead of reactions, you're no longer dependent on what others are doing or not doing.

Giving yourself fully in mind, body and spirit to whatever you do allows you to bring energy and excitement into your life. Self-absorption and ego gratification become meaningless when your passion and self-worth are no longer dependent on the permission or approval of anyone. Every interaction becomes an opportunity for fulfillment, as you experience passionate anger, passionate disappointment or passionate boredom.

The Combative Acquaintance

You may be thinking that fear, exposure and vulnerability are okay to experience with someone you're married to, but how can these principles apply to people you don't even love or trust? Isn't approaching outsiders with an attitude of sameness and acceptance downright stupid? Won't you be opening yourself up to even more pain and abuse? After all, you didn't choose your mother-in-law, your step-kids or your boss the way you did your spouse; they just came as part of a package deal.

The key to assuming an attitude of mutuality with those who have no desire to support or connect with you is to remain much more independent. While the difference game requires reaction and makes you dependent on others for your feelings and desires, mutuality means honoring your own needs so you don't keep bouncing off someone else's.

Once you are willing to accept the unacceptable, you give yourself many more options in responding to others' oppositional behaviors. When you're willing to be inadequate, helpless, selfish or afraid, then combative people lose their ability to put you down or manipulate you around those issues.

Because you embrace, rather than reject, the quality they're criticizing, you no longer have to oppose, argue, defend or prove anything in response. You increase your own power and independence when you're no longer consumed with hiding your unacceptable qualities, and when you no longer live in fear that your inadequacy will be exposed.

The first step toward a mutual approach to difficult people is to recognize that powerlessness is an appropriate response to those who are locked into aggression, narcissism or passivity, and to see that disappointment is a logical reaction to rejection. If you're unwilling to experience these feelings, your actions and emotions will be dictated by the people around you.

The difficult people in your life know, at least unconsciously, that you'll do almost anything to avoid the sense of weakness and emptiness that powerlessness and disappointment instill, and they'll use that knowledge to control and manipulate you. It gives them a great advantage over you if all your energy goes to avoiding these two parts of yourself. When you hold such a reactive stance, you ensure that the drama will continue, and you invariably end up wounded or frustrated.

Think of the combative encounters you have with people other than your spouse. Chances are good that they all tap into your powerlessness or disappointment. Perhaps you feel powerless when your boss chews you out about your inadequacy at work, or when you encounter your daughter-in-law's repeated criticism or selfishness. Maybe your teenager keeps reminding you what a disappointment you are to him, and how you're always letting him down.

Is your usual reaction to these situations to deny your feelings? Do you try to hide your inadequacy from your boss? Do you struggle to regain your power with your children by somehow forcing them to obey, or by bending over backwards not to disappoint them?

Allowing and embracing your powerlessness with a tyrannical or manipulative boss, or a demanding child, is a positive, healthy attitude. And allowing disappointment to exist without labeling it a problem is the best way to take care of yourself when faced with the repeated criticism of an in-law or stepchild. When you can simply acknowledge these feelings, without rejecting or defending them, your true self will remain honored and intact.

As Thomas Moore says in *Care of the Soul*, "Power pours in when we sustain the feeling of emptiness and withstand temptations to fill it prematurely. We have to contain the void. Too often we lose that pregnant emptiness by reaching for substitutes for power. . . . Any exertion of strength motivated by an avoidance of weakness is not genuine power."

Patience is an essential quality for accepting both the disappointment and powerlessness inherent in any impasse. When you and another express opposing needs or desires, and it's impossible for both to be satisfied, you're stuck. When you can exhibit the patience such a situation calls for, you will neither deny your own needs by giving in nor violate the other person's needs by trying to manipulate or control them. And since you are no longer trying to force the situation, there is a greater possibility of something new occurring.

Once you embrace your powerlessness and disappointment and are willing to exhibit patience, you are emotionally ready for a powerful way of dealing with all kinds of people and situations: *utilization*. This tool, originally developed by Milton Erickson, involves using the natural response of others to work for you. You relate to others where they are emotionally, not where you want them to be.

Whenever you simply recognize and express the feelings exhibited by another, rather than judging, denying or attempting to change them, you are employing utilization. Telling a child, "I hear how much you want this," has a different effect than either telling the child to quiet down and stop whining, or repeatedly giving in to unreasonable demands. Utilization is at the core of mutuality, which is built on recognizing, accepting and expressing what's true at any moment in a relationship.

Utilization is a primary component of two very effective movements for responding to manipulative, controlling personalities: *intentional one-down* and *indirect*.

The goal of mutuality is to remove the hierarchy from any relationship and find some basis for connection. When you can eliminate polarization and rejection, the energy is removed from any conflict, and the issue or task involved can be dealt with cleanly. Oppositional people can't continue moving against you when you remove whatever they're opposing.

Intentional one-down means expressing the vulnerable parts of yourself as appropriate responses rather than as problems. "I understand what a disappointment I am to you," you might say to someone questioning your adequacy. "Perhaps I'm not powerful enough to give you what you want."

These statements are made openly and unapologetically, with no hidden stance of better or less. They leave your critic with only two choices: he can agree with you, which isn't something a combative person likes to do, or he can say, "No, you are powerful and you're not a disappointment." Either way you win.

The down position of the difference game is an unconscious reaction to someone's behavior that is designed to protect your image.

The intentional one-down approach is not a defensive reaction, but rather a *conscious* movement that uses the power of the down stance to your own benefit, without any element of judgment or victimization. With the intentional one-down approach, you fully accept powerlessness and disappointment in order to find the most appropriate, effortless and effective way to deal with a situation.

Let's say you're confronted by a boss who repeatedly criticizes your performance whenever tasks are not done to her precise specifications. Your usual responses might be to apologize for your inadequacy, defend yourself by trying to prove you did it correctly, shift the blame to someone else, or exhaust yourself by working even harder to keep from disappointing her the next time.

With an intentional one-down approach, her disappointment and your inadequacy are no longer unacceptable, so you have no reason to hide or defend against them. Instead you honor her feeling and desire, and then find a way to use her behavior to meet your own needs.

Perhaps you respond to her verbal harassment by saying, "I hear that I disappointed you, and you don't think I'm capable of doing this. So would *you* help *me* understand this better? Will you show me how I could do this? How about this? Now if I do it this way, will *that* be satisfactory, or are there other things you need to show me?"

By no longer denying or defending her accusations, you shift her focus to the task. Now your boss faces a dilemma. If she agrees to help you, she'll have to commit time of her own, which she may not want to do. But if she refuses to help, and tells you to go ahead and redo the task on your own (or let it stand as it is), then she's saying you are adequate after all, and her basis for complaining is gone.

Some of you may be thinking, "If I keep admitting my inadequacy, I'll put my job in jeopardy. If she has to keep helping me, I'll get fired."

If your boss sees you as inadequate, she's already evaluating the job you do. Joining in combat with her won't change that. And the idea that her attitude will go away if you don't deal with it is a myth. But once you remove all the noise and smoke from your confrontations, the tasks themselves will get done better and easier, which should put your job in less jeopardy, not more.

By going one-down, you remove the emotion from the situation, and deal solely with the issue or task. You don't object to her objection because that adds resentment to her disappointment. And you don't fight the hierarchy; she is, after all, the boss. Instead you honor her disappointment, but in a way that also honors yourself.

The exception to this approach would be a boss who doesn't really care about the tasks, but wants you there primarily to have someone she can put down and manipulate. In that case, you have to decide if you wish to continue to subject yourself to that or if you prefer to move on to a healthier work situation. If leaving is truly impossible, accepting your powerlessness will still reduce your boss' ability to wound you.

For another example of the intentional one-down response, imagine you have a teenage daughter who constantly berates you for disappointing her. "You never give me what I want." "You two are such losers." "You don't let me do what all the other kids do."

Instead of running yourself ragged, accept her feeling of disappointment and embrace your own inadequacy. Then the next time she asks for something, respond, "We know what a disappointment we are. We'd like to do this for you, but we know if we do, we'll end up doing it wrong and disappointing you again. We love you too much to subject you to that."

Your response cannot be tinged with sarcasm or superiority; if it is, you're just using a clever way to be combative. You must genuinely accept that you're powerless to satisfy your daughter.

As with your boss, this shifts her energy away from you and onto her own attitude and beliefs. If she continues to see you as a disappointment, then she won't get whatever it is she wants. If she still wants you to give it to her, then she'll have to admit you're not a disappointment and that you can satisfy her.

In dealing with people who are very self-absorbed, direct statements of your desire won't work. These individuals count on you going through the front door, so they can rebel against or oppose you. The indirect method asks you to approach combative people through a side door, leaving them without an immediate rejecting response.

Let's say a child demands things from you relentlessly. You're exhausted from repeatedly telling him to stop or from grounding him or sending him to his room. Most parents in such situations frustrate themselves endlessly by futilely trying to change their children's behavior with logical explanations and persuasions.

With an indirect approach, you get out of the way of your child's energy. Instead of reacting to it or trying to diminish it, you respond by focusing on the enormity of the child's passion. You express your honest appreciation for how powerful his desire is.

"Wow! You really want this a lot! I don't know when I've seen so much energy. I'm really impressed by all your passion."

Notice that you have shifted the focus from answering his demands to responding to his passion. You are controlling your interaction without directly confronting him. As long as his demands persist, he is providing you with more energy to comment on.

If his behavior continues, focus on the demand itself, not your refusal to give in to it:

"I hear how much you want this, and I know you're disappointed you can't have it."
"I guess you'd like to be someplace where you could have this."
"I guess you'd like to be with someone who would give you this."
"Are you saying you should get to have everything you want? Would there be any limits to that?"
"I know *I'd* like to be someplace where I got everything I wanted. Where would a place like that be?"

The content of these statements is less important than the shift in energy from one of opposition to one of connection. You honor the child's desires and feelings, and you get him to turn his energy towards looking at his own attitudes, beliefs and desires, rather than toward getting some reaction from you.

Most children will either understand the situation more clearly and let go of the endless demands, or else they'll get bored with a game that has no conflict and move on. Either way the drama has lost its steam.

And as with the boss described earlier, or the combative or unwilling partners in the chapter on divorce, if the child is only interested in battle, you'll at least do a lot for your own sanity by not engaging in such exhaustive behavior.

Shifting Your Perception

Mutuality asks that you see your effect on others as well as their effect on you. When you maintain a difference game stance of superiority and judgment in order to elevate your image of yourself, you often elicit feelings of guilt or shame in others. When someone internalizes your perception of them as not enough, or as having failed you in some way, they usually end up feeling less about themselves. This will in turn propel *them* into the difference game as they struggle to deny these painful, unacceptable and defeated images.

Imagine the effect if instead of judgment, you respond only with acceptance for whatever thoughts, feelings or desires another person expresses. Can a domineering boss be so threatening when his actions are appreciated as passionate expressions of his devotion to work, or if his fear of losing control were seen as the same as your own helplessness? Will a stepchild's combative behavior sustain when he is no longer judged, rejected or accommodated, but is rather respected for his passion and independence? And would your relationship with them, or anyone, not be transformed if your judgment and reactivity changed to acceptance and independence?

By recognizing, accepting and honoring another's feelings as well as your own, you reduce their need to resort to difference game tactics. You eliminate your own intensity from the interaction, and you lessen the chances of getting caught up in the chaos yourself. This shift can only be accomplished by changing your perception from enemy consciousness to loving consciousness.

As you integrate this new approach into all your relationships, you'll begin to respond to the typical obstacles you face without becoming oppositional. With an attitude of mutuality, there are only friends out there, not enemies. Instead of combating the difficult people you encounter, you begin to see each person's positive purpose and contribution to your life. And changing your own behavior and perceptions brings movement to these relationships even when the combative person is unconscious of what you're doing, or unwilling to change their own judgmental attitudes.

Let me emphasize once again, mutuality involves choice, responsibility and independence. Seeing your sameness with others and allowing your feelings of powerlessness or disappointment does not mean sacrificing your own needs and desires, or submitting to any behavior on their part that is hurtful or abusive to you. Mutuality doesn't ignore, camouflage or smooth over anyone's actions. Rather it allows you to clear away all your own drama and protective reactions in order to make a conscious choice about taking care of yourself.

Relationships that are abusive to you in any way, or that push you beyond your own capacity, require you to relate to yourself as a dear friend and not an object. Connection and equality means honoring everyone involved in the relationship, including yourself. Sometimes that means moving on from a job or a relationship rather than allowing your fear of the unknown to keep you in a victimized position.

If leaving a relationship is truly not an option, then you have to accept that it's not a choice for you, and take responsibility for that. If you are stuck with a stepchild or an in-law that you inherited along with your wedding vows, then accept the fact that it's your choice to be in this difficult relationship because it's your choice to stay married. Stop pretending you can keep your husband but somehow make your nemesis disappear.

Whenever you take responsibility for your situation rather than denying it or trying to wish it away, a great deal of turmoil is reduced because you are no longer blowing smoke and making noise about leaving. When you then shift your perception and remove your combative stance, there will be change in any relationship, even one from which you can't remove yourself.

As you read this book, I'm sure the principles and anecdotes remind you of many troubled relationships other than your own. You now have the knowledge and tools to offer an alternative attitude to any friends and loved ones who are themselves caught up in the difference game.

Just be careful. Don't try to analyze or proselytize; friends don't want you to be their teacher or therapist. They want to feel your acceptance, your love and your own vulnerability. They want you to share their real pain and help them move out of their drama. If you offer your strength and support, you can create a safe place for them to bring their own unacceptable parts lovingly into the light. Mutual friends don't judge, criticize, reject or manipulate. They bring honesty, lightness and acceptance to those they love.

MUTUALITY IN THE LARGER WORLD

We live in a world consumed by the difference game.

Every headline, newscast, protest and political debate seems to scream out, *"My group is superior to your group!"*

Congress is mired in gridlock as each political party holds fast to its stance that they are the best. Fear of seeming less prevents any recognition or acknowledgment of the opposing party's principles or solutions.

Wars erupt throughout the world as nations, religious factions and ethnic groups kill to maintain their superiority. Negotiation becomes impossible as each side refuses to acknowledge any legitimacy to the other's stance or any similarity to their wounds, fears or needs.

My country is better. My religion is better. My race, my gender, my language and my beliefs are all superior to yours.

Gays are an abomination to God. The religious right are all homophobic bigots. Abortion rights advocates are killers. Right-to-lifers are sexist fascists. Gun control advocates are wimps. Gun advocates are paranoid fear mongers.

In none of these stances is there a glimmer of recognition that the groups' actions might be based on their particular expressions of love, spiritual belief, independence, reverence, peace or protection. Nowhere is the sameness of their desires for preserving or elevating humanity acknowledged because to do so would be to risk experiencing change, vulnerability, helplessness, disappointment and powerlessness.

Society's need for superiority has become so great that we seem to elevate our models and heroes only to tear them down. For politicians and celebrities, presidents and rock stars, the journey from worshipped hero to scandalized pariah seems almost instantaneous.

And now we seem to have a growing variation of the difference game: the rush to the down position. I'm more wronged, I'm more helpless, I'm more hurt, abused, denied or defeated. I am a victim, and I take no responsibility for my actions.

A single glaring question remains unanswered: in all this drama and all this chaos, with all this judgment and all this denial and rejection, *where is humanity served?*

When the thrust of everything we see and hear of the outside world serves only to frighten us and reinforce our need to be superior or inferior, how can we find the power and commitment necessary to learn and grow and celebrate our humanity? How can we solve the very real problems we face when every thought, word and deed keeps us separate and afraid? And how will hatred, bigotry, war and violence ever subside when we're consumed with proving and justifying our superiority?

Now imagine an alternative to all this conflict and chaos. Look beyond the tabloid headlines and beneath the noisy differences, and think about any positive act of growth or humanity you've ever encountered. In every instance there was a person, a group or a nation that was willing to let go of it's superior stance and find a basis for equality and joining.

Every act of real human progress has grown out of an attitude of love and acceptance. The handshake and the peace treaty, the artist's creation and the scientist's discovery all come out of a commitment to finding the oneness with humanity, life or the universe.

When *"I'm right,"* is replaced with, *"I feel your pain,"* and when *"I'm better,"* becomes, *"We're the same,"* then conflict, prejudice and bigotry can transform into connection, growth and love.

MUTUALITY AND SPIRITUALITY

Spirituality is connection. No matter what the metaphysical or religious orientation, its core principles and beliefs will always celebrate oneness: oneness within yourself, oneness with fellow humans, oneness with nature, oneness with God.

Any time we judge, reject or avoid a particular experience or relationship, whether it's with a person, a plant, our planet or a higher power, we split ourselves off from life. And at that moment, by separating and fighting the object of our fear or disdain, we lose our spiritual nature.

I had an experience recently that really brought this home to me. Health Communications had just agreed to publish this book, and I was feeling high. I felt the need to thank God for whatever role God might have played in my success. So I looked up and said, "I want to thank you, for giving me this moment."

I was shocked by the response I heard in my head. God said, "I don't accept your thank-you."

"Why not?" I replied.

"Because I do not accept a partial relationship with you. Either thank me for all that you are, the acceptable *and* the unacceptable, or do not thank me ?* ill. If you choose to have only a partial relationship with me, you ʌ never see who I truly am."

Mutuality opens the door to our own spirituality. As we shift our perception from judgment to acceptance, from attack to surrender, and from hierarchy to equality, we move into a space where we can join with the universe and experience our lives fully and completely.

When we lose this common basis for joining, our connection to the universe is distorted into one of separation, fear, protection, judgment and bigotry, and its truly spiritual nature is lost.

Everything we think, feel and do allows us to either join with the universe and fully experience our humanity or distance ourselves from it and protect our egos. From an attitude of mutuality and joining we can fully experience the highest nature of our own being.

The ultimate goal of mutuality is not to find a connection you lost. It is to recognize a connection you've always had. When you see yourself and the world through the eyes of real equality, there is nothing to fear, nothing to prove and nothing more you must be.

BIBLIOGRAPHY

Allen, Patricia. *Getting to "I Do"*. New York: William Morrow & Co., 1994.

Anderson, Robert, W. *Solitaire and Double Solitaire*. New York: Random House, 1972.

Anon. *A Course in Miracles*. Tiburon, CA: Foundation For Inner Peace, 1975.

Bader, Ellyn, and Pearson, Peter. *In Quest of the Mythical Mate*. New York: Brunner Mazel, 1988.

Bly, Robert. *Iron John*. New York: Vintage, 1990.

Cabot, Tracy. *How to Make a Man Fall in Love with You*. New York: Dell, 1984.

Carter, S. *Men Who Can't Love*. New York: Berkley Books, 1989.

Crosby, J. F. *When One Wants Out and the Other Doesn't*. New York: Brunner Mazel, 1989.

DeAngelis, Barbara. *How to Make Love All the Time*. New York: Rawson Associates, 1987.

Delis, Dean C., with Phillips, Cassandra. *The Passion Paradox*. New York: Bantam Books, 1990.

Dolan, Yvonne. *A Path with a Heart*. New York: Brunner Mazel, 1985.

Erickson, M. H. "Naturalistic Techniques of Hypnosis: Utilization Technology," *American Journal of Clinical Hypnosis*, Vol. 1:1,3 8, 1958.

Farrell, Warren. *The Myth of Male Power*. New York: Simon and Schuster, 1993.

Farrell, Warren. *Why Men Are the Way They Are*. New York: Berkley Books, 1988.

Fisher, Robert. *The Knight in Rusty Armor*. North Hollywood, CA: Wilshire Books, 1990.

Forward, Susan. *Men Who Hate Women and the Women Who Love Them*, New York: Bantam Books, 1986.

Fritz, Robert. *The Path of Least Resistance*. New York: Ballentine Books, 1984.

Goldberg, Herb. *The Hazards of Being Male*. New York: Penguin, 1977.

Gray, John. *Men Are from Mars, Women Are from Venus*. New York: Harper Collins, 1992.

Hajcak, Frank, and Garwood, Patricia. *Hidden Bedroom Partners*. San Diego: Libra Publications, 1987.

Hendrix, Harville. *Getting the Love You Want*. New York: Henry Holt and Company, 1988.

Hendrix, Harville, and Hunt, Helen. *The Couples Companion*. New York: Pocket Books, 1994.

Kerr, M. E., and Bowen, M. *Family Evaluation*. New York: Norton, 1988.

Kipnis, Aaron, and Herron, Elizabeth. *Gender War, Gender Peace*. New York: Morrow, 1994.

Lachkar, Joan. *The Narcissistic and Borderline Couple*. New York: Brunner Mazel, 1992.

Laing, R. D. *Knots*. New York: Vintage Books, 1970.

McCann, Eileen. *The Two Step*. New York: Grove/Atlantic, 1989.

Miller, Alice. *The Drama of the Gifted Child*. New York: Harper Collins, 1983.

Moore, Thomas. *Care of the Soul*. New York: Harper Perennial, 1993.

Norwood, Robin. *Women Who Love Too Much*. New York: Tarcher/St. Martin's Press, 1985.

Paul, Jordan, and Paul, Margaret. *Do I Have to Give Up Me to Be Loved By You?* Minneapolis: Comp Care, 1983.

Peck, M. Scott. *The Road Less Traveled*. New York: Simon and Schuster, 1978.

Prather, Hugh, and Prather, Gayle. *A Book for Couples*. New York: Doubleday, 1988.

Rhodes, S. *Cold Feet: Why Men Don't Commit*. New York: Penguin, 1989.

Robbins, Anthony. *Awaken the Giant Within*. New York: Summit Books, 1991.

Schnarch, David, M. *Constructing the Sexual Crucible*. New York: Norton, 1991.

Shain, Merle. *Some Men are More Perfect Than Others*. New York: Charterhouse Books, 1973.

Sterling, Justin A. *What Really Works with Men*. New York: Warner Books, 1992.

Stone, Hal, and Winkelman, Sidra. *Embracing Each Other*. San Rafael, CA: New World Library, 1989.

Stone, Hal, and Winkelman, Sidra. *Embracing Ourselves*. Marina Del Rey, CA: DeVorss, 1985.

Tannen, Deborah. *You Just Don't Understand*. New York: Morrow, 1990.

Wapnick, Kenneth. *The End of Injustice*. Tape series. New York: Crompond, 1984.

Wellwood, John. *Journey of the Heart*. New York: Harper Collins, 1990.

Whitaker, Carl. *The Midnight Musings of a Family Therapist*. New York: Norton, 1987.

Williamson, Marianne. *A Return to Love*. New York: Harper Collins, 1992.

310

For those of you who have been touched or provoked by the concepts and methods contained within this book, I'd like to offer you opportunities for further involvement. I would love to hear any reactions you have to the book, or any experiences with the mutuality process you wish to share. And I will be happy to send you information regarding either my schedule of lectures, workshops and couples groups, or my private individual and couples practice.

> Bruce Derman, Ph.D.
> Suite 806
> 22817 Ventura Blvd.
> Woodland Hills, CA 91364
> (818) 375-7194

Please send me information on your programs, workshops, couples groups, and private sessions.

Name: _____

Address: _____

City: _____ State: _____ Zip: _____

Telephone Number: ( ) _____

Interest: _____

* * * * *

For any of you wanting information on Michael Hauge's screenwriting seminars or script consultation service, please contact:

> Hilltop Productions
> P.O. Box 55728
> Sherman Oaks CA 91413
> (818)995-8118 or outside Los Angeles: 1-800-477-1947